o named because
the beach to
Island.

Congress years ago set aside land on the
beach for fish factories here. the factories
are all in ruins now but the land is still
called 'Promised Land'.

"If you pick up the *East Hampton Star,* you'll learn the who, what, and where. The why and how are more likely found in the pages of *Dan's Papers* ... If you want to understand the crazy quilt of art, sand, money, farmland, literature, golf clubs, divorces, sea spray, and the area's remarkable blend of ego, generosity, and dedication to historic preservation, read Dan's book, *In the Hamptons,* and its sequel, *In the Hamptons Too.*"

— Alec Baldwin, from the Foreword of *In the Hamptons Too*

"Dan Rattiner has been chronicling the people and events of the Hamptons for as long as I've been going there (since the sixties). If anyone wanted some insight into what made this area such an interesting place, all they'd need was a copy of *In the Hamptons.* It's as close to rubbing elbows as you can get. Enjoy!"

— Billy Joel

"If there was an honorary mayor of the Hamptons it would have to be Dan Rattiner ... a raconteur with a wicked sense of humor and an eye for detail."

— *Long Island History Journal*

Also by Dan Rattiner

In the Hamptons
In the Hamptons Too

Still in the Hamptons

Still in the Hamptons

MORE TALES OF THE RICH, THE FAMOUS, *and* THE REST OF US

DAN RATTINER

excelsior editions
State University of New York Press
Albany, New York

Cover photo © Christian Sumner / iStockphoto

Published by
State University of New York Press, Albany

Copyright © 2012 by Dan Rattiner

For information, contact State University of New York Press, Albany, NY
www.sunypress.edu

Production by Diane Ganeles
Marketing by Fran Keneston

Excelsior Editions is an imprint of State University of New York Press

Library of Congress Cataloging-in-Publication Data

Rattiner, Dan.
    Still in the Hamptons : more tales of the rich, the famous, and the rest of us / Dan Rattiner. — Excelsior editions.
        pages cm
    ISBN 978-1-4384-4413-0 (hardcover : alk. paper)
    1. Rattiner, Dan.   2. Journalists—United States—Biography.
3. Hamptons (N.Y.)—Social life and customs.   I. Title.

PN4874.R29A3 2012
974.7'25043092—dc23
[B]   2011049984

10 9 8 7 6 5 4 3 2 1

To Rhone and Solange Baker

CONTENTS

Contents

New York

New
Jersey

Long Isl

Long Island

Atlanti

Map created by Kelly Shelley

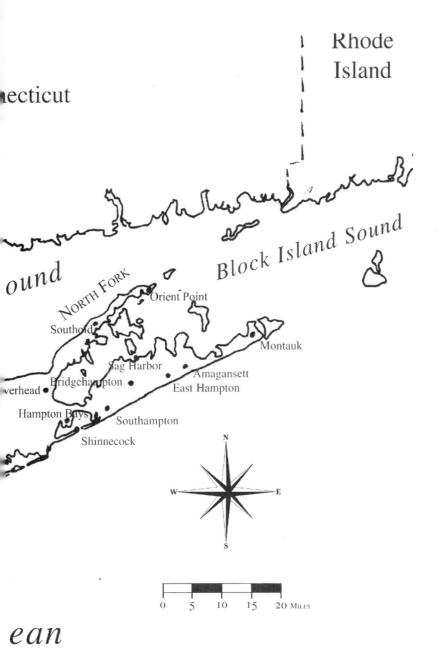

INTRODUCTION

The Hamptons are a string of beautiful old New England towns strung out on the eastern tip of Long Island that around 1980 began to become a glittering resort filled with movie stars, billionaires, Broadway show producers, artists, and writers.

In 1960, I founded *Dan's Papers* as a small, weekly newspaper in this community, and at that time Dwight D. Eisenhower was president, there were three channels on TV, cars had tailfins, gas was forty-nine cents a gallon, and the community of local people largely made their living farming, clamming, and fishing. There were also some wealthy bankers who owned mansions on the beach they came out to in the summertime, and there were a few artists and writers living in seclusion in houses tucked away in the woods. The rest of the people coming out here were tourists. Over the years, *Dan's Papers* grew and soon became the premier newspaper in the community. Also, the Hamptons became "the Hamptons."

Having watched this transformation in fascination, I today offer up in these pages a series of original behind-the-scenes stories about some of the people I have met along the way, both plain and fancy, whose lives intertwined with mine, usually, at first anyway, because I wrote the newspaper.

Here you will read about the Annual Artists & Writers Softball Game with Christie Brinkley, Mort Zuckerman, and Alec Baldwin; about adventurer Peter Beard and the loss of his house to fire; about the attempt to have "the Hamptons" secede from the United States; about the favor done to promote the how-to sex book by Kim Cattrall and Mark Levinson; and about the time Montauk fishing boat captain Carl Darenberg, hired to tow a Coast Guard station on a barge five miles through Gardiner's Bay, had the job go fine until, halfway, a strong wind began to blow and the big house began to head out into the Atlantic on its own.

The people and events I write about are presented here in this memoir in chronological order from 1959 to today, just as I lived them and have remembered them. I hope you enjoy this book, and that it adds to your understanding of what the Hamptons was and has become.

This is the third book in a trilogy of these memories. If you like this book, you will probably also enjoy the earlier ones. *In the Hamptons* and *In the Hamptons Too* are more recollections of my interactions with farmers, fishermen, artists, billionaires, and celebrities in the Hamptons, and both of these books, as is this one, are available either online or at local bookstores.

—Dan Rattiner
January 2012

Driving Out

~~~~~~

Today the Long Island Expressway extends the full length of the island, and it takes about two hours to drive from Manhattan to the Hamptons. Half a century ago, it was very different. Here is how you drove out from New York City to the Hamptons in 1960.

You went out to your car parked right there on the street in front of your Manhattan apartment, and you drove to the entry of the Queens Midtown Tunnel through heavy traffic—the traffic lights were not yet coordinated—hoping there wasn't a tie-up in the tunnel itself. Cars back then were not built as well as they are today and often broke down. When that happened in the single-lane tunnels, they had to be towed. That presented big problems.

At that time, New York City considered itself the center of the world, and it took that responsibility very seriously. It was the largest city in the world in terms of population. It was where world leaders had decided to build the United Nations. The Empire State Building and the Chrysler Building were the tallest and second tallest buildings in the world, and surely there were more skyscrapers assembled in Manhattan than anywhere else. And in terms of money and the arts—with Broadway, the New York Stock Exchange, Greenwich Village, and Madison Avenue—there was little doubt who was number one. The New York Yankees played here, for heaven's sakes.

One thing New York City was not, however, was fun. People would get arrested if they opened a sidewalk cafe. There were not yet banners and ribbons and great busloads of tourists from all over the world. Times Square, not yet family friendly, was a place of prostitutes and peep shows. There were many good neighborhoods around town to be sure, but there were also metal garbage cans that often overflowed, slums filled with immigrants, bad neighborhoods where it was dangerous to walk, and parks filled with weirdos. You didn't go into parks at night. There was also dog poop on the sidewalks. People didn't think anything of it.

In the business district, people wore suits and ties to the tall office buildings, they came in at nine, worked hard, and left at five, left town for the suburbs on filthy public transit systems, and had their two-week vacations in the summertime at the beach. A colorless man named Robert F. Wagner was mayor. There was another man, an exciting man named John F. Kennedy, who was president of the United States. But he was not from here.

And so you would get away to the Hamptons. You would drive through the tunnel and out the newly completed western end of the Long Island Expressway (called Grand Central Parkway), over the booming factories and workers' row houses in Queens—the big neon signs read BALLANTINE and RHEINGOLD and WONDER BREAD—and past Flushing Meadows Park, the place where buildings would soon go up for the upcoming 1964 World's Fair. On the right, you could see the art deco red-brick abandoned structures of the 1939 World's Fair—wasn't it wonderful that New York City had been chosen for a World's Fair *twice* in just twenty-five years? And on the left there were the new structures of the new fair going up—rocket ships pointed at the sky, stadiums, flying saucers held twenty stories in the air by steel pylons, modern domes, and walkways. As you drove through these two fairs—one from the past and one from the future—you drove along the construction of what was surely the largest arrangement of overpasses and underpasses and turnoffs in the world.

You continued on through the outer reaches of the borough of Queens, the superhighway a great sunken gash in the landscape amidst the shattered remains of the road it replaced, the Horace Harding Parkway, just a service road now.

Just past Huntington, the road ended, dumping you off onto the Northern State Parkway. Now you could continue along in a sylvan setting, woods on both sides of the road for a while, and then through villages and farms as you drove out east, until even the parkway emptied into the rather rural serenity of central Long Island. You continued on through a series of two-lane roads with occasional traffic lights in the village centers.

On one occasion, in 1958, my mother and father came to the end of the Northern State Parkway and onto a brand new road that had just opened called the Smithtown Bypass.

It did exactly what it said it did. It bypassed the village of Smithtown by swinging around it to the south and then back up further to the east of the town back on the Jericho Turnpike again. There was absolutely nothing on this road, for its entire twelve-mile length, except for one thing. About halfway, at a particular turnoff, there was a single commercial structure—the first highway fast-food place I had ever seen—called Carvel. We always stopped. At this point, we would have traveled over two hours from the city, and it was a welcome break. My sister and I would get out from the back and run over to the counter to order a swirl of vanilla or chocolate ice cream in a cone. Our parents would follow.

The view in every direction from that Carvel, basically barren and very lightly inhabited, was typical of all of central Long Island at that time. Some of it was farmland. But most of it was nothing at all. Just miles and miles of flat open fields and scrub oaks. The suburbs of New York City had spread out onto Long Island, but hadn't gone all that far out yet. Houses were going up in places with names such as Huntington, Syosset, and Farmingdale, but beyond that—nothing, except a few bars, bowling alleys, delis, hardware stores, and some feed stores. Along this stretch, however, there were often big highway billboards, all identical, that read PATCHOGUE—LARGEST DOWNTOWN RETAIL CENTER ON LONG ISLAND. The suburbanites were coming. As they tumbled farther and farther out, this sign expressed the hope that little Patchogue—a big farm town—would become the center of commerce throughout this large, barren area.

There was a historical explanation for all that nothing in the center part of the island. In colonial times, the Dutch had settled Manhattan and Brooklyn at the west end. And the English New England settlers, coming across in boats from Connecticut, had built villages on the eastern end of Long Island, most notably in the Hamptons. Neither had bothered the other.

Indeed, one of the landmarks in the center of Long Island was Pilgrim State, a grim mental hospital that looked like something out of Dickens. It rose up out of the gloom ten stories high in the middle of nowhere—a facility built in the nineteenth century, far away, I suppose, beyond the eyes and ears of a big city that didn't care about those inside it. Now suburbia was coming. Maybe ten, maybe twenty years away. Would Pilgrim State survive?

My sister and I would look out from the back seat of our parent's car at this facility as we drove along—from ten miles away we could see it across the fields—and it was a scary thing indeed.

We could also roll down the windows of Dad's tailfinned 1959 Buick sedan, look up and see military aircraft in the sky. This was the era of the long, drawn-out Cold War battle with the Soviet Union. These fighter planes glinted in the sun and emitted a thundering roar as they flew by. Often, you could see they were fully armed with guns and missiles. And sometimes you could watch them do tricks and rolls in the sky. These planes were from the Grumman Corporation, which had a 22,000-acre facility just west of Riverhead where they built and tested warplanes for the Pentagon. At this time, the F9F fighter planes, sleek black jets, would be put through their paces and eventually find their way to the flattops of Navy aircraft carriers. Of course, here on the ground, we were told, in the woods of Mount Sinai, there were Nike Missiles. If the Soviets launched a nuclear attack, we were just the push of a button away from a full retaliation.

As you got farther and farther out into eastern Long Island, the roads got even narrower, if that was possible, but at the same time you began to pass down the main streets of some very different sorts of villages. These were beautiful New England affairs. They included Eastport, Center and East Moriches, and Westhampton Beach, each more charming than the one before it. Scattered throughout them as you drove, in the inlets from the big bays to the south, the headwaters came up to the highway between the towns—thereby defining their borders—and allowing the creation of smelly duck farms, long coops of low buildings housing the ducks, grassless stretches of waterfront where they could run around quacking noisily by the thousands. Separating them from the main road was a low turkey-wire fence, often—and especially on windy days—pasted with duck feathers. Cars would stop and kids and parents would get out into this fetid stink, and they would throw bits of bread at the ducks.

To the north, all roads ended at Riverhead, the solid county seat right where the headwaters of the Peconic River meet Peconic Bay. Riverhead had courthouses and administration buildings, lawyers' offices and busy restaurants and department stores. Riverhead was a thriving agricultural market town as well—second only to Patchogue—with produce from the farms brought there and either sold in a big country market or shipped out aboard the freight cars of the Long Island Rail Road to New York City.

In any case, after a three-and-a-half-hour drive along the south shore, you would arrive at this 50 mile long peninsula they called the Hamptons, a series of even more magnificent set-piece New England colonial towns. Bordering them on the north were the beautiful harbors and inlets of Peconic Bay; to the south, the Atlantic Ocean. I soon learned, after we settled in this community, that the local population consisted of farmers, fishermen, merchants, and service people, along with a few artists and writers who just wanted peace and quiet. As for those who drove out from New York City in the summertime, there were only two groups. One of these groups consisted of the "500," the Blue Bloods, who lived sumptuously with servants, friends, and family from June to September in giant mansions behind hedgerows down by the beach. The other was the tourists, mostly white-collar or blue-collar workers and their wives and children, out for their two-week vacations.

Of course, these summertime visitors drove the local economy. The locals suffered high unemployment during the winter. Many went on welfare.

And, as I soon discovered, the tourists were not interested in the Hamptons. They were more interested in a resort and motel town at the very end of the Hamptons called Montauk. The Hamptons were just among the things in their way to get out there. To give an example of how important Montauk was, consider this: On the border of Montauk and Amagansett (one of the Hamptons), the owner of the newly built Driftwood Beach Resort, Sam Weissbein, moved heaven and earth to get a coveted 668 (Montauk 8) telephone exchange instead of a dreaded 267 (Amagansett 7) exchange. He was ten feet into the Amagansett fire district. Who would come to his resort if people reading the travel sections of newspapers in Manhattan saw all the ads for the beautiful Montauk resorts, but the Driftwood resort seemed to be in Amagansett? Where was Amagansett?

And so, we drove that year of 1960 through downtown Southampton, Water Mill, Bridgehampton, East Hampton, and Amagansett, zoomed out of town to the east of Amagansett, and almost immediately drove down a hill onto a long, flat, straight-as-an-arrow two-lane road that headed for Montauk. Immediately on heading down that hill, the weather changed—remember this was before cars had air conditioning—and suddenly it was five degrees cooler, damper, and saltier. To the left and right were low dunes, and beyond them—unobstructed by trees back then—on either side, the water. Napeague Harbor was on the left, the Atlantic Ocean was on the right, and, particularly in the mornings, a salty fog would roll in, sometimes even masking the hundred or so billboards that lined the side of the road right there, advertising one or another of the different attractions in Montauk.

Very often at this time, and simultaneously with this, the reach of the New York City AM radio stations—this was before FM—surpassed their limits. Reception would fade when you came down the hill from Amagansett onto the long straight Napeague. And then there were just the stations from Connecticut.

In just a few hundred yards, the billboards ended and then you could continue down this road, straight for six miles, through a barren wasteland of sand dunes.

After that, the road climbed up into a series of hills and woods to run for the next three miles along the top of a cliff, sharing the views of the Atlantic Ocean with a variety of summer resorts with names such as Wavecrest, Panoramic, Umbrella Inn, Gurney's Inn, Surf and Sand, and the Breakers.

Finally, eleven miles past Amagansett, you descended to the Main Street of downtown Montauk proper. There were clothing stores and real estate offices, souvenir shops and ice cream parlors, a pharmacy and general store (now owned by my father), a liquor store, bars and restaurants, several fish and tackle shops, two churches, and more motels.

In downtown Montauk, particularly along the ocean, were resorts with names such as the Atlantic Terrace, the Ronjo (in Hawaiian motif), the Sands Motel, the Maisonettes, Neptune Motel; restaurants with names like the Shagwong, Trails End, and the Montauk Diner, as well as several gas stations and a miniature golf course.

In an odd way, however, the downtown looked like a Wild West town. The buildings, for the most part, were undistinguished; there was neither street furniture nor sidewalks. And there wasn't even curbing. You just pulled up in front of where you wanted to go.

Also, there were often people on horseback downtown. People from the two ranches out to the east toward the lighthouse often came to town that way. They'd just tie up and take care of their business.

Montauk, in this sense, was a world of its own. Also, as a peninsula fifteen miles long and five miles wide, it seemed to be, geologically, almost a little world in miniature. There were cliffs and dunes, a fishing village full of boats, a lighthouse, a golf course, a yacht club, miles of unpaved rumrunner roads through the woods, a center of town with a small lake where people went out in sailboats and rowboats. There were lots of clam bars. It had the aforementioned two ranches with cattle on them, giant dunes that moved as the wind blew the sand up one side and down the other, a big old hotel on a hill, a boardwalk and surf club on the ocean, ponds, harbors, and miles of beaches. The shiny new motels and inns beckoned. And there were a whole lot of happy sport fishermen. Montauk, it was found, was the "Fishing Capital of the World," with its fishermen holding more titles for record-size fish than any other place anywhere. It was also, with its ocean breezes, "ten degrees cooler than New York," which in the age before air conditioning meant quite a bit indeed.

In those days, in the travel sections of the Sunday editions of the six daily newspapers in Manhattan, there were sometimes two full pages of small advertisements from motels and hotels in Montauk announcing those facts and beckoning families to drive out for a vacation by the sea. COME TO MONTAUK!

The Tycoons

~~~~~~

Often, when I drove from my parents' house in Montauk to East Hampton to buy things I could not get in that little fishing town, I'd come back out the long straight stretch of Napeague and glance up at these two big mansions that looked out the ten miles all the way back to Montauk.

You really couldn't miss them. Today, the hill upon which they sit is overgrown with trees and they are barely visible. But back then, while driving the Napeague Stretch, you could see forever going either way because it was all just beach grass and scrub trees. Those two mansions up there, built in a grand Victorian style, were identical one to the other, with porticos under which you could sit on wicker chairs and see the whole way to the motels and ranches of Montauk and the lighthouse beyond.

But why two? For a man and his wife? For two best friends?

I never went up there, of course. These were private homes. But I sure was curious about them. For one thing, when the wind was blowing the wrong way, there was the smell. There was a fish factory on the north shore of Napeague, at the base

UNLOADING BUNKER FISH AT THE FISH FACTORY
(Courtesy East Hampton Library)

of the hill upon which these mansions sat. Tiny fish called bunker fish were brought in there to a dock to be cooked down into glue for a glue-bottling plant in Long Island City. What an odd thing to do, to build two mansions side by side near to where there was a big glue factory. Or maybe it was the other way around. The mansions first, and then the glue factory. Boy, wouldn't that have been a surprise.

One day, heading toward East Hampton, I decided to go to the library in that town to find out more about the mansions and the fish factory. I loved this library. There was no library at all in Montauk. But even if there had been one, the one in East Hampton would have outranked it by a mile. On hot days, there was nothing better than settling into an easy chair in the beautiful mahogany-paneled reading room to read a book. This was surely the coolest place to be in that town, with the breeze wafting in under the maple trees out back. Meanwhile, in an adjacent room, there was Mrs. King, the librarian, who oversaw the vast collection of local historical material that was stored there. It had been donated by a great Long Island historian named Morton T. Pennypacker. His name was above the door of the reading room.

I explained my mission to Mrs. King when I went inside. She thought about it for a moment.

"I think we have something about those houses," she said. Then she went off and shortly returned with about a half-dozen letters and newspaper clippings to look through. I was amazed. All of this for just two houses.

There had not been just one fish factory. There had been six! They had been built between 1840 and 1860, nearly half a century before the two mansions. Imagine the smell from those six fish factories.

I read a bit more about the fish factories. Each consisted of a brick or metal building in which there was a small office, a coal bin, and stacks of barrels. Outside there was a wooden dock and a giant cauldron of water that sat upon a coal fire burning continuously day and night. A fishing boat would tie up at the dock, the men would roll barrels of little bunker fish over to the cauldron, and men with giant wooden ladles would spoon the fish into it. Twenty-four hours later, the bunker fish, constantly being stirred, would become thick glue, at which time the cauldron would be lifted up with a winch, tipped sideways, and the glue poured into barrels for the trip by boat to Long Island City. All this was out in the open. The stench of all this simply rose into the air.

I then learned that all of this activity was for many years carried out by Portuguese immigrants. They lived in makeshift tiny cottages and barracks buildings on the nearby beach. They were paid slave wages. Then, when their time was done, they'd be sent back to Portugal.

At this time, all of Montauk from one end to the other was owned by a millionaire from Brooklyn named Arthur Benson. There had been Montauk Indians living in the wilds of this land when he bought it. Benson had some of his employees track them down and pay them fifty dollars cash—a lot of money at the time—to leave their homeland and move to Michigan, where they were told was another branch of the Montauk tribe. They could take the long train ride. With a few exceptions, they went.

Benson then used his twenty-five thousand acres of Montauk as his own private hunting and fishing reserve. He'd invite his friends out by horse-drawn carriage. One weekend, those friends were two wealthy industrialists from Detroit named Richard Levering and William Cooper Procter.

It was a weekend in the autumn of 1875. On that weekend the wind was from the south, so the smell wafted out to sea. They all had a wonderful time.

At the end of the weekend, Benson remained camping in Montauk, but the two guests climbed aboard their horse carriage and while passing through Napeague heading back to Manhattan, noticed the beautiful hillside at the most westerly end of Benson's property. Levering wondered if it would be possible to build two beautiful summer mansions at the top of this hill, side by side, facing out onto the vast expanse of Benson's reserve. He and Procter, competitors in business, could be friends on vacation with their families.

When they got back to Detroit, they wrote Benson. Would he allow that? He most certainly would.

And so, letters making arrangements were sent out and, amid this incredible stench, local carpenters, plumbers, and roofers constructed these two identical and magnificent Victorian mansions side by side. The correspondence about how to build them came from Procter and Levering and their architects in Detroit. Sets of plans arrived. Instructions for furnishings were sent, and decorators in New York selected things and had them sent out.

These two homes would be lit by the very latest method: electricity! There were no power lines or lighting company. Instead, the plans called for a small coal-fired power plant with a tall brick smokestack to be built along the stretch of the bay. The coal would be delivered by barge to the dock they constructed there. Fires in furnaces would heat steam boilers. And power lines from the plant would carry the electricity up the hill to the mansions.

There had been a further plan. If there was to be a power plant down by the beach, why not build a small railroad to follow the power lines from the dock to the houses? The Proctors and Leverings could come out by private yacht, tie up at the power plant dock, then take a half-mile train trip up the hill in their own special private parlor car.

The locals were happy to oblige these two millionaires. It would bring them a great windfall of money. And so, in spite of the occasional stench, they labored through the winter and got these homes built until finally, in June, the great day came. The houses were finished, right down to the linens, towels, furniture, and silverware.

As it happened, the steamboat carrying the families and their servants arrived when the wind was blowing the stench the wrong way. The families went down the gangway to the dock, noticed the smell, suggested that it might be bad here but up on the hill it would be just fine, and took their private train up the hill.

It wasn't fine. The next morning, with handkerchiefs covering their noses and mouths, the entire entourage, coughing and gagging, returned to the yacht and steamed back to New York City. They would never come out again.

A lawsuit was filed the next year by Procter and Levering against the owners of these fish factories. Apparently this had been an informal matter. The factory owners had never made any lease with Benson. Benson had simply allowed them to do business there. Why not? As the lawsuit made its way through the courts, the factory owners lobbied the United States Congress to deal with this matter. In the end, Congress passed a law declaring the fish factories legal. The place was to be called "Promised Land," promised to the fish factory owners. The stench continued.

Nearly eighty years later, the stench brought us up short on several occasions when we drove through Napeague. But it was a stench from only one factory. The other five were out of business because the factories were no longer economically viable. The sixth one, called Smith Meal, struggled on, if you can call it that, for about two years after we arrived. Then it, too, closed. And the stench was gone.

As you can imagine, I thought this an amazing story. When I started the first modest edition of *Dan's Papers* in Montauk in 1960 (the *Montauk Pioneer*), I wrote a brief version of this story for it. Five years later, when I opened a second edition in East Hampton, I decided to write a more elaborate version. I had three employees at this time, one of whom was a railroad buff named Ron Ziel. Ron knew everything about railroads and steam engines. He had even written a coffee-table book about the Long Island Rail Road called *Steel Rails to the Sunrise*.

Thinking he might know something about the spur railroad up to the mansions, I asked him about it. To my amazement, he not only knew about it, but also knew someone who had hands-on experience with it. He had been in later years the foreman at one of the fish factories.

"He lives in Bay Shore," Ron told me. "He's pretty old now. I'd bet he'd talk to you."

I could not resist this. I called Louis Martinelli in Bay Shore. He told me he no longer traveled much, but if I wanted to come to him he'd be happy to tell me about his experiences in Napeague. He gave me his address. And so I met him, a small, wiry man with a heavy Italian accent who lived with his wife in a small house on a residential street in that town.

"I came to America from Italy just after World War I aboard what they called 'Liberty Ships,'" he told me. "I was thirty-five. I got a lot of odd jobs in New York. Then I got this job working out in Napeague for the Campbell Packing Company. They put me in charge of the factory and the men who worked there."

"The Portuguese?"

"Most were from Portugal. Others were immigrants from all over. They lived in these tiny shacks nearby. A few spoke Italian. We got along. I was there about a year."

"The smell?"

"Oh yes."

"Was that power plant for the private homes still there when you were there?"

"Oh yes. It hadn't been used in many years. There was also a rusty passenger car and steam engine. You know that little railroad there was a narrow gauge. It was too narrow to attach to the Long Island Rail Road which came later."

"What kind of steam engine was it?" I asked.

"An Airculos. A little steam engine. Worked well, I should think, for what it had to do."

I wrote down the word "Airculos." And when I wrote this story, that is the name I used for the engine.

The day after the paper came out with the story in it, Ron Ziel came into the carriage house next to the post office in East Hampton where we had our offices.

"It is not Airculos," he said. "It's Hercules."

"He said it was 'Airculos.' I wrote it down."

"That's 'Hercules' with an Italian accent," he said.

Carl Darenberg Jr.

~~~~~~

When we moved to Montauk, my parents each handled the move very differently. My mother hated the place. She had her friends in a New Jersey suburb and they meant a lot to her, and she lived for the time when they would come out for a weekend. Montauk, for her, was a place lacking in any culture. It was a small town of fishermen, tourists, motel owners, and blue-collar workers. She spent her time helping my father in the store, keeping house, and playing golf at the local golf course.

My father took to Montauk like a duck to water. As the town pharmacist, he was by definition a respected member of the community. At times, it meant getting up in the middle of the night to fill a prescription. He did that, and he never let anybody down. He joined the fire department. I still have his red fireman's hat hanging on the bedroom wall at my home, and every time I look at it I can see him out there in the middle of the street directing traffic around the fire, wherever it might be, as the younger men in the department, with all their fire equipment, put it out. Dad also bought a fishing

CARL DARENBERG AND ACTRESS LISA KIRKLAND

(Courtesy Montauk Library)

boat, a small, 29-foot affair with an inboard engine and a little cabin and a wheelhouse. He kept it in a boat slip in a marina in Montauk Harbor and loved to go fishing in it for blues out at the point under the lighthouse. He found time to do that with some friends about once a week.

I still remember Dad and I and maybe three of his fishing buddies walking on the dock to the Montauk Marine Basin, and we'd say hello to Carl Darenberg Jr., a man covered with engine grease who owned the place, and then we'd get on Dad's boat and go out. I did this with him maybe twice. The first time when I got seasick I was told it was pretty rough out there. The second time I got seasick there were no excuses. It was calm as glass. I went below and lay on one of the bunks, groaning softly until we got back. Going out in fishing boats was not for me.

What a fate, I thought, as I was assisted up the dock to the car. Here I am, the young newspaperman in a fishing village, not only a fishing village, but a village with the most rod-and-reel deep-sea fishing records in the world—and I can't go out in a boat.

Carl Darenberg Jr. ran the marina with his family, which consisted of his wife and two kids and two black labs. Out in front of the marina, he had a 20-foot steel crane for hauling boats, and also a heavy-duty fish scale. If you caught a 300-pound swordfish or marlin he could haul it up with the scale winch and they could weigh it and take pictures of it. He had a general store on the property and also a garage into which he could haul ships in order to rebuild engines and repair hulls. The Marine Basin was one of eight marinas in the harbor, but it was the largest. And when I asked my father why he chose to dock his boat at that one rather than at any other, he said he didn't know the others, but Darenberg did good work.

Personally, I went to see Carl Darenberg once in the springtime, as I did every other merchant in town in those early years. A tall, thin man, he would listen patiently as I told him of my plans for the newspaper for the summer and what the different-sized ads cost. Sometimes, as I told him about it, I was surprised that he didn't seem to acknowledge my enthusiasm in any way. Others did when I talked about the virtues of the paper. But soon I came to see that this was just how he was. He had been in the Navy in the Second

World War, and like many others who had been in combat during that awful conflict, he had a military bearing and a reserved and quiet way about him. As I spoke, he would indeed give me his full attention. And when I was done, he would be clear with his reply. He would be in the paper. Or not. There was no waffling, no "come back tomorrow." If he was in, he'd tell me what size ad he wanted and for how long. And then he'd thank me for my time.

Around midnight at the beginning of the summer of 1963, fire broke out down at the docks. The siren woke me. I padded to a bedroom window and I could see flames flickering down there. Then I heard my dad banging around in the dark hallway, on the stairs, out the front door, and to the car. He drove off. I went back to sleep.

In the morning, I learned that the general store and repair bay at the Montauk Marine Basin had burned to the ground. I went there and took pictures. I interviewed the fire police, who were still working in the smoldering ruins, and the chief told me that the fire was suspicious.

"We think there might have been somebody who had a grudge against the Darenbergs," he said. I stayed out of it.

No one ever did find out who set fire to the Marine Basin, but the Darenbergs carried on. The renters already had their boats in the slips when the fire happened, although none of the boats were damaged. Certainly, there were other places along the docks where people could get supplies. After a few days, I went to see Carl, who was working out of a trailer. He had signed up for an ad.

"Keep the ad in," he told me. "People have to know we're still open."

Construction got underway in the fall, and by March, it was almost complete. But then, incredibly, one night the entire place burned down again.

I was away at graduate school at the time. It was as bad as the first fire, my father told me. And the next day there was a town meeting at the firehouse. Everyone was there. The town still didn't know who set the fire, but they were not going to put up with it. It was decided that the entire town would raise money and rebuild the place stick by stick, exactly as it had been before. They had the plans and they had the earlier permits. And they would work twenty-four hours a day, seven days a week, and get the job done in thirty days so the Darenbergs could be open by the time the tourists began to arrive in May.

It was, I thought, a remarkable thing that they did.

I went down to the Marine Basin when I came home for spring break to see how things were progressing. I walked around the general store and the repair garage, looking carefully at them with my architectural student eye. They looked fine, although some of the finishing work was a bit sloppy and at least two of the windows had been put in crooked.

Inside, after noticing Carl was not at the counter, I asked where he might be and was told he was up in his office. And so, I went to the narrow stairs at the back of the store and up to the second floor to see him. He was at his desk.

"How are you doing?" I asked.

"We're okay."

I noticed that behind him, on the wall, there was a framed photograph that I had not seen there before. It appeared to be a house on a barge. In fact, now that I looked at it more

CARL TOWING THE COAST GUARD STATION
(Courtesy Carl Darenberg Jr.)

closely, I could see it was the Montauk Coast Guard station, on a barge, being pulled through the water. A young man was on the barge but I couldn't make out who it was.

"That was me," Carl said, noticing I was looking at it.

"I hadn't seen that before," I said.

"Well, I brought it here from home. We had other pictures here—the battleship I was on and so forth. But now they're gone. So now I thought I'd bring a few new ones from home."

"What are you doing with that Coast Guard station?"

I motioned to the Coast Guard station itself. It was right out the window, on its own little island in the middle of Montauk Harbor, a three-story, white-shingled building overseeing everything.

"I'd come home from the war. Didn't know what I wanted to do with myself. And then somebody told me the Coast Guard was looking to move the old Napeague station out to Montauk," Darenberg explained.

"I didn't know there was a Coast Guard station in Napeague," I said.

"It was right on the ocean, about ten miles from here. They had a plan, I think it was from Kennelly, the house mover, to just tow it out across the dunes to the highway and then down the ten miles into town and out to the fishing village. They had a price. Seemed like a lot to me. And then I thought, I could do this better and faster and a whole lot cheaper another way. So I gave them my price."

"You towed it in the bay along the coastline."

"It just seemed like such an easy thing to do. All you'd have to do is tow it a few hundred yards through the dunes, across the highway and the railroad tracks, and you'd be right on the beach at Napeague Harbor. It's perfectly calm there. My dad had a fishing boat—he was running this marina then—and he said he would lend it to me. We'd lift up the station on jacks, build a platform under it, slide axles and wheels under it, and then launch it out into the harbor. In front, I'd have my dad's boat, and with that I'd tow it along the shore of Gardiner's Bay to the entrance to Montauk Harbor. The other way of bringing it to Montauk, along the road, with the problems in the center of town, then turn onto Flamingo Road, then the turn down Westlake to the causeway, then still another turn out onto Star Island, that would take days. We could do this in hours."

"It should work."

"Well, I never had done anything like this before. But I figured, what could I lose? I applied. I won the bid. And so we towed it across the dunes and onto a floating platform we had tied up to a dock at Napeague Harbor. It went fine. But then, out in the bay, it got really scary."

I couldn't imagine Darenberg scared of anything.

"Why?" I asked.

"Myself and my mate were out there, and we had the house about a hundred yards behind us at the end of a heavy rope moving right along, and then the wind came up."

"Oh?"

"And then the rope went slack. The Coast Guard station, pushed by the wind, was gaining on us. We'd been doing about five knots. No sense doing this anything but careful. But now, we accelerated to seven knots and it was still gaining. We went up to eight, then nine, and at ten knots we got the rope taut again. But the engine, under all this strain, was pulling pretty hard. So hard, it began smoking. We could see the entrance to Montauk Harbor about a mile ahead though. I thought, we'll make it. And then the wind picked up even more and once again the house started gaining on us. Fourteen knots was all we had. And it wasn't enough. The house came up fifty feet behind us and was still gaining, and now it was clear there was no way we were going to be able to make the turn into the harbor entrance with this house. In fact, the Coast Guard station was going to pass us and go right out to sea dragging us along behind. It was going to be a disaster.

"But then I thought of something. By this time, the house had pulled up even with us. And seeing it right up close, well, you know how fast your mind works when you are desperate. I told the mate to take the wheel and just keep her steady and close because I was going to jump across to it. And I did.

"I ran inside the house and, quick as I could, opened up all the windows on the ground floor, then ran upstairs and opened the windows on the second floor, and then ran upstairs to the low bunkhouse attic and opened the dormer windows up there. I could feel the breeze. The wind was blowing through. And then I felt a jolt as the rope went taut. The house had slowed and we were under tow again. I looked out. The boat was up ahead, the mate jumping up and down whooping and hollering. So that's how we came through the harbor entrance, with him up front and me upstairs in the house following him in. And there, as you see,"—he pointed out the window—"it is."

"That is a *great* story," I told him.

I had never, ever seen Darenberg smile like this before.

"I think about all this every time I see this picture," he said.

The following year, my dad was flipping through a book of family photographs and he came upon one of his fishing boat, tied up at the Marine Basin, with him and three of his fishing buddies, Brad Marmon, Sol Richer, and Doc Robbins, smiling out at the camera while holding a string of bluefish. Behind them, a bit out of focus, was the Marine Basin, the original one, I think.

"Now that trip, we played a little trick on Doc Robbins," he said. Dr. Robbins was the only doctor in town. He was also my doctor, the doctor I saw when I was home from school.

"After years of urging, we had finally persuaded him to come out on the boat. You know, he worked so hard, he had never been fishing."

"He looks pretty happy."

"He had a good time. But every time he had to do something, hook the bait or net the fish or something, he'd look up at us and ask if he was doing it right, and we'd tell him about your book."

"My book?"

"We'd say he looked pretty good, but if he really wanted to know the exact way to do it, he should read your book. Dan wrote the book, we'd say. *Dan's Fishing Guide.* So he thinks you wrote a book about fishing. The whole town knows you can't go in a boat. But Doc Robbins thinks you wrote a book about fishing."

"He believes it?"

"He never mentioned it to you?"

"I've only seen him twice in two years."

"Well don't ask him about it. Yes, he believes it. Two years, and we still tell him about your bestselling book and he still believes it. And nobody in town is saying a word."

Werewolf Path

~~~~~~

One Friday morning in the summer of 1968, I went into the living room of this little bungalow of a house I had bought on the Montauk Highway in East Hampton, turned on a Rolling Stones album loud, and rolled out an enormous piece of vellum—architect's paper—on the dining room table. The vellum—strong, white, and thin enough to see something under it that you might want to trace—was about three feet wide and nine feet long. It was the kind of paper architects use to draw plans on. It would last a long time.

Unrolled, it fell off the table at both ends, spilling onto the floor.

I was alone in the house at the time. I took a deep breath, rubbed my hands together, and began to assemble things. There was masking tape, to tape the vellum to the table and keep it from sliding around. There were pencils and erasers, there were four different atlases with roadmaps of the eastern end of Long Island, and there was a set of fine German drawing pens that you filled with black India ink and had to wash clean every day so they wouldn't clog. There were pens with

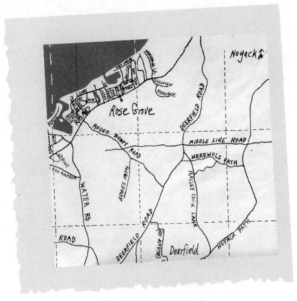

WEREWOLF PATH
(Courtesy of the author)

thick points and thin points. The thinnest point was little more than a needle. The manufacturer, Rapidograph, called it a Triple Zero. I was going to draw a roadmap and it was going to take several days.

About a week earlier, my dad had suggested that I take on this challenge.

"There's no gas station roadmap out here," he said to me. "Everybody's asking directions."

He reminded me of one of the funniest things that ever happened in the store in Montauk during the few years that I had worked there.

A man had pulled up in his car and come in to ask how long it would take to drive from here to the Montauk lighthouse. He had a pile of people in the car.

We told him. It's about four miles to the point. What we didn't tell him, because the lighthouse is so tall and obvious and it's right there at the very tip of Long Island by the side of the road, was that the road there in front of the lighthouse was a big loop. You got the view of the ocean on the south, then the lighthouse, and then as you went further around, the view of Long Island Sound on the north—it really was quite spectacular—and then you were on the same road you went in on, but coming back the other way.

Twenty minutes later, this guy was back, coming through the front door of the store, a bunch of worried faces in the car behind him.

He looked worried. "How much farther is it?" he wanted to know.

Anyway, the idea of drawing a map of the East End appealed to me for several reasons. The main one was that it would give me something else to sell in the fall when I went back to my advertisers to get them to pay for the ad they had run during the summer. I'd sell them a little ad on a strip that ran around the border of the map. I'd put little dots where they were on the actual map and have their names typeset next to the dots. I had worked out the numbers so it would make some money for me, and that would help me bankroll the winter. Then I could go back to the advertisers to sell them the newspaper ads again in the spring.

Another reason I liked the idea was that it was getting increasingly difficult to get free maps of any kind in gas stations. The attendants pumping gas were still wiping your front windshield and side mirrors and checking your oil and water under the hood, but those glossy, full-color roadmaps

that would have the name of the oil company on the front—
Amoco, Esso, Sinclair, Gulf—and which had been distributed
free for a generation, were being discontinued. It had not yet
occurred to any of the people running these companies that
they could successfully charge for a roadmap at a gas station,
as they do today. That would come later.

Finally, there was the whole business of the names of the
roads on the eastern end of Long Island. In Montauk, which
really had been built in the 1920s, most of the names were
pretty common, such as Westlake Drive, Essex Street, and
Grant Road. And these sorts of names I had gotten used
to growing up in New Jersey, where road names included
Ridgewood Road, Greenwood Drive, and Locust Avenue.

But from East Hampton to Westhampton, the names
were amazing. You'd make a turn and find yourself on Widow
Gavitz Road, or Abraham's Path, or Highway Behind the Pond.
Where the hell had these come from? They had come from
settlers who had given them names in the seventeenth century.

And so I began to draw. I started at one end of the vellum,
drawing the shoreline at Montauk Point and the loop of the
road out there. And from there I headed west. I consulted
some of the atlases and books that had roads of the area.
Several of these maps disagreed with one another, and so, in
the weeks before I'd started the drawing, I'd gone in my car
and driven out to see who was right, or play majority rules.
I had four books. If three agreed, that was it. Drawing the
map took me two and a half days.

I took many breaks, and found I could have a consider-
able amount of fun doing this drawing. Many of the roads
in the Hamptons at that time were unpaved and unnamed.

They were just "trustee" roads, two tracks through the woods, connecting one paved road with another. I would differentiate paved from not paved by making a solid line or dotted line. For example, there was a dotted line road that connected Springy Banks Road to Hands Creek Road. I'd name the dotted line road. Why not? I called it Lois Lane. In other places on the map, I named dirt roads Jeep's Folly, or Lost Cow's Journey. If you're looking at oddly named roads all over the place that were real, why not join in? And who names these things anyway? Why not me?

Little did I know that one of my names for a dirt road would stick. It's not quite as creative a name as some of the others, but there were so many that by the time I got to that one I was running low on ideas. It's called Werewolf Path, and it's in the Deerfield section of Southampton, just off Noyac Path, south of what is now named Ruggs Path but which, back then, I cheerfully named Uncle Ed's Romp, which didn't stick.

In any case, when I finished, early on Monday morning, I rolled up the map, put a rubber band around it, and put it into a closet where it would be safe. There was still a lot of work to be done to sell the ads, hire a printer, and get the thing done and distributed. The big cost, I soon learned, was in folding up the map to fit into a glove compartment. There was only one folding machine on all of Long Island that could handle something this big, and the owner knew it. He charged what the market would bear.

I printed fifteen thousand copies of that first roadmap and put them into general distribution throughout the Hamptons early in the spring of 1969. I put another one out the next year.

Everyone seemed to like them. And of course they were free.

Sometime in the early summer of the third year of the map, I got a phone call from Suzy Prudden.

Suzy had opened an exercise studio in Bridgehampton, on Butter Lane. I had gone to see her about an ad and we had become friends. She was about my age. And she was very pretty.

There was also a certain sadness about her. I couldn't quite pin it down, but at the time I speculated that perhaps she felt somewhat competitive with her very famous mother, Bonnie Prudden, and it seemed to get her back up.

I'd never met Bonnie Prudden, but I'd seen her on television. She'd starred in one of the first exercise programs on television. She had written books—ultimately there would be about seventeen books—and she had climbed mountain ranges, some of which had peaks named after her. Then she suffered a serious skiing accident. She broke her pelvis, and doctors had told her she would always walk with a limp, would never mountain climb again, and would never have children. But then she had Suzy, who was now sort of following in her mother's footsteps, but didn't really want you mentioning it to her. So I didn't.

"We're having a party," Suzy told me that day when she called up. "It's Saturday night. It will start around 9 p.m., after dinner, and then we'll just hang out on the deck with everybody for the rest of the evening."

Suzy's house was up in a heavily wooded section of the Hamptons known as Northwest. It would be dark after dinner. There would be crickets and fireflies out on the deck.

It would be a wonderful party. I'd been to her house once or twice, but always in somebody else's car, so I didn't know the way. So now, on the phone, I asked her where it was.

"Bon Pinck Way," she said. "You drive up Hands Creek to Eli Brook . . ."

"What number?"

"Seventeen."

"I'll find it."

I hung up. I'm the guy who drew the map, I thought to myself proudly. And I remembered Northwest being one of the most difficult areas to draw, with roads coming in at all different directions. I had even been up there, to Springy Banks Road and to Old Northwest Road and even to a road called Eli Brook and on to Hands Creek Road because that is where it went. I had it right. Many of the other maps were wrong.

And so Saturday night came, and off I went, into the darkness of Northwest, with the map of mine folded neatly in my glove compartment, to Suzy's house. And I got completely lost.

Several times, I pulled off to the side of the road to open my map, turn on the overhead light, and stare at what I had drawn. Was I crazy? In the dark, here, things seemed to come together differently than they did in the daytime. And what kind of name was Bon Pinck, anyway? I remembered thinking that when I drew it. The road was put in as part of a new development, all houses with decks and sliders and such, in the late 1950s, and some stupid developer had named the roads with these non-eighteenth-century names.

I stopped completely on a road with a sign that said it was Abigail Street. The developer's wife. Did you know that the town of Shirley, at the very entrance to the Hamptons, was named after some guy's wife? So here was Abigail Street and I was hungry and angry and getting angrier. And I would have to knock on a door. Because it was a successful development, there were plenty to knock on, but I didn't want to scare anybody and so I looked for one with a porch light on out front.

Finding one, I walked up the slate path and rang the bell. A woman holding a baby opened it part way.

"I'm sorry," I said. "But I'm lost."

She looked me over and opened the door a bit wider.

"I'm trying to find 17 Bon Pinck Way. I'm going to a dinner party there."

"I'm not exactly sure where that is," she began, "just wait a minute, I'll get a map." And she was gone.

Oh no, I thought.

And indeed, in just a moment, she was back without the baby, and was now unfolding the very map I had myself drawn, looking for the section that had Northwest on it, to provide me with as much help as she could.

"No, no!" I said.

"What?"

"That's *my* map. I *drew* that map. It's *wrong*."

"It is? It just came out."

"I know."

I find it somewhat painful to finish this story. What I had to do was invite myself in to use the phone, which was graciously allowed—and I called Suzy to ask her where Bon Pinck Way was, and she told me. I was late for the party, but then perked up out on the deck with some drinks and music and dancing.

I've never told this story before.

Sometimes, I drive up Noyac Road in Southampton to look at the road I named that became a real name. I look at the sign, and I imagine what might have gone on at the building department all those years ago.

"So you're here with these plans to ask us to consider a housing development."

"Yes sir."

"And you've got the name of the road right, Werewolf Path?"

"That's right. It's on the map."

"There's a legend connected with that going back to colonial times," the building inspector might have said.

"I know. We wouldn't think of changing it."

To get to Werewolf Path, you have to drive past another street name, which fizzled. The day I was drawing the map, I was putting in an unnamed dotted line between Head of Pond Road and Deerfield Road when the phone rang. The sound of it made me put a slight wiggle in the road where it was really straight.

The call was from Michael O'Donoughue, a guy whom I had gone to college with and who worked with me both on the college humor magazine and at the college radio station, where we had a program together. After graduation, he had changed his name. I knew him at college as simply Mike Donahue, and when he got a job with Grove Press doing cartoons for *Evergreen Magazine* (he was later at the *National Lampoon* magazine and even later than that at *Saturday Night Live*), he changed it to something that, he told me, deserved more respect. So Donahue became O'Donaghue.

"Hi."

"Donahue?"

"Yeah. When are you coming into the City?"

Donahue had a loft on Spring Street. That section of the city was practically abandoned back then. I put my pen down, and we talked for a while, and I told him what I was doing and how he had just made me put a squiggle into a road.

"Why don't you name it for me?" he asked.

"Okay."

And so I did. For many years, through fifteen or twenty years of printings, this dotted line road was known as Michael O'Donaghue's Road until some bastard bought it, paved it, put some houses alongside it, and named it Blank Lane.

What the hell kind of name is Blank Lane?

Lazy Lucy

~~~~~~

In early September of 1968, I drove out to Montauk to talk to my dad about what I ought to do that winter. We met in the pharmacy late in the afternoon.

"I don't have any plans," I told him.

"Do what I do," he said. "Things get quiet. Your mom and I go to Mexico for four months and we leave Harvey here to run the store."

Harvey was the year-round hired pharmacist. He stole, my dad found out much later. Dad said it was worth it.

At our meeting, we reviewed what I had accomplished and what I had not accomplished. I had started the summer newspaper in Montauk in 1960 and it had grown and grown. In 1966, I had added a second summer paper in East Hampton. And in 1967, I had added a third summer paper in Southampton and a fourth summer paper in Westhampton Beach.

The winters had not been so successful. After finishing up my undergraduate studies with a degree in 1961, I floundered through graduate school at Harvard for three years, finally withdrawing without a degree. In the winter of '64–'65, I had worked as a clerk in the city room of the *New York Times* but got fired after four days. In the winter of '65–'66, I had worked at an ad agency, but when a new boss came in he fired the whole team, including me. And later that winter, I had helped found a hippie newspaper in Manhattan called the *East Village Other*, but on short notice had run off to St. Thomas with a girl.

"Seems like the only thing you know how to do is run a newspaper," Dad said.

"In St. Thomas, they have a newspaper, but it's very bad. Maybe I could publish one there."

"I think," my dad the guru said, "you ought to stick with what you've got. How about extending the paper a little bit into the fall? And then starting a little earlier next spring? You could expand on your success here. Then go off to St. Thomas in the wintertime as a vacation."

"I could put out two editions this September, and then two editions in April and early May," I said.

"There you go."

The next day, I went to my office, this huge old carriage house behind a real estate office on Gay Lane in East Hampton. It was light and airy, about thirty feet by forty, with big windows all around. I wondered if my dad was right. So I made some phone calls to the customers asking if they would be willing to continue their ads for an extra two issues. About half said yes.

Earlier that summer, I had joined with many other publishing pioneers in producing my newspapers using "cold type." This was an entirely new method of doing things. With the old method, in existence for a thousand years (or at least since 1886, when the first Linotype was installed in the *New York Tribune*), you'd produce a newspaper by pouring hot lead into the top of a Linotype machine and, after it streamed into little brass slots to cool into letters and words, form it into single pages bordered by a frame called a chase. The chase with the lead in it could weigh more than eighty pounds and could only be moved a few feet to a flatbed press on the premises with great effort. All this could only be accomplished in a print shop. I had been using one forty miles away.

The new equipment seemed like a miracle. There were now electric typewriters where typists could, right in your office, produce letters of different sizes and different styles just by changing a small plastic ball. You'd type on regular paper, cut the paper into strips with a scissors, paste them onto boards with rubber cement, one board being one page, and then have a courier deliver the boards to a print shop. The print shop would photograph the pages, burn the image onto a curved aluminum plate, lock the aluminum plate into a rotary press, and then print out a newspaper ten times faster than with the flatbed.

They called this method "cold type." What a treat, being able to control what the paper would look like right in the carriage house in East Hampton.

There was only one problem. If somebody brought in a photograph and wanted that on a particular page in the paper, you'd need to enlarge it or reduce it in a darkroom, with photo paper and chemicals, to make it the exact size you wanted, then dry out the photo paper and glue it into its place. And we didn't have a darkroom.

I could use somebody else's darkroom, which was expensive. I could build a darkroom in the carriage house, which was expensive. Or I could just bring the photos into the printer and let him do it, which was also expensive. And in addition, it would mean spending the day at the printer again to make sure it was done right.

Before the summer had arrived, I solved this problem when I encountered an architect named Gene Futterman at the bar at Bobby Van's in Bridgehampton.

"We have something I'd bet would work for you. It's called a 'Lazy Lucy,'" he said. "It's a metal box about the size of a stove. Architects use it in their offices to resize architectural plans or photographs. It's not expensive."

The next day, I went with Futterman to his office and he demonstrated it. He pulled down the shades. "It has to be dark," he said, "or pretty dark. But not as dark as a darkroom."

He put a photo on a platform on the bottom, slid a piece of photo paper onto a flat glass plate on the top, and closed a lid over it. Then, after making a few adjustments with some metal knobs to get a camera inside focused on the photo, he flipped a switch. A fan inside the Lazy Lucy whirred, a bright light on the camera went on, and Futterman counted out some seconds—two, three, four, five, six—and then he turned the whole thing off. He removed the photo paper, slid it into a metal cylinder with chemicals inside, let it develop, and then, at the other end, slid it out. And there it was, a bit damp, but a picture resized and ready for a newspaper.

"Cool," I told him as he shook it to get it completely dry. "How much does a Lazy Lucy cost?"

LAZY LUCY
(Courtesy *Dan's Papers*)

"They're cheap compared to a darkroom, that's for sure. I could find a used one for you for about five hundred dollars."

"Sold," I said.

When it arrived, I tried to set it up in our carriage house, but soon realized that we could never get the room dark enough. There were too many giant windows. And none had shades. We'd need a fortune in window treatments, unless we wanted to black out the windows, which I didn't want to do.

Where it wound up for the summer was in the two-car garage of my house, about three miles away. Electricity in this garage consisted of a wall switch leading to a single light fixture on the ceiling with a lightbulb screwed into it. I took the bulb out, screwed in an extender with two female sockets and a pull chain, put the lightbulb in the end of that, and then plugged the Lazy Lucy into one of the sockets on the extender. I flipped the switch to on. It would work.

We gathered up photos in batches and, once a week just after sunset, went over there and developed them all at once. As Futterman had said, it worked.

The two editions of the paper I published in the fall both featured two wonderful events. The first was the auctioning off of the giant oceanfront mansion, owned by the Minskoff family, on twenty-four acres abutting Lily Pond Lane in East Hampton. It sold for $225,000.

The second, out a week later, featured an account of a high-speed auto race at the Bridgehampton Race Circuit. Down in the pits, I took close-up photos of the cars, the auto mechanics, and racing cars, and the drivers, such as Sam Posey, Dan Gurney, and Bruce McLaren, in their fireproof uniforms, all sweaty and exhausted and covered with grease. Back out into the race, the cars screamed around at one hundred and fifty miles an hour. What a day that was.

I took these pictures to the photo shop, and after they were developed, took them back to the house and tried to develop them in the Lazy Lucy. It didn't work. I called Futterman.

"It's a chilly night," he said after I described the problem. "And your chemicals are too cold. Turn up the heat there."

"There is no heat," I said. "It's a garage."

"Well take the whole rig and do it in your house."

"I don't want to disassemble this thing and drag it into the house. I have to do this now. I need the pictures done for the morning."

"Then you'll have to get some heat out there, or some other way to warm the chemicals."

That, as it turned out, resulted in one of the most remarkably awful evenings of my life.

I had an electric heater in the house. Also a hot plate, an extension cord, a clothesline, some clothespins, and a teapot. I brought them all out to the garage. It was now 10 p.m. and it was a very chilly night.

And here was my plan. Wearing a sweater against the cold, I would use the heater to heat the garage where the Lazy Lucy and the box of photo paper were, put the chemicals in the teapot, and heat them on the hot plate. Then I'd develop and resize the pictures on the Lazy Lucy. Then I'd hang the photos on the clothesline with clothespins, to dry.

Between the hot plate, the Lazy Lucy, and the heater, of course, there were three different plugs, but the extender above the lightbulb with the pull chain only had two different sockets, which is why I had brought out the extension cord.

I plugged everything in, turned everything on, and bang, blew out the fuse in the house controlling the electricity to the garage.

I went into the house, replaced the fuse, and went about figuring out what would work fine and what would overload the system. Five blown fuses later, I had figured out a way to do this.

Over the next two hours, I produced eleven pictures. I treasure these pictures as they appeared in the paper, all bright and smart, to this day. Here is the procedure I followed for each one.

1. Turn on the light.
2. Fill the teapot with cold chemicals.
3. Put the teapot on the hot plate.
4. Turn off the overhead light.
5. Turn on the hot plate.
6. Turn on the electric floor heater by the photo paper.
7. Wait five minutes for everything to cook.
8. Turn off the hot plate.
9. Turn on the overhead light.
10. Pour the chemicals into the developing cylinder from the teapot.
11. Take out a piece of photo paper from the bag next to the heater.
12. Put the piece of paper in the top of the Lazy Lucy.
13. Put a photograph of Bruce McLaren (or Sam Posey, or Dan Gurney) in the bottom of the Lazy Lucy.
14. Turn off the floor heater.
15. Turn off the overhead light.
16. Turn on the Lazy Lucy.
17. Count slowly to seven.
18. Turn off the Lazy Lucy.
19. Slide the photo paper into the cylinder.
20. Turn on the overhead light.
21. Turn on the floor heater.
22. Take the photo paper out of the cylinder and clip it onto the clothesline to dry.
23. Turn off the overhead light.
24. Pour the chemicals back into the teapot, put the teapot on the hot plate, and turn the hot plate on.

25. Wait five minutes in the dark.
26. Turn off the teapot on the hot plate.
27. Turn on the overhead light.
28. Repeat as necessary.

It took eighteen pieces of film, six of which were mistakes, to develop the eleven photos correctly. Surely it was like patting your head and rubbing your tummy, then patting your tummy and rubbing your head. When I was done, I unplugged everything, went back in the house and fell onto the sofa where I slept until morning.

The next day, the Lazy Lucy got covered with a sheet for the winter. A month later, I was in the Canary Islands. In the spring, for April and May, the Lazy Lucy got its own bedroom in the house.

My friends coming over wondered what the hell that was all about.

Dick Sandford

~~~~~~

In 1969, I bought a house on Main Street in downtown Bridgehampton to turn it into the offices of *Dan's Papers*. It came about this way. I had started a third edition of the paper in Southampton the year before. The carriage house in East Hampton was now not big enough for all of us. Perhaps I ought to look to find something in Bridgehampton. East Hampton would be on one side, Southampton on the other. It would be a perfect location.

One day, a friend told me his uncle might be willing to sell his house.

"It's right on the highway," he told me. "It's a private home and the guy hasn't put it on the market. But he told me if somebody offered him $38,000 for it, he'd part with it. But it would have to be $38,000. Not a penny less."

I tried to bargain with him.

"Look," I said to Mr. Dumpkowski, for that was his name. "There's no broker involved. A broker would get $2,000. So I'll pay you $36,000. Okay? That's $38,000 to you."

The elderly Mr. Dumpkowski, who, as it happened, was in his morning bathrobe and had not yet put in his teeth, tapped one of the Greek columns.

"Rock solid," he whistled. "$38,000."

"Okay, $38,000," I said.

At the closing, I discovered that the water there came from the Bridgehampton Water Authority. You would pay for it monthly.

"I thought everybody had wells," I said to one of the two lawyers. "With a well, water is free."

I had never paid for water before.

"It's city water on Main Street," Frank Dumpkowski said. "You get it from Mr. Sandford."

"Maybe I'll have a well dug in the back," I said.

My lawyer spoke up. "You better do it fast," he said, "because tomorrow, if you don't sign up with the Water Authority, there won't be any water there when you turn on the faucet."

I looked at Dumpkowski. No offer for water was forthcoming. "Well, I'll meet this Mr. Sandford, whoever he is."

"Atta boy," said my lawyer.

After the signing, I had lunch with my friend Elaine Benson, who owned an art gallery about five houses down from my new office home. It was something of a celebration.

"My treat," she said. We were at the Candy Kitchen Luncheonette, further down Main Street.

She told me that the house was absolutely perfect for a newspaper office. Her house, a big old Victorian about the same size as mine, was an art gallery on the first floor. She and her husband occupied the apartments upstairs.

We talked about new developments in the town and how, though it was a farming town with a feed store, a hardware store, and several gas stations, there were slowly but surely inroads being made by avant garde artsy types from out of the area. Finally, our conversation came around to water and Mr. Sandford.

"As you know, we bought our building three years ago," Elaine said. "He came around. And I told him we wanted him to just transfer over the account from the people we bought our place from. He said he doesn't do that. New people, new account, is what he said."

"Was that a problem?"

"I had been warned about him. His family goes back to the Revolution. He lives right there." She pointed to the Sandford house. It was a white house with a porch, three houses up from hers, and just next to mine.

"People told me if he likes you he charges you one thing; if he doesn't like you, he charges you another. You get the bill once a quarter."

"And he liked you?"

"No. He charged us $50 a quarter. Everybody else he charges maybe $12 or $15."

"How do you know that?"

"I asked. Or anyway I asked a few people I knew. I didn't want it getting back to him that I was asking around. He might have raised the price even higher."

"I guess I should go see him," I said.

"He'll come to you. Probably before the day is out. He knows what's going on. And don't worry. He'll probably *like* you."

Around three, back up the street at my new office, there was a knock at the front door. I had cleaned up a bit. But the knock still made me jump. I knew it was him. There was an old beat-up panel truck parked outside. I'd seen it around town.

Dick Sandford was tall, a bit stooped over, about fifty years old, and wore blue overalls and a blue cap that made him look like a railroad man. He had a long, sad face. And that was it. "Water company," he said.

He took off his cap and looked past me to scan the interior of the house. Then he made a motion with his head which was a clear request. Could he come in?

I motioned him in with a big sweep of my arm.

"Changin' anything?" he asked. He was already past me and walking along, talking to the wall in front of him.

"Nope," I said.

He walked through the living room. No water. He walked through the dining room (also no water) and then into the kitchen, where there was water. Then he found the lone bathroom on that floor.

"Still the same bathroom upstairs in the hall?" he asked, following the pipes from the toilet that went up through the ceiling.

"Yes."

"And the spigot outside where it was before?"

I looked at him anxiously and nodded.

"I think it's fine," he said. He took out a pad and pencil. "Just spell your name for me." Then he licked his pencil.

I walked him to the front door and then all the way out to his truck. I thought things had gone well. But maybe not. Perhaps I should have offered him something to eat or drink? He had lingered for a moment by his truck, eager, it seemed, to engage me in a little conversation. And I obliged him, leaning on the window of his truck as he leaned on it.

"How much will it be?" I asked.

"Oh I don't know." He looked up at the sky. Then he looked down and spat on the ground.

He did not seem to be in any hurry.

"Want to see where the pipes meet up?" he asked.

"Sure."

"It's right over here," he said. He pointed at a round metal plate on the asphalt apron of the street just in front of his truck. Then, from the back of his truck he slid out what looked like a long, metal crowbar and walked with it over to the metal plate.

The plate, about the size of a dinner plate, had the words BRIDGEHAMPTON WATER AUTHORITY in raised letters on it. The words were formed in a circle completely surrounding a small slot next to a bolt in the center of it.

Sandford set the crowbar against a tree, squatted down, and with a pliers he had in his overalls, removed the nut. Then he stood up, put the business end of the crowbar in the slot, and, with one motion, lifted it up and placed it alongside.

"In there," he said, indicating that we both squat down, which we did. He took out a flashlight and shone it down into the darkness to something wet and metallic.

"There it is," he said, the light wavering on it.

"Yup," I said.

Sandford put everything back after that, returned everything to his truck, and then left. And I waited three months.

Occasionally, Elaine Benson would ask me if I got the water bill, and I told her I had not. Then she'd change the subject.

When it came in the morning mail at the office three months later, with the address on the front handwritten in the same pencil writing he had used when he paid me a visit, I opened it with quivering hands. And I looked.

My personal office was upstairs, in what had been one of the bedrooms. I went up there and dialed Elaine.

"I got the bill," I said.

"And so?"

"He likes me," I said. "Thirteen dollars a month."

There was a silence.

"I don't get it," she said. "Why do you suppose he doesn't like me?"

"I don't know," I said. We discussed that it might be because she was Jewish. But I was Jewish. Maybe it was because she was a woman. Who knew?

"Maybe he just doesn't like art," I said gleefully.

We decided we really didn't know. Perhaps the discrepancy was because of something he ate or something.

Dick Sandford provided us with water for the next twenty years, and to a certain very limited extent, I got to know him. He was, I was told, a very strict, very churchgoing man, with a wife and daughter who was, at the point I met her in our yard shortly after we moved in, about eleven.

I never did see him out at any of the local events during those years, not at the Fourth of July Parade in Southampton, not at any of the pancake breakfasts at the firehouse, not anywhere. I did see him, pretty often, out on the street some place or another with his crowbar, always with that same old truck, working at something with the pipes underground in town. He always wore the exact same thing. And he always worked completely alone. I thought he wore those overalls all six days of the week, and then on Sunday, he probably had his suit for church. But I never really knew.

At night, when I'd leave work, I'd often see that old truck parked right in front of his house next to mine. Hedges separated us. But I could see a few lights on inside. I imagined him in there with his wife and daughter, and I imagined him very quiet but very strict. But I never really knew that. Sort of.

One day a few months after I met him, a strange thing happened. At two in the morning, a vicious lightning storm passed over the community and woke me at my home, five miles away. I watched it from a window for half an hour, then had trouble getting back to sleep. At seven, with the sun rising, I drove to work to find Sandford's daughter curled up on the sofa in our front office fast asleep. There was a blanket over her.

I woke her up, gently, and she sat up and got her bearings and said she had been very scared by the lightning storm, saw the light on in our office, and so had come over, hoping somebody was there. At that time, I employed a man named Ben Lynchman as a handyman. He lived way up the island and was an older retired man, and on some nights he would sleep in our attic, on a cot up there that I had set out. He had been there that night, and I knew he was still there because, out back, I had seen his car when I had come in.

I wondered where her parents were, but didn't think it was my place to ask. In any case, she said she should get back to her house now, and so she got up and just left.

Up in the attic, Ben, who I also woke up, told me the exact same story. He said he thought it was strange too, but he said she was shivering so that he had held her and rocked her there on the sofa until she fell asleep.

"She's eleven years old. She was terrified. I couldn't send her out into that, and I wasn't going out into it either. When she fell asleep, I went up to the attic. What was I supposed to do?" he asked. I told him I didn't know. And I didn't.

The Sandfords lived in that house on Main Street next to mine for many, many years. Once, I heard, the Suffolk County Water Authority had made Dick Sandford an offer that he couldn't refuse. And he refused.

Some years after that, Mr. Sandford passed away, and though Mrs. Sandford lived on there, the water company was sold to the Suffolk County Water Authority. Years later, Mrs. Sandford died and somebody else bought that house, and that was the end of that.

Everything changes. Nothing remains the same. Except maybe *Dan's Papers*.

Charlie Vanderveer

~~~~~~

In the early 1970s one of my favorite things to do was to go up to Charlie and Gypsy Vanderveer's 300-acre farm on Scuttlehole Road in Bridgehampton. The Vanderveers lived just a mile away from me and my wife, up a dirt driveway past their potato fields to an old dusty farmhouse, where there was always something really odd or hilarious or strange going on. Charlie had, shall we say, an inquiring mind, and I found myself enormously entertained by it.

One summer evening, we went up there for dinner. Gypsy was a good cook. We were told to show up at seven. There would be ten of us, myself and my wife, our two kids (ages four and two), and their four (also four and two, but also two daughters twelve and ten). It would be a family evening.

We did the best we could getting everybody ready, but wound up coming twenty minutes late. When we pulled up to the house, a cloud of dust from the driveway trailing behind us, I noticed that all the lights were on inside, but everything was very quiet. This seemed strange. Inside I could see everybody setting the table and setting up for dinner. But something was amiss. We walked to the front door. Beside it was their television, all smashed up in the bushes. This did not look good. We rang the bell and Lowie, the twelve-year-old, opened the door. She had this very strange look on her face, as if she was spooked.

"Hi," I said. She nodded. She motioned us inside and then followed us in and sat down quickly at her place at the table with a plop. Gypsy was at the stove. The food was about ready to be served. We had just made it.

Charlie walked into the dining room from the bathroom, wiping his hands on a towel. He was a huge man, six foot five, maybe three hundred pounds. He had wavy, very unkempt black hair, a thick nose, a broad face, and very prominent eyebrows. He wore his usual flannel shirt and suspenders.

"What's with the TV?" I asked.

All four of their kids were lined up sitting in their seats at the table, their hands on the table, looking straight ahead.

"Good thing you didn't come a few minutes earlier," Gypsy said from the stove. She did not look up.

"Yeah," said Bondie, age ten. "You'd a been hit."

At that, everybody started snickering.

Gypsy explained further.

"The food was ready. I saw the dust coming up the drive. I called everybody to come down from upstairs. I kept calling and calling, but they wouldn't come. So I told Charlie to do something."

"We were watching TV," said Lowie. "It was cartoons."

CHARLIE VANDERVEER WITH HIS KIDS
(Courtesy of the Vanderveer Family)

"You're not watching TV now," Charlie said.

"Yeah," Lowie said, "because you came up and threw it out the window."

Charlie sat down. He waved a fork. "Okay, everybody, let's eat."

And so we did.

After dinner, with the kids playing in the living room and my wife and Gypsy cleaning up, Charlie showed me the toilet seat that had been painted by Willem de Kooning. It was in a large open cardboard box on the floor. It was among many cardboard boxes on the floor. At this particular time, Charlie Vanderveer, in addition to running his farm, was the town auctioneer. He'd clean out houses being sold. He'd tag items and bring them over to the church for the auction. His two older daughters would hold stuff high while he sold it to the highest bidder. He worked at high speed, a man in charge, a man possessed. I loved watching him.

Some things he'd buy himself. He had stuff not only in the living room, but also on the floor and shelves in the dining room, in the three closets in the bedrooms upstairs, and in much of an old front room they called a parlor. There was more stuff outside, all around this hundred-year-old farmhouse.

"I'm keeping this," he said, leaning over and pulling the toilet seat out of its box. "Bought it for fifty dollars."

It was made of wood and it had abstract expressionist splash painting all over it. It sure looked like it could have been painted by Willem de Kooning.

"Where did you get it?" I asked.

"At the old Herrick house on the Montauk Highway."

"Which one is that?"

"You know it. It's that old falling down Victorian with the porte cochere on the north side, down the road east of the monument."

"You went in that mess?"

"It's been sold. New people coming in to fix it up. So I went in there with a crew to clean it out. It was a lot of work. We found this seat in the old outhouse out back."

"What makes it a de Kooning?"

Charlie, who had been out in Bridgehampton for many years before I moved there, knew everything and everybody. Half a dozen painters rented there one summer in the 1950s, he'd once told me. De Kooning and his wife Elaine, the

Slivkas, Abraham Rattner, and Bob Freedman, the art critic for the *New York Times*. Those who painted, painted out in the barn or in the bedrooms. They'd fought. They'd partied. He'd joined them sometimes.

"Rose Slivka told me about this," Charlie said. "She'll vouch for it. De Kooning, one night, just for fun, took some of his paints out to the outhouse and painted up the toilet seat and the whole interior of the outhouse."

"And Slivka remembers this?"

"She sat on it while it was still wet, she says. I have to tell you, you can see where the rest of the outhouse got painted, too. It's pretty faded and peeling now. But not the toilet seat." He patted it. "I cleaned it up," he grinned. "You ought to write an article about it in the paper."

The next day, I did.

One night, dinner was at our house. We had bought a big house on a residential street in Bridgehampton called Lumber Lane, a walk from Main Street, by this time. Gypsy showed up in their regular car with the kids, but no Charlie. I was out on the front porch when she pulled up.

"Charlie will be right along," she said, rolling down the window. "He wants to show you something."

As she and all the kids climbed out of the big car, a tiny, tiny bright green 1950 Nash Metropolitan pulled up into the driveway. This already was a twenty-year-old car. You know the Mini? Imagine something even smaller than a Mini, a car that Donald Duck might drive. The Nash Motor Car Company made these for three years in the early 1950s. It pulled up, this old automobile with the little tiny tailfins,

CHARLIE VANDERVEER
(Photo by the author)

and out of it slowly unfolded six-foot-five Charlie, first an arm, then a leg, then another arm and another leg and a head.

"I wanted you to see I could do this," he said when he had gotten his whole self out to stand on the lawn.

"You gonna keep it?"

"Naah."

The year of the thrown-out television was the year that Charlie turned one of his barns into a preschool. He and Gypsy had their two little ones at the Hampton Day School on Butter Lane the year before, but he didn't like how they were being taught there. He and Gypsy were on the board. There was a big fight at a board meeting. They had stormed out. They'd start their *own* school, they said as they left, and they did.

My daughter, when she was four, went there for a semester because Charlie asked that we send her. He also asked that my wife work as one of the monitors. One day, I was a monitor. I still recall it. The teacher went off to the main house for something, leaving me in charge of twelve kids playing with blocks. My job was to make sure nobody got hurt or fled the building. During that time, I realized the importance of seeing to it that my daughter did not get hurt or flee the building and, while I was at it, I might as well also keep an eye on the rest of them too, whoever they were.

The following year, everybody was back at the Hampton Day School.

Sometimes I'd go up there just to ride around on a tractor with Charlie as he planted or plowed. I knew he had inherited the farm from his father. He once told me about that.

"Dad farmed about half of Queens," Charlie told me. "It had been handed down from father to son from the days when New York was New Amsterdam. Anyway, the farm was enormous. We were very rich. We had a chauffeur and several open cars. Then Dad had a heart attack. I was ten. He recovered, but the doc told him he shouldn't work so hard. So he had the farm subdivided into housing developments. He built thousands of houses, houses so close together that if you wanted to bring your lawnmower from the front yard to the back, you'd have to take it through the living room instead of along the side yard.

"After he did that, the doc told him he was too sedentary. He needed to go back to farming. Mom didn't want to do that, so Dad decided to just pick up and buy this farm here in Bridgehampton and move out. It was 1945. I was fifteen. I came out here with him as his helper. There was no running water, no electricity, no heat. We chopped wood for heat in the winter, used kerosene lanterns. There was a well not far from the house. We carried water."

"Potatoes?"

"First year, turnips. That failed. Next year, potatoes. Every year after that, potatoes."

There was a big wooden shower in the middle of the farm field. It consisted of a wooden enclosure, wooden planks on the ground, a big metal bucket of water overhead on some beams across the top, and a rope. On a hot day, you'd pull the rope and some holes in the bottom of the bucket opened and the warm water heated by the sun would sprinkle down. At the end of the day sometimes, we'd get naked, the two of us, and take turns in the shower. Two grown-up heterosexuals, laughing and giggling.

"What's the biggest auction you ever had," I asked one day out in the fields.

"The Rose mansion in Southampton, no doubt about it. It took me six days to just mark everything. Old Mrs. Rose collected everything. Toothpaste. Cans of soup. Whatever. And not just everything, but two of everything. She'd go shopping with one of her servants and whatever she'd buy she'd get two. The auction itself took three days. You know what I got?"

"I can hardly wait."

"I'll show them to you. You know that porno woman Marilyn Chambers from the green door movie? And how she had been a model and her face was on the Ivory Snow soap flakes box before she went into porno so they fired her? Well, I've got two of those boxes. From 1959. She was eighteen. Neither ever opened."

At the most northerly end of Charlie's farm, there was a hollow about a hundred acres in size. Charlie had it planted in potatoes, but sometimes he'd be riding his tractor through it and he would look longingly at it, imagining the hollow as an open-air stadium where he could hold a rock concert similar to the one at Yasgur's farm in Woodstock in 1969. I kept steering him away from that idea. The town, I knew, would never allow it.

At first, Charlie thought he'd just hang onto the toilet seat for a while. De Kooning was in his early eighties at this time.

"Nothing personal," Charlie said when we talked again about the toilet seat, "but things artists do are worth more when they are dead."

"De Koonings are already selling for hundreds of thousands," I said.

"I know," Charlie said. "But it is a toilet seat."

After my article about it came out in the paper—it included a picture of a smiling Charlie peering through it—he had a different idea.

"Rose Slivka called. She wants to partner with me because of your article. Says she told me about it so she's entitled to some of it. Matter of fact, now we're four partners. It's a committee. Maybe we'll make a corporation. Four people at half a million bucks, it's still a lot of money."

Once up at Charlie's house, I came upon two entire shelves of *English Country Magazine*, in chronological order, for the prior four years. Came from somebody's house, obviously.

"You know what's in the most recent issue?" Charlie asked, watching me flipping through one. He took it out and turned to the page. "They've got this entire barn just outside of Chichester, England, for sale. Built in 1542. I'm thinking of buying it. They take it apart over there, ship the pieces over here, I assemble it on our property."

"Why?"

"Because I don't like those holier-than-thou Ladies Village Improvement Society women with the blue hair in East Hampton. So what if they own those old saltbox houses from the 1600s. They think those are the oldest houses in the state? Not when I'm done with them."

Charlie never got around to doing that, though.

Then, a few years later, came the news about Arlan Ettinger. Ettinger owned Guernsey Auctions, a Manhattan company that held the largest auctions in the city of New York. He'd rent one of the big armories in Manhattan. In it, he'd auction off the entire contents of the *Queen Mary*. Or the stuff found in the attic of Jacqueline Kennedy's apartment after she died. He was famous in New York. And he had a house in Westhampton Beach.

The news was that he was going to hold a big auction with thousands of paintings from hundreds of abstract expressionists from the Hamptons. Potentially there could be a sale of $50 million. It was getting a lot of press in the newspapers.

"He's gonna auction off the toilet seat," Charlie told me.

Charlie was showing me his new collection of homing pigeons at this particular time. He'd built a coop in the barn next to the old preschool and he had thirty pigeons, all of whom he had named. They were all cooing and bobbing and weaving, anxious to get at the corn from the master.

"What you gonna sell the toilet seat for?" I asked.

"Arlen says fifty thousand and up. Under that, no sale. This one with the hook beak is the prize winner," he said. It looked at me with yellow eyes. "They flew to Linden, New Jersey, two days ago," he said. "This guy won first prize. Did I tell you what happened with Billy DePetris last night?"

"No."

Billy DePetris owned a bar in town.

"You see way down there by the road at the end of the field where there's the berm?"

"Where the tractor turns and the dirt piles up?"

"Yeah."

"What are all those tire tracks in there?"

"From the crane, getting the car out of the field. I wake up this morning and there's this big white Cadillac convertible plopped in the mud about fifty yards into the potato field. I get dressed and walk down to it and behind the steering wheel, snoring away, is Billy DePetris."

"He drove into the potato field?"

"No. He flew. He came up Lumber Lane, must have been after he closed the bar in the middle of the night, and he must have fallen asleep at the wheel with his foot on the accelerator. Was going ninety miles an hour when he hit the berm."

"How do you know that?"

"Police pointed it out to me. No tracks. Splat. Did the math."

"He okay?"

"Oh yeah. Very well rested."

Charlie and I drove Charlie's pickup truck into the city to opening night of the big auction at the Sixty-Fifth Street Armory on Park Avenue. This was in 1989. Gypsy wanted no part of it. My wife wasn't interested either.

On the way, rumbling down the Long Island Expressway, I asked him what it was like growing up in Queens.

"Well, we were rich," he said, "like I told you. I went to private school. In my senior year, I had a motorcycle, a Harley."

"Of course. Did you ever have to get a job?"

"I was a roofer, once."

"A roofer?"

"They were building Levittown. About four hundred houses I think it was, all at the same time. Just after the war, for all the returning vets. I had a friend who worked there. He said you ought to come down here and see this. There's about a thousand of us kids building all this. So I drove down on my Harley. I was eighteen at the time. And we were standing around talking—he was a carpenter and they let him take a break for a bit because I came there—and we're talking and suddenly there is this whooshing sound and a thump and right next to me there is this guy with a tool belt lying on the ground moaning. He'd been up on the roof.

"We called the foreman over. People gathered around. Somebody said we ought to call an ambulance. And the foreman said, 'All right, all right, who here knows how to do roofing?' And no hands went up. So I raised mine. He asked me my name. I told him. So the foreman, he bends down and unhitches the big leather belt with the tools on it this guy was wearing and handed it to me. 'You're hired,' he said. 'Break's over. Get up there.'"

We howled.

"Did you hear what happened last Sunday with that shower I have in the field?" he continued.

"No."

"Most of the farmers out here, as you know, bring up black migrant workers in the fall for the harvest. Well, I don't do that anymore. I have Mexican workers come out from Queens. They're wonderful people. They live here through the harvest, and every Sunday we make it Mexican day. We have a big party. Music, dancing, food, the works.

"So on Monday, the day after one of these parties, I'm in this shower and I look out and see across the field this cloud of dust from behind a car coming up the driveway. Who could this be? They get closer, and then they pull right up to me there in the shower and I see it's the pastors and ministers of each of the four churches in town. It's the council of churches. They stop. And they just sit in their car. 'What can I do for you?' I ask. 'We've been told that you are having your farmhands work on Sunday, on the Lord's Day,' one of them says. 'And we don't think you should do that.'

"So I think about this and I say 'let me tell you about this' and I open the door and walk over dripping wet and buck naked and boy you should see how fast they got that car in reverse and burned rubber backing down the driveway. They never came back."

About five thousand people attended opening day at the armory. The toilet seat did not sell that day, though. In fact, it didn't sell at all. But it did get a lot of publicity in the newspapers.

Henry Geldzahler, the former curator of twentieth-century art at the Metropolitan Museum, was quoted in *Newsday* in an article by Karin Lipson.

"We don't know if de Kooning said it was art," he said. "We do know that his wife Elaine did not like the idea. But I will say it does have some value. It's not the equivalent of another toilet seat. It is somewhere between a toilet seat and a painting."

Lipson also interviewed Michael Covett, an art collector and recording industry executive. "If you close the holes," he said, referring to the outhouse, "it's a painting. If he had just been looking to paint an outhouse, he could have painted it white."

Ten years later, I was having dinner with my twenty-year-old son at Bobby Van's in Bridgehampton and there, a few tables away, was Charlie, having dinner with his twenty-year-old son, Stuyvie, the one who was a preschooler when Charlie threw the television out the window. I hadn't seen Charlie in a few months, and I thought isn't this sweet, two father-and-son dinners, and I waved at him.

Charlie came over and stood at the side of our table as people sometimes do in restaurants.

"Have you heard?" he asked.

"About what?"

"I went to the doctor last Thursday and he told me I have six months to live."

"Stop joking."

"No, I'm serious."

"You can't be serious."

"I have lymphoma. He just told me that, just like that. I have lymphoma and I have just six months to live."

I stared at him.

"What are you doing about it?" I asked.

"What do you mean what am I doing about it?"

"Are you going to have treatment?"

"No. If it's time, it's time."

"Charlie, that's crazy."

"No it's not."

"You've got to do something about this. Get medical treatment." I began to cry. "I don't believe this."

"Look, you have your lifestyle. I have my lifestyle. So when it's over, it's over. If I can't be me, if I can't have my lifestyle, then I'm done. I've had my life. It's been wonderful."

Tears rolled down my cheeks. My son looked at me in amazement. Charlie tousled my hair.

"Look I've got to get back to my son," he said. "You'll be fine. We're talking about arrangements."

And then he was headed back to his table where I now noticed that his son looked exactly, *exactly*, like him. Six foot five, the whole thing. But no bushy eyebrows. Not yet.

I didn't see Charlie after that, for a while anyway. I found it too upsetting. But one day, about three months later, a friend called and said Charlie wouldn't have much more time, and I ought to go see him. And so I did.

The house was a mess. Charlie was in a bathrobe, and he sat on his bed with his head propped up, but otherwise seemed perfectly fine. His girlfriend was not there—he and Gypsy had split up years before—but a woman, apparently a nurse, was there, and she went off to get a Coca-Cola for me when Charlie asked what I wanted.

"You look fine," I said.

"Well, I'm pretty good. I sleep a lot. I have to be careful when I walk around. If I bump into a tree, apparently, I'll die. Can't stop the bleeding when it starts. Big problem."

He laughed for a moment. Then a drip of blood appeared under his right nostril. Charlie stopped it with his hand.

"I'll get the nurse," I said.

When Charlie died two weeks later, I felt I had lost a great friend. He was only sixty-four.

David Willmott

~~~~~~

The house on Main Street in Bridgehampton that I bought in 1969 for *Dan's Papers* became the offices of the newspaper for the rest of the century and up until this day. It was a two-story home with two bedrooms and a bathroom upstairs, and a front hall downstairs that led into a living room, dining room, and kitchen. Fluted Greek columns held up a front porch that wrapped around the house. There was a garage in the back. A picket fence out front. A gravel driveway. It was all together a very pleasant affair on a half acre.

We had fifteen employees at that time. I could have gotten a suite of offices in a one-story office building somewhere, but the truth was I liked the idea of working in shirtsleeves in a converted house. I'd seen houses like that on Brattle Street in Cambridge when I was in grad school at Harvard seven years earlier. They were filled with filmmakers, artists, sculptors, and architects. Here in Bridgehampton, I would make my living room the front office, the dining room the bookkeeping office, the kitchen the production rooms with the typewriters and big layout tables. Upstairs would be my office and, next to it, an office for reporters. We had three salesmen. I figured they should be out on the street, so why should they need desk space? I had two delivery vans. The garage in the back would be a storage area for newspaper bundles. We put a sign out front that said DAN'S PAPERS just behind the white picket fence. Above the crossbar at the top of the sign there was a smaller sign reading PUBLISHING TOWER.

Things went very well in the first two or three years at Publishing Tower. At the time, and this is sort of a confession, the paper was being printed at a big plant in Freeport, Long Island, that printed about fifty different newspapers, of which forty were X-rated. It was an odd thing to go to this plant and see these publications with bare naked ladies in various provocative positions next to copies of *Dan's Papers*, but the owner of the plant, Mark Dreyfus, who was a really nice guy, never said anything one way or another about it. So I didn't either. But it did throw me off. And occasionally, a few of them, lurking on the press room floor, got packed up into our bundles from time to time. I'd hear about it occasionally from an upset customer.

"What the hell are you doing?"

I'd explain what was going on at Dreyfus and that Dreyfus had given us the lowest price and so we could print the most copies and I'd tell them to be more careful and that was usually the end of it.

Not only did I like Mark Dreyfus, I actually admired him. He had been crippled by polio as a young man and could just barely get around with leg braces and canes. But he ran this whole plant with a firm hand and a mild manner. He was a testament to how someone could overcome a disability.

In 1976, I read that there was a shortage of newsprint, which is what we were printed on.

"We're running out of it," Mark told me one week. "I've got about a four-week supply. Just letting you know."

"Oh, you'll find some more somewhere," I said.

"I'm trying," he said.

The weeks went by. He'd gotten another week's supply. Now that was running down.

"Just to let you know," Mark said one day at the plant, "if I don't get anymore newsprint by Monday afternoon, I won't be able to print you on Tuesday."

I had such confidence in Mark's ability to get through things that it came as a terrible shock on Monday when he told me that the next day there would be nothing to print me on.

He told me this by phone on Monday morning. And after it began to sink in, I became terrified.

"What do I do?" I asked him.

"I think you've got to find some other printer with paper," he said. "Look. I'll call you if I can get something later today, but don't count on it." Mark gave me the names of half a dozen other printers that could do this job.

Downstairs, we were laying out the paper onto cardboard flats, getting it ready to take to the printer. I would be taking it. I'd be leaving in the afternoon. But to where?

I tried the other printers. There were seven of them. Six said they just barely had enough for their current needs and were very sorry they couldn't accommodate me. A seventh, in Westchester, said he would print me, but the cost would be nearly four times what I was currently paying. I felt sick to my stomach.

Now I tried some of the publishers I competed with here on the eastern end of Long Island. It's an odd thing in publishing, the relationships you have with your fellow publishers. It's very much a standoffish affair. If they're on one side of a room you walk into, you generally stay on the other side. The reason is that all publications are just so public on the street. You can count the ads, see who turned you down and went with the competition. Had they low-balled the price? Had they stolen it away?

Editorially, you might come upon an editor telling some big lie, but then you could never criticize him. If you did, he could criticize you. Then you both look terrible, and a third publisher and editor benefit. What a mess.

In any case, I tried the four other publishers in the area. None were forthcoming. Their responses went from "I'd help you if I could" to "Forget it." Nobody said anything like, "Well, that's what you get when you print at a pornography plant."

At three in the afternoon, the flats were given to me in a big folder and I went out to my car with no place to go. So I drove west, toward New York. We didn't have cell phones then. I'd stop periodically and use a pay phone to call somebody who had given me a glimmer of hope. But again, there was nothing doing.

On Sunrise Highway, about an hour to the west of *Dan's Papers*, I pulled over to the side of the road and began to cry. When that stopped, I went over in my mind everybody I had already called and remembered that one of my competitors, a man named Dave Willmott in Riverhead who published a pennysaver called *Suffolk Life*, had said he did have paper and he was holding onto it as if it were gold and would surely help if he could, but he didn't want to jeopardize his own publication. And I remembered the last thing he said to me.

"If it's absolutely your last resort, call me. Maybe I could do something."

And so now, I did. I called him and I bawled and cried on the telephone and told him about Dreyfus and the pornography and all the people who had been mean to me and particularly the man who said he would charge me quadruple to print my paper and I absolutely would not do that, and he heard me out.

"Well, come back over here," he said. "I said if it was a last resort, call me. Whatever I've got, I'll share with you. We'll be in it together. Whatever happens to me happens to you."

This was just so totally unexpected. I thanked him profusely, turned the car around, and drove back to Riverhead. On my way, I realized I had never asked him what he would charge. Whatever it was, I guess, I would pay it.

Dave Willmott's publishing operation was in a former airplane parts factory on Riverhead Road in a town called Speonk, just to the south of the town of Riverhead. I pulled in and took my pack out and went inside.

DAVID WILLMOTT
(Courtesy of the Willmott Family)

Willmott had, years before, bought presses for his operation. His pennysaver publication, delivered through the mail, was at that time the same size as mine physically, but about eight times the size of mine in revenue, advertisers, and circulation. Its circulation, delivered into mailboxes, was 350,000 copies in twelve different editions all up and down Long Island. Willmott himself was a big, friendly Irishman with red hair and a clumsy looking Irish setter who sprawled fast asleep and snoring by the doorway of his office when I arrived there.

I stepped over the dog and went inside. In the large space in the back, I could hear a newspaper press thundering away.

"Let me see what you've got," he said, offering me a seat.

I spread out my flats on the desk between us, and he looked them over. He asked me the press run and I told him: 58,000.

"How much is this going to cost?" I asked.

"Tell me what you're paying now. That's what you pay me."

"That's it?"

"I said I'll share what I've got. I meant it."

About a month later, the paper crisis eased up and Willmott told me everything would be fine from then on. "I'm just so glad I squirreled so much paper last year," he said. "I had a hunch this might happen. And it did."

During the next two years I continued to print at *Suffolk Life*. And in that time, I got to know more about Willmott. I had seen *Suffolk Life* around town before all this, of course, but I didn't know the history. The year after I started my paper in Montauk at the age of twenty, Dave Willmott, at the age of twenty-five, started his paper in Riverhead in a storefront office.

We had the same story, but we were cut from a very different cloth. He was from a blue-collar Irish background in Riverhead. I was from an upper-middle-class Jewish background in suburban New Jersey. From my perspective he was like an older brother who had achieved great financial success in the field I was in. From his—and he kept telling me this—I wrote these wonderful fanciful stories he never could. He just covered politics and gave his opinions about the politicians in the one column he wrote every week in the front of his newspaper. The hell with competing, he once said.

Two years later, when a new printer opened up and gave me a tremendously lower price than I had been getting from either Dreyfus or Willmott, Willmott didn't say anything like, "Oh you owe me" or "You should pay more for me because we're friends." He said he couldn't match it and that was that, and we could still be friends.

And so we were friends, although not close friends. We were so different that we didn't socialize, but we'd run into each other from time to time and have lunch and catch up.

One time, I opened my mail to find a death threat about something I wrote. It said not only me but my wife and family would all be killed. The writer said he knew where we lived, and, because there was my home address, he sure did.

I turned this over to the police and they watched my house for about two weeks until, as they said, they thought the danger had passed. I called Willmott at one point.

"I carry a gun," he said.

"You do?"

"I get these all the time. I keep a gun in a shoulder holster. You never noticed?"

Willmott had this wonderful promotion for *Suffolk Life*. You got it free in your mailbox, but at the beginning of every year, he would insert a small return postcard in the paper asking that you send in a donation "subscription" to *Suffolk Life*, and for the upcoming year, they would use all that money entirely for reporters and editors. "The more you send, the better the stories will be," he wrote.

One time, I got some idea to run a promotion where people could buy two ads for the price of one and get a little gift of some kind. I wasn't sure it was a good idea. I thought I'd ask Dave. At this point, Willmott was operating *Suffolk Life* out of a giant shopping center in Riverhead up on Route 58. I'd been up there a few times to have lunch with him. He had bought the entire center. Now he had more room than he could possibly use. It was quite amazing.

Willmott asked an odd question about my sales promotion. "What does your sales force think?" he asked.

"I haven't presented it to them yet."

"Here's the thing. If it turns your salespeople on, it will work. It doesn't matter. It could be horsefeathers. If the salespeople like it and get all enthusiastic, that's it. Don't even ask what the customers think of it."

In 1978, Apple Computer came out with their first Macintosh. It was a big jump to doing the paper by computer, but I had a production manager named Allison who knew the Macs and said everything would be fine.

"Trust me," she said.

We ordered seven Macs and they came and some techies came and Allison huddled with them and they figured everything out.

"All hooked up," she said after they were gone. "Tomorrow I'll show the rest of the staff how to use them."

Tomorrow came and there was no Allison. Not at home, and nowhere that anybody could locate her. She never did come in. And Willmott had not yet gotten his Macs in so I couldn't ask him for help. That day and the next, still without

Allison, we had to muddle through with Apple technicians talking by phone to five of our production people for half the day getting them up and running.

A few days later Allison did come in, and said it was some family matter. I thought, well, screw you, but then I thought we can get through anything, I guess.

Two weeks later, I looked out the window from my upstairs office to see that out in the parking lot, Allison was looking suspiciously in all directions while putting rolls of company toilet paper into her trunk. I recognized it because of its wrapping. I fired her the next day.

Nothing, however, was going to save us from Hurricane Donna as it rolled up the Atlantic during August of 1983.

I did think we were invincible by this point. We had never *not* published on time. But Donna roared through eastern Long Island with 110-mile-an-hour winds, ripped up trees, flooded farmland, knocked down electric wires, and shut the power down throughout the Hamptons for what would turn out to be eight days.

I had come to work during the storm and we had all just stood around. There was nothing we could do. No power meant no newspaper. By late in the afternoon, with portable radios telling us that this sure was a big one, our local lighting company declared they had done all they could with their repair force and pleaded with neighboring companies to send their repairmen and trucks. Soon they were able to announce that repairmen were on their way from upstate New York, Pennsylvania, and as far away as Ohio and Indiana, but it might be quite a while.

Then someone commented that they had heard that some people up in Riverhead had power. And so I called Dave.

"Hi," I said.

"Wonder what you want," he said.

I told him our situation.

"You can have our entire front lobby," he said. "It's a big room. The entrance to the mall in the old days. I think it's about twenty feet by forty."

"You wouldn't mind?"

"Hell no. How soon can you get here? We'll get it ready. We've got plenty of tables."

And so our fifteen employees unhooked the twelve computers and cameras, piled them one upon the other into our two delivery vans, and, in a great caravan of cars and trucks, headed west down the Montauk Highway toward *Suffolk Life*, thirty miles away. We passed stores with all the lights out, restaurants that were giving away the food—we were a newspaper caravan on the move.

As we drove along, what came to my mind was a television show called *The Beverly Hillbillies*. We were the Oakies, all packed up in our trucks, heading down the road from Appalachia to the promised land in California—if the trees blocking the roads didn't stop us.

Up at Dave's shopping mall, we settled into the front lobby, which was all prepared for us with tables and chairs and even an urn with fresh coffee. We unpacked, set up the computers, put out the flats, plugged in the telephones, and at that point, Willmott walked in. He stopped and put his hands on his hips.

I just looked at him. What the hell do you say to somebody at a time like this?

And the next thought that went through my mind was—I hope he doesn't see the lead story on the flats. It's ours exclusively. We've got to get this out before he does.

Nell Robinson

~~~~~~

In the spring of 1974, I met a wonderful woman named Nell Robinson.

Nell at that time was about sixty years old, had bright red hair which she dyed, was slender, handsome, and still very beautiful.

Nell also was a member of that WASP set that came out in the summertime. But she was not liked. I was never sure why, because I was not part of that set. But when you'd see members of this group together, for example at the Ladies Village Improvement Society Fair, or at the Members Outdoor Clothesline Art Show at Guild Hall, both of which I covered for the newspaper, it was quite apparent. All the other women would be formal and proper and well behaved. And there'd be one woman laughing and telling jokes and bossing people around and that would be this woman with the red hair. The other women stared at her.

I don't think I ever said two words to her. But just watching her in action, I liked her. On a cold day in March, drawn by something I saw in the window of an antique shop on Main Street in East Hampton, I went inside. And there she was, behind the counter. Women in the WASP community *never* ran antique shops.

"Oh hi," she said, "I know you."

I was standing alongside a marble statue of a naked woman with her arm upraised, and next to an armoire that was draped with a cloth with a gold fringe. Everything was dusty.

"I have a bone to pick with you," she said.

"What was that?"

"You sent a reviewer to write about the play I directed at Guild Hall last fall. Thornton Wilder's *Our Town*. You know this is community theater. You shouldn't hold us up to such high standards. We had lawyers and waitresses and piano teachers out there on stage. A pat on the back might have been in order instead of such a big pan."

"I'll talk to her for next time. I promise. But what are you doing running an antique shop? And in the off-season?"

"Well, my husband died," she said, very matter-of-factly.

"I'm sorry," I said.

And so, we talked. And she talked, and I listened. And she talked and I listened. I spent about two hours with her—nobody at all came in because everything was quiet on Main Street in those days during the heart of the winter—and we got to be friends.

At one point, we talked about how slow business was out of season, and she commented that she'd already been approached by the Chamber of Commerce to become a new member, which she had agreed to do.

"Honestly," she said, "this place is so beautiful—our windmills, our beaches, and our farms—I don't see why we can't be busy with tourists out here in *all* the seasons—spring, summer, and fall."

A silence settled over us for a moment as we both realized what had come out of her mouth, or what had not come out of her mouth, which was the dreaded word "winter."

I learned that Nell was not a native New Yorker, or even anyone particularly acceptable to the New York upper crust, until she had met her husband Bartholomew Robinson.

"I was a Ziegfeld girl," she said. "You know what that is?"

"A dancer on Broadway."

"And Mr. Robinson, this big show producer, saw me in the chorus line, and he picked me out and I married him. I loved him. And he loved me."

Her eyes welled up.

"Where are you from originally?"

"Columbus, Ohio," she said.

And so this hot red-headed number—I could easily picture her in my mind—had come to join the world of Palm Beach in the winter, the Hamptons and Newport in the summer, and Manhattan the rest of the time. No wonder she wasn't particularly popular with the other ladies.

What I later learned was that when Mr. Robinson had passed away two years earlier, it turned out that he was not as rich as everybody thought. And so she had rented this space to sell off some of her stuff. But I was never really sure of that. Perhaps she just wanted a place on Main Street where she could socialize.

The third time I came to the antique store, I fell in love with something. I can't really explain it. Nell had to break off talking to me to wait on another customer for a while, and so I started looking around and, up front, in the picture window, along with silver combs, a pair of riding boots, a silver serving bowl, and several old wooden tennis rackets, there was, facing into the store, an oil painting.

It was about two feet by three feet, it was placed on an easel, and it was the face of a girl. She was perhaps eighteen, had big black eyes, black hair pulled back into a bun, and this look on her face that I find very hard to describe: trusting, innocent, curious to be standing still to be painted, relaxed. She was not quite sure of herself yet, this girl. People surely must have told her that she was absolutely beautiful. No doubt about that. But, I think she didn't believe it quite yet. The painter had captured her just at that point, maybe just a month before that would happen. It was a most amazing portrait.

Nell was standing alongside me.

"She has that effect on everybody who looks at her," she said. "It's by Thomas Moran."

"Who was he?"

"One of our great American masters. He did his best work in the late 1880s," she said. "Landscapes. He traveled out west and painted magnificent scenes of Yosemite and the Grand Canyon and the Rockies in Colorado. He's quite famous."

"And the girl?"

"It's from earlier. It's dated on the back. He lived out here for several summers teaching painting to the old biddies."

Aha, I thought, so this young girl had had that effect on Moran too.

"I think the girl must have been from here. Would you like to buy it?"

I had never been so smitten by a painting before.

"How much?"

"Three hundred dollars."

In today's money, that would be about a thousand dollars.

"That's too much for me," I said.

'I'd sell it to you for two hundred dollars," she said.

I was certainly tempted. I had never spent two hundred dollars on a painting in my life.

"I have to think about this," I said. "I'll come back tomorrow."

"I'll hold it for you till tomorrow," Nell said. "I think you should have it."

That evening, I told my wife about the painting. We talked. I did have to tell her that I was in love with this young woman in the painting, and she was very nice about it. "If you get it," she said, "hang it in your study." An eighteen-year-old girl, long dead from old age, would be just fine with her as the other love in my life.

And so I decided to get it.

As I drove into town the next morning, however, I saw blinking red lights in front of Nell Robinson's store. I parked and walked over. The brick frontage of the store was all blackened with smoke. Broken glass from the show window was scattered about on the sidewalk. There were still firemen there with a few hoses out, but they were just standing around, talking and drinking coffee. The fire was out. The painting gone.

I tried to walk in. "Nell?"

"You can't go in there," a fireman said.

"I'm over here," Nell said. She was behind me, standing by the front grille of a fire truck. She looked so sad.

"I'm so sorry," she said. "It's just the stuff in the show window. They got here as quickly as they could."

"Is there anything? A charred canvas? The frame."

"It's gone," she said.

The store was fixed up and stayed open for the rest of that summer, and then the next. Nell continued to direct the plays of the community theater for the next year, and I instructed our reviewer to go lightly on them, considering where all the actors had come from, and she did.

But then there was some sort of controversy between Nell and the director of Guild Hall. It was in the local papers at the time, and although I don't remember the actual topic, I do remember it had something to do with what Nell felt was artistic integrity and what the director felt was something else. Yelling at the actors or something. So now Nell was out of that job.

After that, I didn't see much of Nell anymore. Every once in a while, I'd be driving down Main Street under the great elms that arched over the road, and I'd see Nell walking briskly along on the sidewalk, this red-headed elderly woman with ramrod straight posture, accompanied by a little white toy poodle on a leash who had to trot to keep up.

Where she was going I did not know. But once, as I went by, I honked and waved, and she looked up and smiled and waved back, and it meant a whole lot to me.

Grey Gardens

~~~~~~

Every community I lived in growing up had a haunted house. In Millburn, New Jersey, where I spent my childhood in the 1940s and '50s, the haunted house was a block and a half from where I lived, at 854 Ridgewood Road. It was right on the corner of Ridgewood and Myrtle, high on a hill, an English Tudor home just like ours—they were all English Tudor along that street—except that everything was overgrown and nobody lived there. We kids would go up there sometimes and sneak around. There was still furniture in some of the rooms, and we thought that maybe if we looked carefully enough we would find a dead body or something. We'd stay as long as we dared, and then somebody would scream and we would all run away.

Here in East Hampton, the haunted house was in the most unlikely place imaginable. It was located south of the Montauk Highway, on the corner where the most exclusive streets in that community, Lily Pond Lane and West End Avenue, meet. On that corner there was this grand abandoned mansion so thick with foliage and vines and unmowed grass that it was falling in on itself. It was 1967 and I was twenty-seven years old the first time I saw it, and I had been publishing this newspaper for seven years, so I was no young kid.

A long time before, I had passed where these two streets met, and just thought there was an empty lot there, so thick was the foliage. To the right was the Revson mansion (he owned Revlon), and to the left was the Minskoff mansion (of the Minskoff theater chain in New York). And down at the very end of West End Avenue was the mansion owned by Juan Trippe, the founder and chairman of Pan Am Airways. But then one day I saw there really was some wreck of a house in there. I asked around. The house, now abandoned, was once owned by the family of Jackie Kennedy, the former first lady of the United States. She had grown up in East Hampton, the daughter of "Black Jack" Bouvier, and she had a younger sister, now the Princess Lee Radziwill, who still lived here, though surely not in *that* house.

Once, just after sunset of a summer's evening in July, I stopped briefly in front of this haunted house. Should I go inside? I got out of the car, began to walk through all the vines and foliage, and then thought—how can I accomplish this without drawing attention to myself?

I turned back and had retreated to my car when something happened that brought me up short.

High up in this mansion, at a third-floor window with the glass broken in, an electric light switched on.

There have been two young women born and raised in the Hamptons who have gone on to be first ladies of the

United States. Julia Gardiner, born in a house on Main Street in East Hampton, went on to marry President John Tyler in the White House in 1843. She bore him eight children. The other was Jackie Bouvier. She was born in Southampton, and she spent every summer of her childhood in East Hampton, and when she was in her late twenties, she married John F. Kennedy. There are photographs of the two taken in town in the early 1950s. In some of the pictures, the two are seen with Jackie's younger sister Lee. Both sisters are strikingly beautiful. In one picture, Jackie and Lee are photographed alone out near the Montauk lighthouse when Jackie was twenty-two and Lee was eighteen. The two look gloriously happy, the children of wealth and privilege.

Jackie was thirty-two when her husband was inaugurated. She was the youngest first lady in history, except for Julia Gardiner, who was nineteen when she married President Tyler.

As for Lee Bouvier, when she was twenty years old, she married Michael Canfield, a wealthy New York publishing executive, but divorced him six years later, something people in high society did not do in those days. Just a few months later, she married a prince, Prince Stanislaw Albrecht Radziwill of Poland. And she would stay married to him for twenty-five years. In the first year of her marriage to her prince, however—Jackie had become first lady at that time—she went off to Chicago to pursue a career on the stage. She acted in two shows and was universally panned in both. Then she starred in a movie and was panned in that. So she gave up the idea of that career, and returned to New York and set herself up in high society, attending concerts and fundraisers as Princess

JACKIE KENNEDY AND LEE RADZIWILL AS TEENAGERS
(Photo by Peter Beard)

Lee Radziwill. But there was a twist to it. In keeping with her reputation as the artsy one of the two sisters, the princess began to keep company with many offbeat New York writers and artists, including Andy Warhol, Larry Rivers, Edward Albee, Truman Capote, and Peter Beard, all of whom had summer homes on or near the ocean in Montauk or the Hamptons. In fact, she maintained an oceanfront residence near them in East Hampton in later years, a beautiful three-story thatched-roof home next to the Maidstone Club.

In 1971, approaching forty, Lee Radziwill decided to engage two documentary filmmakers, David and Albert Maysles, to make a film of her life growing up. She had learned of these two through friends who had seen their work. To accomplish this, she gave them a list of some of the important events and people in her life, and they were soon out in the Hamptons doing some preliminary filming. When Lee saw these films, she hated them. She told them not to proceed. The filming was cancelled.

That autumn, a young man, newly employed at Fedi's Market on North Main Street in East Hampton, delivered three bags of groceries ordered by phone to a home at the corner of West End Avenue and Lily Pond Lane in East Hampton. And, unlike other deliverymen, who couldn't have cared less, he was disgusted by what he saw. The house was in terrible disrepair, covered by vines and overgrowth, and when he got through and across the dilapidated porch to the front door, he found two old ladies living in the house amid a terrible smell. There were cats everywhere.

Two weeks later, the board of health sent an inspector to the house. He gave a summons to the two ladies, informing them that the house was unfit for human habitation, and that they would have thirty days to clean it up. If they didn't do that, the house could be condemned and bulldozed to the ground.

The two women were a mother and daughter, both named Edith, and known by friends and family as Big Edie and Little Edie. The last name was Beale. And they were an aunt and cousin, respectively, of Jackie Kennedy and Princess Lee Radziwill.

The two of them were also number thirty-two on the list of forty important places and people that Princess Lee Radziwill had given to the Maysles brothers. And so, when

LITTLE EDIE *(LEFT)*
(From the author's collection)

an item appeared in the papers, including mine, about the state of affairs at this mansion right in the middle of the estate section of this town, the Maysles took their cameras, picked their way through the underbrush, and knocked on the front door.

Little Edie, who met them at the door, decided on the spot that these two would be the best thing that ever happened to her. They would make her a movie star. And they would launch her out to Hollywood. The millions that would ensue from this would enable her to take care of her aging mother and to restore them both into the good graces of society.

But why were two women from the wealthy WASP set living in these awful circumstances?

"And why don't their relatives do something about this?" I wrote one week. "They can afford it."

"Is it perhaps that this is the way these two women *want* to live?" I wrote another week. "And is it just possible that the town should leave them alone? Isn't a person's home their castle?" I really had no idea what was going on.

Of course, I also had no idea that a couple of filmmakers from Ohio had also decided to get to the bottom of this and were in this house day after day, filming the two Edies.

In the late summer of 1972, armies of repairmen, hired by Jackie Kennedy and Princess Lee Radziwill, came to the house and fixed it all up. And the following year, the documentary called *Grey Gardens* appeared in theaters. It was the most critically acclaimed and most popular documentary the Maysles brothers ever produced. But it never did make Little Edie a movie star. Instead, she and her mother remained in the house, and a few years went by and Big Edie died. After that the family was finally able to coax Little Edie out of the house, and it was sold in its fixed-up state to editor Ben Bradlee of the *Washington Post* and his wife, reporter Sally Quinn.

As the years went by, *Grey Gardens* came to be considered one of the best documentaries ever made. It has been taught in courses at universities, and it has been shown and reshown on television. The two filmmakers are almost totally invisible in the movie; it is Big Edie and Little Edie, mostly Little Edie, who come to define this very strange, somewhat sick relationship in total squalor. It is, in the end, a film about hopes dashed, disappointment, blame, love, and attachment.

About 1995, I began a small twice-a-year film festival called "The *Dan's Papers* They Made the Movie Here Film Festival," held at Southampton College or the Ross School or the Westhampton Beach Performing Arts Center. We'd show about a dozen films made in this community every year, and every couple of years, we would include *Grey Gardens*.

In 1997, I interviewed Albert Maysles at his Manhattan studios. His brother David had since passed away. But Albert was still making movies. Among other things, I asked him what Princess Lee Radziwill thought about them making the documentary about her aunt and cousin.

"There wasn't much she could do about it," he said. "The Beales willingly allowed us to make this film."

Meanwhile, there was more trouble for Princess Lee Radziwill. In 1988, she had married the prominent Broadway director and choreographer Herbert Ross and was spending increasingly more of their time at the thatched-roof mansion on the beach next to the Maidstone Club.

The trouble came with the purchase of the adjacent four acres of sand dunes next to her home by a willful, wealthy, and stubborn widow named Alice Lawrence.

Mrs. Lawrence soon broke ground on her new home there. It was more than twice the size of the princess's house, and it was, unfortunately, not only just a few hundred feet from her house but designed in a brutal modern style with a roof that many said was reminiscent of the TWA terminal at Kennedy Airport. Personally, I hated the house. I tried to get an interview with Mrs. Lawrence, but she declined. According to what her assistant told me, this was her house, she'd build it any way she wanted, and it was nobody else's business.

I did interview the architect for the house, a man named Rafael Viñoly. He told me he couldn't exactly explain the philosophy of the house. "You run into problems with words," he said.

What turned into a five-year legal battle with the princess, however, was an enormous concrete wall, twenty feet high, that the builders for Mrs. Lawrence constructed between the Lawrence house and Princess Radziwill's house.

When the house was first being built, it was immediately apparent that though the Lawrence house was absolutely not in keeping with the half-timber Tudor and Old English homes in the community, it was at least set back from the ocean roughly the same distance as the Radziwill house. Then came the wall.

The wall started at the corner of the Lawrence house and ran straight down toward the ocean right to the back of the closest dune. At twenty feet high, it completely blocked any view of the water eastbound from the Radziwill house. And in the late afternoon, in the few hours before sunset, it put the Radziwill house in shadow.

The lawsuit was filed by Herbert Ross and Princess Lee Radziwill. It claimed that this wall was decorative and, though attached to the house at the back, was not part of the house. It therefore had to be legally considered as a wall. And walls over four feet high between neighbors were against the law.

Attorneys for Mrs. Lawrence argued that it *was* a part of the house, an extension of it, a great arm stretched out toward the ocean, welcoming the ocean to Mrs. Lawrence and Mrs. Lawrence to the ocean. It was part of the architecture. It could not be removed. As a matter of fact, should the Rosses win, there would have to be something done very seriously with jackhammers to have it removed.

In the end, after four years and hundreds of thousands of dollars in legal costs, the Rosses lost. The wall remained and remains to this day.

From time to time during this period, I would attend events at which Mr. Ross and the princess would be in attendance, and the sight of them would immediately bring to mind this terrible wall. I also was told that the couple was now not getting along at all, and there were frequent fights between them. In 2001, Herbert Ross died of a heart attack. But two months before he died, Princess Lee Radziwill won a divorce from him.

In 2005, a Broadway producer decided to make a Broadway show out of the film *Grey Gardens.* It had its world premiere at Guild Hall, right in East Hampton, "on the road" as they call it, working out the kinks in the hopes of taking it to Broadway.

I chose not to go see it. I thought it was ridiculous to make a musical out of *Grey Gardens*, which is what they said they were doing. After that, it opened Off Broadway for a while, ran for three months, and then closed. It then reopened on Broadway and ran for over two hundred performances, with smashing reviews.

The play is in two acts. The first act is set in 1938 in the house known as Grey Gardens in East Hampton. Mr.

Beale has just left a few years earlier and the place is aglow in candlelight and guests and servants. It is the coming-out party for Little Edie. During this act, two girls, age eight and four, run in and join the guests, then tell their aunt and cousin about their riding adventures down at the stables. They are, of course, Jackie and Lee.

The second act takes place in 1971 amid the squalor of what Grey Gardens had become. Christine Ebersole, who played Big Edie in the first act at the age of fifty-two, now plays Little Edie, who is now fifty-two. And of course, the two little girls are now grown and, as it happens, make no further appearance in the play.

Grey Gardens opened on Broadway on November 4, 2006. Because this had been loosely based on events that had happened in East Hampton twenty-four years before, it seemed to me that I ought to go see it and write about it right away. I had low expectations for it, as I said.

I was unable to get tickets for opening night or for a few nights after that, but we did get tickets for November 22. And so my wife Chris and I went. At the end of the first act, as we got up and walked up the aisle to the bar, we passed an elderly woman sitting at an aisle seat a few rows behind us who I thought I recognized. Our eyes met, and then she looked away. It was Lee Radziwill.

I didn't say anything for a little while as we walked the rest of the way to the back of the theater. But as Chris and I stood in line, I turned to her.

"Princess Lee Radziwill is here," I said.

"Where?" she asked.

"She's sitting about five rows behind us, on the aisle."

At the end of the intermission, the lights flashed and we returned to our seats. But the princess was gone. And her seat remained empty for the rest of the show.

Four months later, the star of the show, Christine Ebersole, won a Tony for her performance in *Grey Gardens.* And the show was universally acclaimed as one of the ten best Broadway shows of 2006.

In 2008, another movie called *Grey Gardens* came out. Produced by HBO, it starred Drew Barrymore, Daniel Baldwin, Jessica Lange, and Jeanne Tripplehorn as Jacqueline Kennedy. It was not a musical. It ran more closely along the lines of the documentary. After its run on HBO, it went nationwide into theatres, where it enjoyed a successful run.

Then, there was a photo spread about Grey Gardens in *Vanity Fair.* It was in the October 2007 issue of that publication and it features Mary-Kate Olsen and Lauren Hutton as Little Edie and Big Edie.

Then the children of the Maysles brothers published a book, which consisted of memorabilia about Grey Gardens. And then a woman who was a friend of the Edies published a book about them.

Finally, there was this other book. It was not about Grey Gardens. It was written by Princess Lee Radziwill, and it is about her growing up in East Hampton in happier days. If you want to learn more about what it was like to live in privilege and excess, just pick up a copy.

It's called *Happy Times.*

Oceanfront

After sixteen years of running the newspaper, I decided the time had come for me to live in a big house right on the ocean. I couldn't afford it, of course. I wasn't a millionaire. But now, in 1975, there was a new way to live oceanfront even if you didn't have the money. When the summer ended and all the parties were over, all the summer people went back to their apartments in New York City. The oceanfront homes, many of them large mansions, lay vacant, rather forlornly as a matter of fact, until it was time for the locals to get them ready for the next summer.

What I found out earlier that summer of 1975 was that, for the first time, the people living in these houses were willing to rent them for free in the wintertime. The deal was it had to be somebody they knew, and the person living there would have to pay the utilities bill, which was no big deal. (Oil was five dollars a barrel.) That was it. Just live in it. And keep an eye on it. From the owner's perspective, it was essentially free house-sitting.

As for me, it seemed the perfect time. I had gone through a divorce and was footloose and fancy free. That summer, I had lived on a friend's touring yacht, but now I had to move on. When was I going to find another time to live on the ocean? Through friends, I learned of a man named John Arnett who owned an ad agency in Manhattan and had a handsome oceanfront house on Sandune Court in Sagaponack. I never did get to meet him. But he knew me. The guy who runs the summer newspaper? I know *Dan's Papers*. Reliable? Responsible? He and his girlfriend? Sure.

The house was a modern affair, with sliding glass doors and decks, of a design they called an upside-down house. The ground floor, built out of stone, was the garage and the bedrooms. The upstairs, where the sun would stream in through all that glass, and from which you had a panoramic view of the ocean, was the public living area, which in this case consisted of a kitchen, dining area, study, and living room. It was in a row of oceanfront summer homes, right in Sagaponack, with the sand dunes between the house and the sea, and with a vast potato field behind.

What a wonderful house.

The day we moved into the house was September 10. It was a wonderfully warm day, warm enough for swimming, and my new girlfriend Ann and I got into our bathing suits and ran down this wooden boardwalk to the beach and jumped into the ocean.

That was the last time we did that. The next day there was a chill in the air. We stayed in the house.

ANN NOWAK
(Photo by the author)

And for the first month or two we really enjoyed it, with friends over, visitors out from the city, dinner parties, even jam sessions of banjos, guitars, and a washtub bass on Saturday nights in the living room. We had hoped we might have had the first one out on the deck, but it was too cold at night by then.

On a Sunday morning in early October, I had in the house a guy from the city named Mike Goldstein, who was the publisher of the *SoHo News*. This was a free paper in the city, just like mine. Goldstein was a wild man.

"Let's call Larry Rivers and have him over for brunch," Goldstein said. "He lives in Southampton year-round, doesn't he?" Goldstein picked up the phone.

I was horrified. "You can't just call him up," I said.

"Why not? We both have newspapers. Don't you know him?"

"No."

"If he's free, he'll come over," Goldstein persisted.

There was no answer at the Rivers house.

By late October, however, I had come to the conclusion that living on the ocean was not all it was cracked up to be. For example, there was fog in the morning. I'd drive into town and discover on my way that just five hundred yards further inland from the house was a bright and shiny day. But here at the beach we were socked in.

Another thing was that there wasn't a view of the surf or the beach. The sand dunes out front blocked it. There was a view of the ocean and the horizon—but that soon became quite boring. A blue area and a sky area. Occasionally, it would feature a fishing trawler going by or a large oil tanker way out there, slowly making its way to New York Harbor. You could get a good view of the tanker through binoculars. And it was surely quite something, though it didn't really fit into the rural idea of the Hamptons.

You could clearly hear the ocean crashing on the sand, though. And you could go out the boardwalk and see it, but it was altogether pretty damp and cold by that time, so you didn't do it for very long.

There was also a constant accumulation of what looked like white salt on everything—on the deck furniture (which we soon brought in), on the sliding glass (blocking the view), and on the windshield of our car every morning (blocking that view).

By November, with nobody home in any of the other houses and with the wind coming through the cracks of the sliders, we began to think it might be a good idea to go some place warm for a while. Not that we didn't love our oceanfront house, of course. But hey, even in paradise, nothing's perfect.

The trip I outlined for early January involved something new and something old. The new was Hong Kong and Tokyo. Neither of us had been in either of these places before. The old was a two-week stop in Hawaii. I had been to Hawaii three years before in happier times for three months when I was married. I had fallen in love with it. It was so colorful, so filled with birds and waterfalls and rain forests, with people who were just so gentle and loving. Wherever you went, people greeted you with a smile and an aloha. I had made many friends there, and I thought Ann might like to meet some of them. Specifically, I thought Ann might like to meet a guy named John Grayson, whom I had befriended in Maui. Grayson had founded and was now in his fifth year of publishing a year-round free newspaper called the *Maui Sun*, which was a lot like *Dan's Papers*. I'd visited him in his offices in Wailuku and given him one of my papers. I'd been back to his office a few other times to help get the *Sun* to the printer. I wrote a few articles for his paper, free of charge.

And so, at the beginning of January, with my newspaper shut down for the winter, we went on this trip, and had a great time. Three weeks later, at five o'clock in the afternoon in early February—and in the middle of a snowstorm—the second in command of *Dan's Papers*, Ron Ziel, picked us up at Kennedy Airport to drive us back to Sagaponack. We were

RON ZIEL
(Photo from the author's collection)

in serious jet lag and very tired, but all suntanned, happy, and feeling very goofy looking out at a world blanketed in dazzlingly white snow.

"So what was it like?" he asked. We were on the Belt Parkway.

"Amazing trip," I said. "Hong Kong looks just like Manhattan, with these great tall buildings. I never knew there was another place that looked like Manhattan. Tokyo was something else. I can't even begin to explain it."

"Did you see Grayson?" Ron asked. He knew about Grayson because Grayson and I had been mailing our newspapers to one another over the years.

"He wasn't there," I said. "He was on the mainland."

Ann was in the back seat, fast asleep after the long trip. By the time we arrived in the Hamptons it was dark.

"Is my car at the office?" I asked as we approached Bridgehampton. We were just two miles away, now.

"It's in the back, but it's snowed in. I'll take you home, and then I'll come back for you in the morning. We can dig it out when it's light."

"Okay. But I want to stop at the office," I told Ron.

"You do? It's eight o'clock at night."

"We're going right by it. Just pull up. I want to pick up all the mail. There's got to be a whole lot of mail."

"There sure is," Ron said. "It fills a tote box. You sure you don't want to do this in the morning? We can get it then."

"Just pull up. I've got the keys. I'll just run in and be right out."

The tote box was filled to the brim. I slid it in next to Ann, which awakened her.

"What's going on?" she asked.

"We're almost home," I said.

Ron slowed as he came down Sagg Main and onto Sandune Court. The streets weren't plowed as well as they were up on the highway. And then he pulled up into our oceanfront driveway, which was not plowed, and crunching through the snow, he came to a stop by our front door.

We got out, or I should say Ron and I got out, leaving Ann still fast asleep in the back seat, and in a biting wind, we unloaded the suitcases from the trunk and walked them the few feet to the door, which was covered with ice. I hacked away at it enough to loosen the lock and I opened it up, and we carried things inside.

"Good to be home?" Ron asked. There was something wrong.

"There's a white puff of smoke coming from your mouth," I said. "That's odd."

We thought about this for a moment.

"Yours too," Ron said. We were both all bundled up in scarves and mittens. "I think there's no heat in the house."

"Down here there isn't."

We went upstairs. There was no heat up there either. And indeed, we could feel the wind coming through the cracks. There was also no electricity.

"Do you have electricity at your house?" I asked.

"I did when I left to get you," he said.

We both looked out one of the sliders to see if there were any lights on in any of the neighboring houses. There weren't any. But of course, there were no people there either, so you really couldn't tell.

"I wonder how long this has been going on?" I asked. "And I wonder if the pipes are frozen."

Ann was still asleep in the car with the engine running. We walked through the house. Upstairs, we found the water flowing in the kitchen sink and also in the bathroom. Downstairs, however, the bathroom was frozen solid. There was ice in the toilet. It looked like a very scary situation to me.

"What do you want to do?" Ron asked.

I looked around. There was a big stone fireplace we had used a few times there in the ground-floor master bedroom. And there was lots of firewood. On the mantle were matches and candles.

"Bring everything in here," I said. "I'll build a fire. And we'll be okay until morning. I think the phone works when the power is off." I picked up the receiver of the phone on the night table. There was a dial tone. So I could make calls in an emergency.

I built a big fire in the fireplace, lit some candles, carried in the rest of the luggage and the tote box, and then Ron and I woke Ann and she came in, too. I explained everything, and that we had a bathroom upstairs that worked.

"This is very nice," she said, looking at the candlelight and the fire. "But I'm going right to bed if that's all right. Okay?"

"Okay."

"You sure you'll be all right?" Ron asked.

"Yes. And thanks for everything," I said. "I'll call in the morning."

He left. I sat there quietly on the bed, next to the tote basket of mail, listening as he drove off. It occurred to me that we were very, very much alone.

Behind me, Ann was in her nightclothes climbing into the other side of the bed and under a thick blanket.

"Mmmm," she said.

"I'm going to call the electric company," I said. "They have an emergency number. Also the heating people."

"Okay," she said. She snuggled under the covers.

I got through to both places, and told them the problems. I also told them I had built a fire, had plenty of wood, and everything was all right for the moment. We discussed the fact that when they got everything back on, a burst pipe could cause a flood. It might be best to do everything in the morning when we could have a plumber standing by. I told them that would be a good idea. They both agreed to send somebody as their first stop at 7 a.m.

But now I was up. Behind me, Ann was fast asleep, even in the flickering firelight. And here, in the tote box on the bed, was this mail. I wondered—what did I get?

One at a time, I quietly opened each letter, careful not to wake up Ann. There was enough light from the fire to read each piece. Here was a bill from the phone company. I would be happy to pay that. Here was the printing bill for the winter issue we had printed just before Christmas. The paper would be on the stands until April. I'd pay that. Here was a check from Don Clause Real Estate for the summer advertising. Thank God for that. Here was junk mail. A catalog with things inside I could buy. Here was more junk mail, a request I send money to an orphanage in time for Christmas (too late). Here was an offer from a magazine to save two dollars by extending my subscription for another year.

I wasn't going to do anything about any of this mail, really, but I wanted to read it all anyway. I was curious. What I did find was that I was separating the mail into two piles. One pile was the junk mail, all of which basically requested that for some reason I part with my money in some new way I had not thought about before. The other pile was the real mail: the checks, the bills, the requests for information, the late Christmas cards. Someone had sent in a short story for me to consider for the paper. There was a letter from my mother, with a ten dollar check inside for Chanukah. And there was a letter from Hawaii. But the firelight was dimming. Before I read it, I got up and put another log in the fire.

It was from a woman who said we had met a few times at the office of the *Maui Sun* years before and she had taken my phone call about Grayson when we had recently called. The paper is thriving, she wrote, but Grayson has decided he wants to stay up in Oregon and so he wanted me to ask you if you would like to buy it. He would sell it at a very good price.

Now that is an exciting idea, I thought. An opportunity to have a business in a place I had fallen in love with. I've got to think about this. And I set the letter down on the pile of the real mail.

I continued on. The piles grew and grew. Boy, this is a lot of mail. I wasn't even halfway through.

And then I came upon a second interesting letter. The envelope was cream colored and of a high quality, my name and address carefully typed on the front. There was an embossed return address at Greenwich Street in New York City. I opened it. It was a formal business letter.

"Dear Mr. Rattiner," it read. "I have been reading your newspaper for several years, and have admired the progress you have made with it. At the present time I am buying properties, and I would like to buy your newspaper. If you have any interest in selling it, please contact me."

It was signed by someone I did not know, a man with the last name of Cardinale.

I turned it over and over. I read it again. Then I scrumbled down into the pile of the real mail to find the letter from the woman at the *Maui Sun*. I found it and held that up. I had the letter from Hawaii in one hand, the letter from Manhattan in the other. What I had here was an opportunity to change my life, presented in a way that had "fated to happen" all over it. My heart was racing.

This would be so easy, is what I thought. I could live in that land of waterfalls, surfing, sunshine, palm trees, luaus. I *loved* Hawaii.

But then I thought I loved the Hamptons, too—the farms, the sea, the changing of the seasons, the classic old villages and towns, Manhattan just a short distance away. And I thought of the people, all my friends and my family, my kids. My two little kids. I cannot do this. I don't think I can do this. It would be a full-time year-round job in Hawaii. Here, I work hard in the summertime, then there is the winter and I can travel and see the world, see Hawaii whenever I wanted.

I set the two letters down, one on top of the other, on the pile of the real mail, and was about to dip back into the tote box, which was now about one-quarter full, when I realized that the fire was beginning to dim again. And it gave me an idea.

I'd throw the junk mail into the fire. Get rid of it, which is what it deserved, and at the same time make the light brighter and further warm the room. What a good idea.

I scooped up the junk mail, walked across to the fire and threw it in. And then returned to the bed to look at—I could hardly believe this—the junk mail.

It took me a moment for it all to sink in.

I was shocked. I leaped up, ran across the room again in a single bound, and began as fast as I could to pull the real mail back out of the fire. It came tumbling out into the room. I stamped on it to tamp the flames, reached in and grabbed some more and stamped on that. Black smoke and soot flew into the air, and then, Ann sat up straight in bed, wide eyed.

"What's *happening?*"

"I got most of it," I shouted out to her.

At 3 a.m., I woke up, cold, and threw more wood on the fire. There had to be a deep psychological meaning for what had just happened with the mail. But I had no idea what it was.

Marty Shepard

~~~~~~

The spring of 1976 was a time of great anticipation in America. On July 4, 1976, the country would celebrate the two hundredth anniversary of its birth. There would be a parade of tall ships up the Hudson River that, from early indications, would draw more than two hundred four-masted schooners from all over the world. The mayor of New York City announced that on that evening, which was a Friday, there would be the largest fireworks display in the history of mankind in New York Harbor. There would, of course, be parades and celebrations everywhere.

I thought long and hard about what I ought to do in my newspaper to celebrate what came to be called "the Bicentennial." And then one day I saw a movie starring the English comedian Peter Sellers called *The Mouse That Roared.* Sellers plays several roles in this movie, sometimes with two of him talking to one another at the same time—a neat thing because this was before the advent of computer animation. All of them were characters in this tiny backwater of a kingdom in Europe about the size of Lichtenstein that had somehow

MARTIN SHEPARD
(Photo courtesy Judy Shepard)

survived World War II unscathed. There was a queen, a duke, a court jester, and lots of men with lances and swords and suits of armor, and also a big problem. The treasury was going empty. They got this idea. They would declare war on America, deliberately lose, and then, because America offered financial help to all countries it defeated, receive enormous amounts of cash in reparations, thus saving the kingdom.

"I hate to do this," said the queen (Peter Sellers in drag and falsetto). "But I must do something for my poor subjects."

And so, I decided that in my newspaper the Hamptons should secede from America, declare war, and be defeated. Thus, the potato farmers in the Hamptons, the owners of almost all the open land on eastern Long Island and in the beginning stages of the great siege by New York City developers, could thereby get the financial means to survive.

I told nobody about this. But when the time came, I ran the story about the war on the front page over four consecutive issues. The first one ran three weeks before the Fourth of July with the headline HAMPTONS SECEDES, the next one US DECLARES WAR, the next one WAR RAGES, and the last one, after the Fourth of July celebrations were over, an issue with a twist: US SURRENDERS.

It was an ingenious way to celebrate the bicentennial, if I do say so myself. And it did seem to me to be very much in keeping with the sorts of civil rights demonstrations and antiwar protests that were prevalent at that time.

In that series of issues there was this crucial battle. The U.S. Marines attempted to make an amphibious crossing of the Shinnecock Canal to enter the heart of the Hamptons, but it was thwarted from the other side by this ragtag group of farmers who had developed a secret weapon—the potato bazooka. They would fire it, and a potato would fly across the canal and fall into the midst of the soldiers, causing panic. After numerous potatoes had landed, they fled.

After the war ended with the surrender ceremonies, and with the Hamptons now a new country receiving, even in victory, all sorts of financial help from the United States, I got a call from somebody named Marty Shepard, who said he lived in a house in Sagaponack and wondered if I would like to come down there because he and some friends were planning to announce the secession of the Hamptons from the United States for real, sort of.

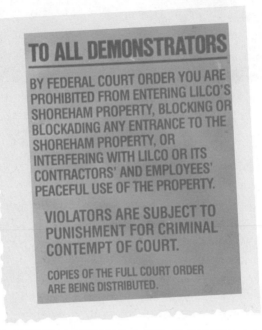

TO ALL DEMONSTRATORS

BY FEDERAL COURT ORDER YOU ARE
PROHIBITED FROM ENTERING LILCO'S
SHOREHAM PROPERTY, BLOCKING OR
BLOCKADING ANY ENTRANCE TO THE
SHOREHAM PROPERTY, OR
INTERFERING WITH LILCO OR ITS
CONTRACTORS' AND EMPLOYEES'
PEACEFUL USE OF THE PROPERTY.

VIOLATORS ARE SUBJECT TO
PUNISHMENT FOR CRIMINAL
CONTEMPT OF COURT.

COPIES OF THE FULL COURT ORDER
ARE BEING DISTRIBUTED.

SIGN OUTSIDE A NUCLEAR PLANT AT SHOREHAN, L.I.
UNDER CONSTRUCTION
(Photo by the author)

"A group of us were inspired by your series of articles," he told me. "But it's not news to us. We've been fooling around with this idea for some time. We'd like you to come over and see what we're up to."

Marty met me at the front door of his house, which was a modern affair set in the middle of a vast potato field. He was a slender, good-looking man, with a suntan, cut-off jeans, a flowered shirt, and sandals. He brought me inside, where I found about a dozen people, some in colorful headbands, who had just finished up a summer barbecue on the deck and were now drinking coffee or passing around some pot.

It was in that era when people smoked pot. It seems hard to believe today, but in many places, this was the norm, and it was also the norm to go see X-rated movies that were playing at a movie theater near you, even in the Hamptons, right along with the G-rated stuff. The Ladies Village Improvement Society of East Hampton had no idea of what to do with that fact.

In any case, Marty Shepard introduced me. "This is Dan Rattiner, who writes *Dan's Papers*," he said. A few people waved or said something about the sequence of articles I had just written. Nobody got up, however.

And so we talked about the plan to form a new country, to be called "The Hamptons." I got right into it. It was a fairly ambitious but comical idea, based on the fact that the Vietnam War had just ended and you still couldn't trust anybody over thirty, though now Jimmy Carter had been elected president and Richard Nixon was in exile and disgrace in his retreat in California, so there was hope. Maybe secession was the thing to do.

We could have our own money, somebody said. We could have our own foreign policy. We ought to design a flag, somebody else said. Life would be good.

"It should have Jimi Hendrix on the flag," somebody said, pointing to a poster of the performer up on the living room wall.

Outside, a potato farmer on a tractor was plowing a field, sending beautiful brown dust into the air. Beyond that were the dunes and the beach and the wild surf of the ocean.

I had a wonderful time at this tail-end-of-a-barbecue party, and in a subsequent issue, I did write about this nascent but hilarious plan. But the most interesting thing that came of this was the birth of a friendship with Marty.

Marty was a New York City psychiatrist. But he also *wasn't* a psychiatrist. He had had a brilliant college career, had become a doctor, then a psychiatrist, and after a number of years working with patients had come to the conclusion that, in his personal opinion, psychiatry was a big waste of time. He also thought it was corrupt, with, among other things, a vast army of psychiatrist friends he knew who administered therapy at the same time that they slept with their patients. In fact, he had written a book about it and had described how he himself had done exactly that. It had created a huge stir. But Marty wasn't practicing psychiatry anymore. He was practicing what he preached.

"I should write an article about all this for your paper," Marty said. And he did.

One afternoon, having lunch at Bobby Van's in Bridgehampton, Marty and I elaborated on the plan to secede by drawing on a tablecloth. Marty's idea was that we should bring in to our new country all the "islands" that exist off Long Island.

"We need to think bigger," he said. "We've got Nantucket, Martha's Vineyard, Block Island, what else?"

"There's Fisher's Island," I said. "And Shelter Island."

"Have you ever been to Fisher's Island?" Marty asked.

I told him I hadn't. It was a strange thing, Fisher's Island. About two hundred people lived there and it was just a few miles off the coast of Connecticut. But it belonged to New York State. What was that all about?

Marty had a way of talking very calmly about the most inflammatory things. I liked that about him. It was the attitude of a psychiatrist, is what it was. Unleashed.

"All of these islands have something in common," I said.

"What?"

"They all have windmills on them. Old English windmills from the eighteenth and nineteenth centuries."

"Even Fisher's?"

"I think even Fisher's."

And then I got another idea. "In the Caribbean they have the Dutch Antilles and the French Antilles. Do you know what Antilles means?"

"Not a clue."

"Me neither. But our country could be the 'Windmill Antilles.'"

"Yes it could," he said.

Later, Marty's wife Judy designed a flag. It was a flag with an upper horizontal bar in white and a bottom horizontal bar in blue, with a red windmill in the center. I published a picture of it in the newspaper.

And then—and Marty thinks that he thought of this and I think that I thought of it—we came up with the idea of a t-shirt that would parody the poster of UNCLE SAM WANTS YOU, where a stern and bewhiskered Uncle Sam with the stars-and-stripes hat points out at the viewer, urging him to enlist in the army.

Our t-shirt mimicked this exact poster, but our Uncle Sam had curls coming out from under his hat, and long lashes and lipstick. WINDMILL AUNT TILLIE WANTS YOU, it said.

(Photo by the author)

An article about all of this made it into the paper, and it got picked up by the *New York Times*. Lots of people were wearing these t-shirts for a while in town.

In the end, though, the plan sort of fizzled, as we all had certainly expected it would. It had been fun, though.

I really had no idea how Marty and Judy Shepard made their living at this point, except that I knew that Judy was a soap opera actress on television occasionally, and I thought maybe Marty had money left over from his psychiatrist days. But I soon came to realize that Marty earned a living by buying a small piece of farmland, building a house on it, living in it for a while, and then selling it and using the money he made to buy another piece of property to put a house on.

He only did one house at a time, and I saw little harm in it, but it did occur to me that on a very small scale he was cutting into the land that the farmers owned. Well, I rationalized, *somebody* has to look out at the farmland.

On the other hand, there were environmentalists coming into the community now, joining with the developers and saying the farmers themselves were destroying the environment. They were using pesticides on the land. The farmers responded by saying that they only used pesticides they had been assured were safe to use. For example, they used Temik, the most advanced of the chemicals, and now the only effective chemical for killing crop-ruining potato bugs. DuPont had assured them that although Temik was strong enough to kill the potato bugs in the soil, it was designed to chemically break down after a few days, turning into a harmless substance in the soil that was soon dissipated by rain.

Some farmers did acknowledge that their parents had used dangerous sprays. But at that time, nobody knew about these sorts of dangers. Some of these farms had been in families for the whole two hundred years we'd been a country. The Suffolk County Board of Health waded into this conversation by saying that everything the farmers were using now was okay, and there appeared to be no damage done.

One day, Marty called me up to tell me that a building contractor had bought about fifteen acres of farmland just off Daniel's Lane, was putting a dead end road through, and was going to turn it into seven two-acre building lots.

"He's going to call it Amy's Lane, after his wife," Marty said. "I'm buying two lots. He's just about to put the project on the market at $35,000 a lot. But if you want one now before he does, you can reserve it with him for $25,000. I thought you might be interested. It's quite a deal."

I was disgusted by this idea. But I went to see the lots. I couldn't help myself. The road had been driven with a bulldozer, but was still dirt. The property was staked out. I had the money. And the lot I liked the best viewed directly out across a potato field at the ocean. The price of $25,000 was almost a steal. Forget $25,000 or even $35,000. Home sites were selling for $80,000 and $90,000 and rapidly heading upward.

The increased land value meant the farmers had to pay higher taxes. So this was even more pressure put on the farmers to sell part of their holdings.

But I could not make this purchase. And I did not. It made me angry with myself that I had even considered doing this. The idea was to save the potato fields.

The property is probably worth three million today. And we're practically out of potato fields.

Soon after this, however, Marty and I, inadvertently, and without wanting to, helped accelerate the collapse of potato farming in the Hamptons.

"I'd like to write another article for the paper," Marty said the next day, after I told him I wasn't interested in the land purchase. "You pick an idea. I just miss writing. Haven't done it in a while."

I thought about it. The Windmill Antilles was old news. But then, I remembered something from my days at Harvard. Among the other courses I took there was one on city planning. It was not a good idea to build a housing development next to a big farm, the professor told us. Farming makes a lot of dust, and there's a lot of spraying of chemicals. It doesn't happen but a few times a year, he

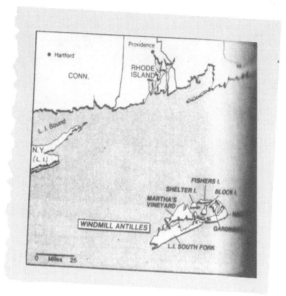

THE *NEW YORK TIMES* ILLUSTRATES THE WINDMILL ANTILLES
(*New York Times* May 29, 1977)

continued, but when it does, and if the wind is blowing in the wrong direction, whatever it is can get into the homes. And that is not good.

"You live in a farm field," I said. "Did you ever check your water to make sure it's good?"

"No," he said.

"Have the county check your water. I know they do it. They do it free of charge if you ask. And then write about it."

"Okay."

Two weeks later, Marty called me back.

"The county came and checked it," he said. "It's perfectly fine. There's no story here, really. Iron is high, but it's within normal range. And there are some other things. But it's all normal."

I asked Marty to read me the list of things the county checked for and he did. And as he did, it became apparent to me that all the pollutants they were checking for were poisons that a factory might leave behind, not poisons that farms might leave behind.

I have a reporter's instincts.

"Call them up and ask them to check for farm chemicals," I said.

The next day he called back again.

"They don't do that for free," he said. "But they *will* do that if you pay them fifty dollars."

"Let's spend the fifty," I said.

And so we did. And that's how the roof fell in on potato farming. It was the Temik. It was in there. And it had *not* decomposed. Marty and Judy were drinking contaminated water. Now they shifted over to bottled water. And again he wrote about it.

This story was picked up by *Time* magazine, by the *Wall Street Journal*, and NBC as well as the *Washington Post* and the *New York Times*. It ran around the world.

In the days that followed, the county came in and found Temik in a lot of wells, including many in farmhouses where the farmers lived. And then DuPont rushed in and said they would stop producing Temik and free of charge would put filters on all the wells where Temik could be found. They would change the filters and monitor the levels indefinitely into the future. They did this for years, until, at long last, the levels of Temik were gone.

I have often wondered what the potato farmers thought of me for having brought everyone the bad news about Temik. I knew potato farmers. And I still know some of the few that remain today. And yet, nobody ever said anything about that article. Who wants poisons?

Ten years later, on a warm day in August, I walked into the backyard of *Dan's Papers* to where the delivery drivers were loading the bundles of papers onto the trucks. It always amazed me to see all these tens of thousands of copies of what I wrote every week getting separated and prepared for distribution.

That day, one of the drivers was wearing a battered old baseball cap that said TEMIK on it. I could hardly believe it. Temik had been banned from the market almost immediately after the article had appeared in *Dan's Papers*. I had never seen the word anywhere, on a can or bottle or a hat. This was a leftover.

"That's quite a valuable baseball cap," I said.

"It is?"

"Temik hasn't been made in years. Where did you get it?"

"I don't know."

"I'll buy it from you."

"Sure."

"Twenty?"

"You said it was valuable. How about fifty."

"Okay."

And so I bought it. I have it today. But I have never worn it out in public. I just can't.

Potatohampton

~~~~~~

At 8 a.m. on the sunny morning of June 4, 1978, my girlfriend and I and several other employees of *Dan's Papers* threw into a delivery van some banners, folding tables, chairs, registration forms, cash, and an empty cigar box and drove it all up to the parking lot of what is today the Kmart Shopping Center in Bridgehampton.

Our starting gun would go off at nine (runners who had urged me to have this race said the runners were dedicated souls who would want to start early), and since we had been advertising it in *Dan's Papers* so vigorously for three weeks, I figured there might be a hundred runners or more, so maybe we ought to start it in a big parking lot nearby. That would be what is now Kmart. We'd be in and out in half an hour before they opened. They'd never know we had been there.

But we didn't have *one* hundred people who wanted to run in this race, we had *five* hundred. And by five minutes to nine, with those registered waiting in astonishment at the long lines of other runners hoping to still do so at our single registration table in the parking lot, everybody began

START OF THE FIRST POTATOHAMPTON
(Photo courtesy *Dan's Papers*)

to get angry. The ten-dollar registration fees had been going into the cigar box (the charity was Southampton Hospital). We had numbers we gave out, but they ended at 200, and we had run out of pins to pin them on with, and as I stood with Marty Lang, the Southampton town supervisor (he would make a speech and fire the starting gun), we watched all this in alarm. Then, suddenly, one of our editors stood up by the registration table and took matters into his own hands, literally.

"That's *it!*" he shouted. He simply grabbed the registration slips, lists, numbers and the cigar box and simply heaved them up in the air to waft down in great fluttering pieces.

I moved toward that crowd of people. Then stopped.

"Everybody over to the starting line," he shouted. I forget this fellow's name, actually I have never forgotten this fellow's name, but I am not going to tell you who he is even now.

And with that, everybody—both registered and unregistered—ran over to the starting line, which was located at the eastern entrance to the shopping center where it spills out onto Snake Hollow Road, and made a big crowd facing north. They already knew the route. I had printed up two hundred eight by eleven sheets of paper and folded them into four-page booklets with the map as one of the items on it, and so there it was.

And they were off. They whooped and hollered and ran north up toward Scuttlehole Road. Marty and I, quite a bit behind all these athletes and still in the parking lot, looked at one another. Marty had brought the Town Recreation Department Starter Pistol.

"Just aim it at my head," I told him. Neither of us laughed.

Well, the more responsible members of my staff, mostly the women, were now walking around picking up the litter of the failed registration, and so that was being taken care of. And so, with that, I told Marty "thank you very much," and then my girlfriend and I got into my car, and we went out onto Snake Hollow Road and soon caught up to the runners where that road turns into Mitchell Lane and heads for a mile or so up to Scuttlehole. They were beginning to spread out behind a leader in a long line of pumping runners in various colorful costumes, and they were kind of a blur as we went by and off to the open road ahead.

MITCHELL LANE IN BRIDGEHAMPTON, 1961
(Photo by the author)

There were no signs on trees about where to turn for this race. There were no police officers at any of the turns. There were no water stops anywhere. Unaware of the protocol of running a race—this was the first public race ever held in the Hamptons—I had no idea of what I was doing, was just making it up as I went along, and was now just so blissfully happy to have created this monstrosity, so much larger than what I had conceived, and so roared on.

It was my girlfriend who was driving, actually. I had my camera with me, a long lens Canon, and I was leaning out the window taking pictures of the crowd thundering along behind.

But then, a dark thought came over me. I had discovered this big problem just a week before the race. And it might be that people could get killed.

"Pull way ahead," I told my girlfriend. "Turn left at Hayground. We've got to get to the railroad crossing fast!"

Here is what I had done a month before the race. I had set out a route that would take runners past some of the most beautiful scenery we had. My idea at the time—this was long before we were jammed with summer visitors; at that time we wanted *more* visitors—was that if I brought the runners past the beautiful scenery on a Sunday morning right during Memorial Day weekend, at the end of the race, they'd tell their friends and family and more people would come out to the Hamptons, meaning more $$ for the merchants and after that more advertising for us.

I had selected a route heading off north through the farm fields of Mitchell, left onto Scuttlehole, past the three magnificent ponds and potato fields there, left onto Hayground, past the dairy farm, across the railroad tracks and south to the Montauk Highway, and then down into Sagaponack to the beautiful little bridge and the old Sagaponack General Store and two-room schoolhouse and the windmill. It would be just a dazzling display for those running in this race.

And crossing the railroad tracks would not be a problem. There were two crossings, actually. The first was just a hundred yards north of the starting line, when there was no train coming. They'd be in a big clump. As for the second crossing, at Hayground, well, what were there, anyway, two trains a day? What could go wrong?

But then as race week approached I thought about it. Maybe I ought to check. And so it was, a week before the event that, just to be sure, I called the railroad to find out when those times would be at those crossings, at Snake Hollow going northbound and at Hayground going southbound, and what I found out was that the train would pass going eastbound full steam ahead at 9:14 a.m., just fourteen minutes after the start! The runners would be crossing southbound for the second time, at Hayground, exactly when the train was coming through!

"Can you ask the train to wait?" I asked.

"No. It has to keep to a schedule."

"What could you do?"

"We could have it slow way down and honk a lot."

I actually wrote about the possibility of the train in the race program. The map noted the two crossings. "If you get to the second crossing at Hayground and the crossing gate comes down indicating the train is going to shortly pass through," I wrote, "just jog in place."

What else could I do?

We drove swiftly west down Scuttlehole and turned left onto Hayground heading south. The railroad crossing was about half a mile down. Two hundred yards beyond was the busy Montauk Highway with the police with their flashing lights ready to stop the traffic so the race could cross over and head down into Sagaponack. I saw that the railroad crossing gates were still up. I crossed my fingers that we could get across before they came down, and we did. Now we were down near the melee of the police cars and flashing lights. I tried to make a U-turn to go back to the railroad gate, but an officer wouldn't let me. He tried waving me on.

"Race is coming down Hayground," he told me. "You can't go back. Just come on through." He was indicating the Montauk Highway.

"I'm running the race," I said.

He nodded, motioned for me to park on the grass there, and in a flash we were out of the car and running up to the railroad gates. The leaders, three of them, were coming down Hayground toward us from far away. They were going to make it. No they weren't.

CLANG, CLANG, CLANG, the gates sounded. The lights flashed. And there it was, the gates slowly lowered. Then I could hear the horn of the train, and then there it was, slowly just as they said it would be, coming, and coming and now about to come through. At this point, the runners were obediently running in place right on the other side of the gate. And then I couldn't see them anymore as the train began crossing the road.

But now I couldn't bear to face them when the gates would come back up. I had screwed up their rhythm and planning.

"Let's run back to the highway," I said.

And so we turned around and ran off, with the train still coming slowly through, just as that man had said it would, and so it was that we got back to the highway before the lead runners and I was able to take a picture of them as they came down.

I surveyed the scene. There at that crossing of the Montauk Highway, a half dozen policemen had completely stopped all the traffic on Route 27 in both directions. And then here came the leaders now, past us, the five of them (two stragglers had caught up at the gate), in a bunch and safely across the Montauk Highway with the police holding all the traffic up and down Newlight Lane and on into Sagaponack.

There was a big space after these first five. And then a few more runners came and then a few more. After three or four minutes, about thirty runners had come through, and you could see up the road that there was this endless line of runners all spread out all the way up almost to Scuttlehole.

I looked at the sergeant who was standing on the white line of the highway in charge of the shutdown, and all the runners coming at us from as much as half a mile away, and he looked at me.

"I thought they were coming in a group all together," he shouted. "We can only do this a few more minutes."

"Aaaargh," I said.

And so, five minutes later, he did just that. Now—and I was standing there watching this in horror—it was just the cops slowing down all the motorists and the runners weaving between the cars coming through individually and in packs and I just prayed that nobody was going to get killed. I waited there watching this for only another five minutes. I couldn't bear to watch it. And so we got in the car and left to go to the finish line. If somebody died, I just didn't want to be there.

This was long before people sued you over the slightest thing.

Well, I will end this commentary here. I will tell you that the race was won by Marcel Philippe, who was a member of the French Olympic track team. He commented to me as he crossed the finish line in just over thirty minutes flat that he could not possibly have run that fast.

"Your course is too short," he said. "It's not 10K."

"I drove it and measured it on my car speedometer," I told him. "That was 10K." He looked at me blankly.

"You need professional people," he said.

Other people complained to me about other things—the lack of water stops, the train, blah blah blah—and I thought, what a bunch of wimps. But then a whole lot of other people congratulated me and told me what a wonderful thing this was and I should just concentrate on fixing it for next year.

So that's the story of the first Dan's Potatohampton Mini-thon Race ever, back in the day when the New York Marathon was in its infancy and us pioneers were not yet deified for what we did to start the running-race industry—though I do bow down to the Boston Marathon, of course, which had been going on a long time by then.

Since then, we've run the race more or less smoothly. It's no longer a 10K, it's a 5K. In the past, we've had potato farmers show up at the finish line and hand out sacks of potatoes to the participants. We've had a psychiatrist on duty at the Sagg Bridge, which on the day of our race was in a weakened state about to be repaired and closed to car traffic and it was the psychiatrist's job to see to it that the participants tiptoed across. (The psychiatrist came from a research division of Stony Brook University Hospital, which was the beneficiary that year.) That went well. There was the time people came in costume and ran as, for example, a couple of baked potatoes.

And there was the time when we ran it in 100 degree heat and the leader of the race collapsed just a quarter mile before the finish line. (He lived.) And there was the time when the entire community was flooded with torrential rains and although on race day it was sunny we had to cancel because the route was in some places something you would have to wade waist deep through.

It's all been great fun. See you this year at 8:30 a.m., in the little two-acre Militia Park on Ocean Road in Bridge-hampton, just fifty yards south of the Montauk Highway on the west side behind what is now where Almond Restaurant has just reopened.

We don't cross the tracks anymore. Good idea, that decision, too.

The Cannon

~~~~~~

On a Saturday afternoon in June of 1986, a group of summer people with sailboats in Sag Harbor held an impromptu regatta beginning at 5 p.m. A horn was sounded at that hour, and whoever showed up in the next fifteen minutes at a starting line, marked off by a white buoy in the harbor, was in it. The rules were that there were no rules. Any size boat with any number of people on board could enter. And the winner would be whoever could get all the way down to another white buoy and back three times.

This regatta was so successful that the yachtsmen decided to hold it every Saturday at five all summer, and when they did that it became a story for the newspaper.

When I went down there to Long Wharf to cover it, pad in hand, I was startled to hear, exactly at 5 p.m., the very unmistakable sound of a cannon. I asked somebody about it. This was not a horn.

"They're now using a cannon," a man said. "It starts the event."

"They have a cannon?"

"Oh yeah," he said. Then he chuckled.

The chuckle made me think—this must be some cannon. I imagined it looked like a revolutionary war cannon. People would put cotton in their ears, light a fuse, then turn away and clap their hands over their ears. What did I know?

A few years later, I came to learn that a regatta cannon did not need to be anywhere near that big. I was not in Sag Harbor but on Shelter Island, at a cocktail party in the main dining room of the Shelter Island Yacht Club. The sun was setting. As it did, a cannon was fired from the deck of the yacht club to celebrate that fact.

Curious, I wandered out to look. The cannon was about two feet long and one foot high, and the man who fired it had pulled a string attached to the back of it while pressing one foot on the top of it to keep it from jumping around.

And now I thought—I ought to have a cannon at my house. I live on a hillside. A road passes down below in front of the house, and on the other side of that road, backing almost right up to it, there are boats rocking in their slips. Beyond that, across one mile of water, the sun sets over the far shore every evening.

I have kids ages fifteen, twelve, six, and four, is what I thought. And I'm a kid age forty-seven. From the time the oldest was in a stroller, we had gone to Disney World every year. They'd love a cannon.

And so I bought one.

I got it at Preston's Nautical Store in Greenport—the only store on the East End to sell cannons—and when I did, I told this skinny kid who was my salesman that I did not

THE CANNON
(Photo by the author)

want to have to put my foot on the top of it when I fired it. It seemed undignified and unfair to the cannon.

The kid looked at me funny. He was chewing gum and he blew a bubble. "It does have quite a kick," he said.

"What if I bolt it to the deck railing?"

"You could do that. Just make sure you use strong steel bolts. I would recommend at least a quarter inch. There's a hardware store just across the street."

"How far away can you hear it?"

"With ten-gauge shells? Four miles. You have a yacht club?"

The cannon he sold me was a chrome-plated-steel affair with a two-foot-long barrel on wagon wheels, with the string you pulled at the back. It came with ten-gauge shotgun shells—blanks, of course—along with earplugs and a whole lot of other gear.

At 4 p.m., I drove home from Greenport by taking the little ferry ride from Greenport to Shelter Island and then, after crossing Shelter Island, another ferry ride to the Hamptons. I was very excited. I had a cannon in the back.

Sunset, here we come.

My four kids were all for this. Their mother was not. She folded her arms. But the kids raced around, fists in the air, whooping and hollering as I described where on the deck railing I would put it and just how loud it would sound.

"You can hear cannon fire from four miles away," I said, repeating what the salesman had told me.

"Yippeee!" the four-year-old said.

"Don't worry," I said, addressing their mother. "It will be bolted down." I showed her the bolts and the drill. "It will only be fired at sunset. And you can keep the shells in the filing drawer with the lock and key."

That seemed to satisfy her.

During dinner, the kids repeatedly asked me if it was time to fire off the cannon. Each time, I pointed at the sun to note that it still had a ways to go. They were pretty impatient about how long it was taking.

Finally the time came for what would be the first firing. This was a few minutes before eight.

"Earplugs in?"

All the earplugs were put in. Everyone was standing around in a big semi-circle, the four kids, the mom, and the two dogs. I fiddled with the cannon, cocking the trigger, sliding the shell all the way in.

"Step back please," I said. "I want everybody far away from this."

Now the sun was right at the point where the last sliver of it was almost set behind the far shore. I gripped the string, closed my eyes, and pulled.

WHAM!!!

I heard screams and howls. I blinked open my eyes to see a cloud of white smoke and two midsize animals that looked like my dogs go barreling past me and out into the yard and up the hill. The younger kids were bawling. The mother was holding them tightly to her.

"Cool," said one of the older kids.

Out on the street, I saw a car that just happened to be passing by when I pulled the string, pull over.

"Everybody inside," I shouted.

This man got out, looked around, apparently didn't see the white smoke that was still hovering over our deck, and then walked around his car, a white Toyota, examining all four tires. Then he got back in and drove off.

For the next six months, I fired the cannon every night at sunset except when it was raining or all clouded over. Slowly, it began to sink in on the yachting community that there was some guy sending out a salute to the sunset every once in a while from the head of the harbor. Those in the immediate neighborhood, I suppose, could see the puff of smoke if they looked at the appropriate time. Those farther away would have no idea who it was.

I ran into my neighbor once and talked about it. I only had one neighbor there. He was Cliff Townsend, and he lived on the other side of some underbrush that separated our properties. This was about two hundred yards away. He said he rather liked it.

"You always know it's coming, maybe," he said.

There was a problem that came up after a while, however, with the yachtsmen who had the boats directly across the street. The yachtsmen were not there all the time of course. They would only be there for a while, either coming or going. After that, there'd either be an empty slip or an empty boat in the slip bobbing around for another day or two. It was just that sometimes, the sunset would begin to set up just as some yachtsmen and their guests were messing around on their boats.

BOOM!!!

"Ahh, hey, guy hold off, would ya?" two of them shouted up at us the first time this happened.

Well, the sunset was the sunset. "It's all over," I shouted down. Then I thought about it. "Tell you what," I continued. "If we see you out there and the sun is about to set, I'll shout out a warning for you."

"Okay."

As for the kids, I now had a rule that everybody had to be inside behind closed door sliders when I fired the cannon. And the dogs had to be further into the house in one of the bedrooms. The kids could take turns being with the dogs.

In mid-August—this was now seven weeks later—a police car came up our driveway just ten minutes after I fired the cannon. The kids, who were playing in the yard, looked at the policeman wide eyed as he got out of his car and, in his full uniform, came up onto the deck.

"Are you the people who are firing some sort of cannon?" he asked.

You could still smell the gun powder.

"Yes."

"We've had a complaint. I can't tell you who. One of the neighbors. You can't be firing a cannon on Three Mile Harbor Road."

I stood my ground. "It's not like I fire it all the time," I said. "I fire it only once a day, at sunset. It's a sunset cannon. That's what you're supposed to do with it."

He looked at it closely. It really didn't look like much of anything.

"It's what they have at yacht clubs," I said. "And it only fires blanks, of course."

That was a lie.

He thought about it for a minute. Then, finally, he spoke. "Yeah, I guess that makes sense," he said. "Just make sure you fire it *only* at sunset."

"Okay," I beamed.

The kids cheered.

I continued on, firing the cannon through the autumn. But then I began to tire of it. At this point, it seemed to me, it was getting to be a job. There were no boats in the water. Very few cars to try to fire between. And as a matter of fact, the sun was now setting so early that it was getting hard to get home in time to fire it with any regularity at the proper time. In fact, now, I was only firing the cannon when I happened to be home when the sun came down, which was now four in the afternoon.

But boy did it make a roar at that time of day, late in the year. Without the leaves on the trees, it would make the big bang and then echo not once but twice, up and down the harbor. It must be something you could hear for ten miles or more.

About the tenth of November, I gave up.

One day in early May of the following year, however, there was the most beautiful sunset imaginable setting up at the end of the day. I could not resist it. I closed all the sliders, got the dogs in the bedroom, told everybody to get the earplugs in, shoved a shell into the breach, looked left and right to make sure no cars were coming, looked down to make sure there were no people in boats—well—there were actually *no* boats yet for the new year, and then, WHAM! Another sun successfully set.

Welcome to the summer season of 1987, I thought.

Chris Johnson

~~~~~~

In the 1970s and 1980s, Chris Johnson was the best-singing troubadour in the Hamptons. He had a great repertoire of songs he played on guitar or mandolin, and he was always in demand for parties.

I got to meet him at one of these affairs, a book party for a local author. There he was, fingering with dazzling speed through "Rocky Mountain Breakdown" and "Tennessee Traveler."

He was an imposing figure. He was six foot two, thin and lantern jawed. He had a friendly face and a great shock of black hair. And he sang effortlessly through his songs with a fine smile and this very strong and soothing baritone voice.

He also wrote songs, which were either about local history or local events. My favorite was an upscale, joyous number called "Acres of Clams." He was often asked to play it. He made a 45 record of that song, which I still have. If I could find out where he was playing, I'd try to get myself in just to hear him. I loved listening to Chris.

THE AUTHOR WITH CHRIS JOHNSON
(Photo donated by Chris Johnson)

It was about this time that somebody bought me an autoharp, which is a triangular stringed instrument you lay across your lap and strum with your fingers. I considered learning it a challenge and, after a while, got pretty good at it.

One evening, I heard that Chris was going to do a set at the Stephen Talkhouse coffee house in Amagansett, and so I brought my autoharp down there in the hopes he'd ask me to play it with him. He did. We played together seamlessly, with him out front and me behind him, backing him up. The second and third time I did this with him, I added a kazoo and a tambourine. It was even better.

Thus a musical acquaintanceship began between Chris and me, not strong enough that we might consider creating a little band, because I was not good enough, but because we just liked playing together.

In 1978, Perry B. Duryea, a Montauk lobsterman who had become the powerful speaker of the house up in Albany, announced his candidacy for governor. He faced the popular incumbent Hugh Carey, and to defeat him, vowed to spend three months touring the state and shaking tens of thousands of hands. Among those he asked to accompany him was Chris Johnson. Johnson would sing at every village and town and introduce Mr. Duryea. He wrote songs about Mr. Duryea. Perry, forthright and true, he came off of his lobster boat to run the state for me and you. And he'd warm up the crowd from the back of the campaign train they hired for the occasion.

But when Duryea lost—in a landslide—Chris came back changed in an odd way. He seemed a bit harsher, perhaps a bit politicized. After that, he seemed to lose interest in his work as a troubadour.

"There are many issues facing this great nation," Chris would say. His jaw was thrust out. I didn't know what to make of it.

Johnson, it seemed to me, was going through some sort of midlife crisis. I had seen a sign of it the year before when he was in a patriotic play put on by the local theater group. He had a small role: Abe Lincoln, and he was, in real life, beginning to sound like Abe Lincoln.

But then he apparently stopped being Abe Lincoln. I didn't see him for a while, but when I did, a few months later, he was now talking like a man from the colonial era named Francis Hopkinson. I didn't even know who Francis Hopkinson was. Chris explained it.

"Francis Hopkinson was a signer of the Declaration of Independence and the designer of the first American flag. Most people think that Betsy Ross designed and made that first flag, but it's not true. Hopkinson designed it. And he never got credit for it."

Then, I began getting letters from Chris Johnson. This was very unusual. Nobody wrote letters. You just picked up the phone and called someone. The letters Chris wrote were in bold script made with a quill pen. Sometimes he'd sign the letters "Chris Johnson," and sometimes "Chris Johnson a/k/a Francis Hopkinson."

"I know I haven't seen you in a while," he said. "I've gotten a job playing Francis Hopkinson at a restaurant in New York City. We perform five times a week. Come and see me." He enclosed a picture. He was dressed up in colonial costume. He had a fake beard. You could see the diners at the table in the foreground.

"Hope you're well," he concluded. "Your humble servant, Chris Johnson, a/k/a Francis Hopkinson."

Over the next ten years, I would get a letter from Chris every six months or so. He had moved to Philadelphia. He was performing as Francis Hopkinson all over town. There were newspaper clippings of Francis Hopkinson in historical dramas. There were pictures of Johnson as Francis Hopkinson taken at parades going through downtown Philadelphia, at the table celebrating the birthday of someone playing Benjamin Franklin, and so forth and so on. On rare occasions, he was Lincoln. Most pictures were of him as Hopkinson. Hopkinson was where it was at.

Philadelphia was, of course, home to the Continental Congress. It was where the Declaration of Independence was signed. It was where the Liberty Bell was. Chris was in heaven.

At his invitation, I went down to visit him once. He put me up in a bed and breakfast rather than where he was living. He was living with a girlfriend at her house, but apparently he did not have personal-guest privileges. We did eat together though. I found his girlfriend to be very intense and strong willed. But Chris liked her.

"Do you play guitar much?" I asked.

"Once in a while," he said. "Mostly, though, I'm Hopkinson. Hopkinson is real popular here. He came from here."

I knew that.

Chris, remaining in Philadelphia, continued to write to me in East Hampton. On occasion I'd write him back, though briefly. Then one day, five years later, I got a letter from Hopkinson, not Chris. It really brought me up short. The address to me on the front was very elaborate and flowery. Playing at Hopkinson was one thing. *Being* Hopkinson was another. Had he gone off the deep end?

I tore open the letter and read it. There was a *reason* he was Hopkinson.

"Dear Sir," it began. "Having read your latest newspaper article about the American flag and the role supposedly played in its creation by the treacherous Betsy Ross, I have to tell you that you leave me no recourse but to challenge you to a duel. You have offended me greatly Sir. I will see you on Saturday, November 14, 1987, at the central point of the western footbridge of 17th Street leading down to the harbor here in Philadelphia at dawn. I am your humble servant, Francis Hopkinson."

What had I done? I had indeed written about the history of the American flag, harmlessly mentioning the role supposedly played in its creation by Betsy Ross. It was an article about a new store that sold Americana: tablecloths, napkins, flags, bunting, and so forth. It was unusual to have such an establishment in one of our downtowns.

Had it come to this?

Chris Johnson, the real Chris Johnson, was still living with the same woman and in the same house as five years before, though now he had graduated to being allowed guests. I got there the night before the duel, and they welcomed me warmly. I was to stay over, they had said. I was offered something to drink and a dinner of chicken croquettes and peas. His girlfriend, Sherry, who was now his common-law wife, he told me, went up to bed at a reasonable hour while we stayed downstairs with the cats in the living room and talked.

After a while, I asked him if he continued to play guitar.

"I sold it, actually," he said. "I wasn't playing anymore and we needed the money. It's okay."

Late that night I wondered about that. The conclusion I came to was that Francis Hopkinson, who had invented a wind bottle instrument and several other niceties for the eighteenth century, besides designing the flag, was not a guitar player. I'd heard the last of "Foggy Mountain Breakdown" from him, anyway, whoever he was.

A cold wind was blowing on that footbridge over this 8-lane highway that dark November morning. I had brought a windbreaker, but it wasn't doing any good. And, as instructed, I had obtained the services of a second. He was a full professor of psychology at the University of Pennsylvania by the name of Sonny Klausner.

It was a fitting choice. Sonny was my second cousin, someone I had known since I was born, about ten years older than me, and an adventurer. He had been born in New York City to my mother's brother Ed and his wife Bertha, and had been a bombardier in World War II. After that, he went to Palestine and joined the Haganah to fight for the creation of Israel. To me he was a war hero and a brave and amazing role model. At the time of the duel, I was fifty years old. Sonny was sixty-five.

As instructed the night before by Chris Johnson, I was to wear present-day street clothes, while Francis Hopkinson would be dressed in his colonial garb.

"There is to be no fooling with history here," Chris had told me as we sat on the sofa together. "You are a modern newspaper publisher who has offended a colonial American founder of this country. We will each dress appropriately."

I asked Chris if he would be taking me to the duel in the morning. It was a sort of test to see if Chris and Francis were separate. But he would have none of it. In the dark just before dawn, he said, my second should pick me up and drive me to the site of the duel.

"I will leave you with written directions if you like," Chris said.

I told him that wouldn't be necessary. "Sonny has lived here for thirty years, he says, and he knows where the bridge is."

Up on that bridge, a stone affair that spanned this 8-lane highway, Francis Hopkinson and I stood, with our seconds, facing one another in the predawn darkness, about fifteen feet apart. Between us, there was a referee, a heavyset man also in colonial garb, who apparently had been recruited by Hopkinson to keep us apart and issue us instructions.

"Mr. Hopkinson, having made the challenge, shall present Mr. Rattiner with his choice of weapon," this referee said with some elaborate pre-Revolutionary flourishes. "Shall you step forward, Mr. Hopkinson?"

Hopkinson had his own second, who was carrying this wooden box. They stepped forward. Hopkinson's second held it out and indicated I should open it, so I did.

The referee lit a lantern and held it up so we could have a better look. Inside, on a velvet pillow, were four weapons. There were two identical colonial flintlock pistols, and two plastic water pistols, one green and one red. The choice, apparently, was mine.

I thought about it only briefly. It would be water pistols. I took the red one and Hopkinson, after I took mine, took his, which was the remaining green one.

"We shall forego the flintlocks," Hopkinson said with a flourish.

"Gentlemen," the referee said, "you may consult with your seconds for a few moments. And then the duel shall begin."

We retreated to the opposite sides of the bridge where we had been before.

At this point, about six people who had been walking across the bridge at that early hour stopped to see what was going to happen. Dawn had not yet broken, but it was getting light. I looked to speak to one of these people.

"Ssshhh!" Sonny said. "Talk to *me*."

I stared at him. He came up close to me and, cupping his hand over his mouth, whispered to me, "Get off the first shot. And aim to the left to account for the wind."

"Okay, break it up!" shouted the referee. "Would the combatants please step forward?"

The four of us assembled in the center of the cobblestones again.

"Mr. Hopkinson, are you ready? Mr. Rattiner, are you ready?"

We both nodded. Behind my opponent, fifty feet below, flocks of automobiles and trucks were now noisily moving along the highway. This was so ridiculous.

"Seconds to your corners. Combatants, please turn around back to back. Point your weapons upward in the cocked position. I will count to ten. And as I do so, please begin pacing off the steps. At ten, feel free to turn and fire. Are you ready?"

We were ready.

"One. Two. Three." A plan was beginning to form in my mind as I took the appropriate steps. "Four. Five." I wheeled around and faced Hopkinson who, at the very moment had also wheeled around. And we both fired. I missed. He got me. I could feel the sprinkle of water.

"No, no!" the referee shouted.

But it was over. I clutched my chest and spiraled down to the ground, on my back, dead. As I landed, I apparently hit my head on a cobblestone jutting up from the road. I saw stars.

The next thing I saw were a dozen or so people peering down at me, with looks of concern on their faces. I blinked. My face was wet. It had started to rain. There were drops on my glasses. Where did this come from?

"You're bleeding from the back of the head," Sonny said.

"I'm disappointed that no press showed up," Chris in his Hopkinson suit was saying. "I sent out releases. Maybe we did this too early."

He held out an arm. "Let me help you up," he said.

As he did so, he blew a breath over the end of his water pistol, cooling it down and dispersing the smoke from the end of the barrel.

And so I lived to fight another day.

J. J. Johnson

On a hot day in July of 1981, I got in my twenty-two-year-old English sports car and drove it about two miles to the junkyard owned by J. J. Johnson across from the East Hampton Town dump. J. J., a slender black man with a perpetually dazzling smile, was on the phone at his battered old desk inside the shack there. In a second shack, attached to the first, was an old car prepped for painting. J. J. did body work.

"A '73 Pontiac Grand Prix sedan? I think I got one of those. You come on down and have a look. I'll be here all day and I'm pretty sure. Yeah, it's a four door. A '74, actually. But I think that's about the same as the '73. Yeah."

Then he hung up the phone.

"Hey *Dan*," he said. He always shouted my name when he saw me. He always shouted everybody's names when they first would come to his attention. "I guess I know that old sports-car sound," he said. "Pretty, pretty. So you brought it by. Let me have a look."

J. J. JOHNSON
(Photo by the author)

Out front, we walked around my little red sports car, admiring it. That's what people did in the 1980s, men anyway, when they came upon an old sports car from the 1950s.

It was a little bit of a thing. It had an open cockpit with two black leather bucket seats side by side. Behind the buckets was a tiny, narrow bench, a sort of joke for a back seat. One person could sit back there, if he or she sat sideways. In front, a long low hood with two headlights jutted out from grandly leaping front fenders. And below the hood in front was a grille that had a round hole in its center. If your battery died, you could insert the metal crank that came with the car in that hole and turn it manually to start the engine. I'd never done it, but it was nice to know.

From inside the cockpit, you pushed a button to start the engine. There was a stick shift on the floor and behind the cockpit a tiny trunk with little protruding red taillights. It was—and is—the cutest thing. The car also had a top you could put on if it rained. It sat in the tiny trunk, folded up like a blanket, a black leather blanket you could button onto a metal frame that lifted up and over the cockpit from the back and then attach to the outside of the cockpit with snaps. It was really hard to put on. But the alternative was just to drive real fast through the rain and huddle up against the front windshield. The mist would swirl around.

Something utterly unique about this car was the fact that if you sat in either of the two front bucket seats, you could reach out above the front doors, turn your arm down and touch the street with the palm of your hand. At speed, that would be a real stupid idea, of course. But the possibility was there nevertheless. There has never been a car built before or since that has this feature, as far as I know.

"So that's what's propping the driver seat up," J. J. said. He was pointing to a soft, square nautical seat cushion that was wedged in between the back seat bench and the front seat. The bench was providing support.

"Take it out and the seat backs just fall back into the bench," I said. "That's why I came here. The seat collapsed backwards yesterday. You can't drive without the cushion in back of it."

"Not good," J. J. said.

"I figured there must be a metal frame in that seat. Figure you can open it up and reinforce it. You know what's in there? Look."

J. J. squinted at a seam in the leather seat that had partially come undone.

"Horse hair," I said.

"Hmm," he said.

J. J. put his hand up to his chin. "I'll have a look," he said, "but it's probably rust. Maybe nothing left in there to attach any reinforcing to."

"You can do it."

"I'll have a look."

"I'm sure there's something you can do."

"Hmmm. Need a lift home?" he asked.

"Wouldn't hurt."

J. J. took the BE RIGHT BACK sign off his desk and hung it on the screen door. Five minutes later, we were up my driveway in his old Cadillac sedan and by my front door. I got out.

"Call me next week," he said. "But don't get your hopes up."

"I have a lot of faith in you."

He drove off. Frankly, I was very concerned about this front seat. It was the driver's seat, after all.

The car was a 1959 Triumph TR3 that I had bought when it was seven years old from the owner of a nightclub called Charlie Brown's in Hampton Bays. I'd paid eight hundred dollars for it. A used car. There were lots of English sports cars around in those days. The GIs had brought them home from England after the war twenty years before. At the nightclub, where the sports car had been with a FOR SALE sign on it, there were pictures of Charlie Brown, the comic book character from the *Peanuts* cartoon everywhere. But it also turned out that was the owner's real name. It was right there on his car registration when he signed the car over to me.

The car had been in perfect working condition. Amazingly, nothing on it ever broke, not for years and years. These sports cars were famous for breaking down. But not this one. I changed the oil periodically. I serviced it every three thousand miles. It just kept going and going. Now the seat had broken. And that was a worrisome problem.

Before I went to J. J., I called a company I'd been told about that sold TR3 replacement parts. It was called Moss Motors and it was located in Petaluma, California. Seats were no longer being made for that car, they said. And whatever stock of them they had was now gone.

J. J. did not wait for me to call. Four days later, he called with the bad news.

"It's just all rust in there," he said. "I looked in the other one too. That one is just about to go. Nothing I can do. You've got to get new seats."

"There aren't any," I said.

"Let me look around," he said, referring to the twenty acres of his junked car lot. The next day he called back. "I've got two front seats from a Thunderbird that would fit in there. Just give me the word."

This was the worst idea I ever heard. And I told him so. "It would just look awful, an old English sports car with Thunderbird seats."

"Well, I got 'em," he said. "You know what? I'll make some calls around and see if any other junkies have seats for a TR3. But that's a long shot. What you really want to do, I think, is find somebody who's got a broken-down TR3 who wants to sell it for junk. You could use it for a parts car. A lot of people with old sports cars have parts cars."

"I don't know anybody that has one," I said.

"Well then, keep that cushion in there and you'll be fine. And I'd get a mate for it. You'll be needing a second one soon enough."

J. J.'s idea that I find a parts car was something I had not thought of. There were lots of rich people in the Hamptons. Maybe somebody had one. Amazingly, someone did. I had put an ad in the paper. And I got a call from a summer resident who had a TR3 good for junk. He gave me his address, which was in Napeague, and I drove over there to have a look.

The address was a little A-frame house with a small garage attached. I knocked on the door. The man, a small fellow of about forty with stooped shoulders and black hair, opened it and, instead of inviting me in, motioned me around to the attached garage on the side.

"I'll meet you there," he said. Then he closed the door.

Shortly, he raised the garage door up from the inside. And there it was, his TR3, just like mine, except that it was bright yellow. It looked pretty good, too, except for one thing: every piece of glass on it was smashed in—windshield, taillights, dashboard gauge covers, headlights, everything.

"How did that happen?" I asked.

"We were having a fight one night," he said softly. "She took a tire iron to it."

Neither of us said anything for a while. I listened for sounds of a wife somewhere. Nothing.

"How much you want for it?" I asked.

"Three hundred dollars and haul it away. And I'll have to set it up for you to come. We'll make an appointment."

I had a pretty good idea what that was about.

"Deal," I said.

Ten days later, I came back with the money, a friend, and a heavy rope and towed it back to East Hampton and up into my driveway. It sat there next to the garage for about a year, a tarp thrown over the cockpit to protect the two seats from the rain. There was no folded-up leather top in the trunk. I'd get around to taking those precious seats out and putting them in my car one of these days.

One day, a year later, J. J. called.

"I was thinkin'," he said, "you got such a nice house up there, and there's this piece of junk in the backyard because it won't fit in your garage with the other TR3 and it's such a shame, lookin' at that every day. I thought maybe we could tow it over to my place and just leave it in the back here. When you get around to changing the seats out, I'll have it. I got lots of room. No charge to you."

"That's a nice offer. Thank you, J. J."

I towed it over.

More years went by. Because I knew I had the two seats I needed, now there was no hurry putting them in. I'd think about dropping my TR3 off from time to time, but there was always some reason I didn't. It was raining. There was a party I wanted to drive it to. Really, the seat cushions wedged in there worked fine. You never really noticed them unless you were looking directly at them.

On the other hand, I was a frequent visitor at J. J.'s junkyard just because I liked hanging around with him. He was such an interesting guy. He had been in the Korean War when he was young. He came home to the black section of the Hamptons and went into the taxi business. He had five station wagons at one point. Then he'd opened J. J.'s Autobody, at first just to repair his taxi fleet but then for just anybody. He became a respected member of the merchant community. Then he decided he wanted to run a nightclub. He found an old run-down bar in town that was out of business and transformed it into a great nightclub called The Pipe Dream, where locals from the black neighborhood in town would mingle with locals from the white neighborhood. The girls flocked to him over there. But after three years of that, he bought the old junkyard, moved the bodywork operation into the garage, and got married. In his shop, he'd tell wonderful stories. I'd come over. We'd sit around in his office drinking Cokes and eating potato chips and stuff. These were nice times.

One day, after I was there for about a half hour, he just happened to mention that there had been a problem with my junk TR3.

"Sorry about this," he said. "The bulldozer guy was over here last week to flatten part of my lot. I have to thin the herd, you know, when it comes to that. Don't keep around what isn't being used. Comes every six months or so. And—this was an accident—he flattened yours. I'm real sorry about that. It's been four years. You just never brought over your car."

I thought I might cry. "The whole thing? The seats too?" I said.

"I told him about the yellow sports car. But he did it anyway. It was in a whole group of other cars."

I stood up. "Can I see it?"

He stood up. "Sure."

We marched out back, him in the lead, and he was saying maybe the seats were off to one side but he doubted it and we went over first to one place, then another, and for a while I thought he didn't know where it was, but then he found it.

What a sad business. It was about six inches high, things sticking out of it at odd angles, and flat as a pancake. You could see in one place the curve of the old seats. There was a piece of the stick shift. Here was the metal frame of the windshield. An old English sports car, thirty-five years old, mashed.

"This is awful," I said.

"I'm really sorry about this."

"It cost me three hundred dollars," I said, although I immediately regretted saying that. I just kind of blurted it out. It was not his fault.

"You're gonna get those TR3 seats from somewhere," he said. "I know you will. And when you do, I'll put them in for you free. On me."

And he gave me that dazzling smile.

The next day, I began a monumental effort to scour the country to somewhere find myself a pair of TR3 seats. I called Moss for starters. I knew they didn't have any. But I had another idea.

"What about some of the auto body shops you deal with?" I asked. "You sell them parts for TR3s. Somebody must have a car with seats."

The salesman at Moss gave me a list of fifteen different auto body places around the country they dealt with, the fifteen most likely, he said, that might have a TR3 seat. I called them all. They were in Kentucky, California, Massachusetts, Florida, wherever. Back then, long-distance calls were expensive. I didn't care. I was going to find TR3 seats somewhere in the country come hell or high water.

No dealer had a set. But one of them did give me a lead. It came from an auto body shop in Charleston, West Virginia.

"We had a guy who worked here who I think had them," one of the mechanics told me. "He had an Austin Healey from that era, and it came with an extra pair of seats. But as I recall, the extra pair didn't fit. They were for a Triumph TR3."

"Do you have this guy's name and phone number? Maybe his address?"

"No address. And no phone number. But his name is Joe McBain. He doesn't live here anymore. He moved."

"To where?"

"Last I heard he was working as an orderly in a hospital in Dayton, Ohio."

"Know the name of the hospital?"

"I dunno. Dayton Memorial Hospital?"

I tried getting a phone number for Joe McBain in Dayton, Ohio, from information, without success. Then I asked for the names and phone numbers of every hospital in Dayton.

There were four. The third one had a Joe McBain who worked there. But he was on the night shift.

So I called back at night, and I got him.

"Joe McBain here."

I introduced myself, told him where I was from, and then got to the point.

"Somebody told me you might have two bucket seats for a TR3," I said.

"Who told you that?"

I told him.

"Well, it's true. And I still have them. They're new, never used. Wrapped up in plastic. I have 'em in my garage. You want 'em?"

"Yeah."

"Well, I guess you'll pay me a pretty penny for them. Whatever I want." He giggled.

A long silence followed this statement.

"How much you want for them?"

"I wouldn't take less than fifty dollars for them," he said. "Each."

What I said at that moment qualifies as one of the most remarkably intelligent things I have ever thought to say on the spur of the moment.

"How far are you from the Dayton airport?"

"Not far. Why?"

"Turns out," I said, "I need to be in Dayton tomorrow to make a speech. I get in around eleven in the morning and I fly out of there about three. I don't have the exact time the plane takes off, but I could call you back and give it to you exactly. Could you bring me the seats to the airport? I'd have the fifty dollars."

"Fifty dollars each," he said.

"That's what I meant. I could give you the money right there, in cash, and take them off your hands. I'd fly them home as luggage. Nothing to it."

"Give me a time," he said, "and I'll be there. I work nights, so I could be there during the day."

Today, the two seats from Dayton Ohio are firmly bolted into the floor frame of the TR3. I drive the car everywhere. They're holding up fine.

J. J. isn't at the junkyard anymore. He closed that business about 1990 and went back into the taxicab business. I see him once in a while and I ran into him the other day at a celebrity fundraiser I was attending. He was supervising the valet parking. Now he's in the car valet business.

He walks with a cane now. He was in a very bad car accident about five years ago. His hair is a little grayer. But he still shines that big smile.

"I'll handle this one, boys," he said when he saw me pull in with the TR3. He turned to me. "Hand over the keys."

"Absolutely," I said.

He hopped in, set his cane down in the passenger seat, spun the gears, shifted into first, and, spinning the gravel a bit, was off.

Manny Quinn

~~~~~~

Early on running the newspaper, I came to the conclusion that it would be a good idea to give the police the benefit of the doubt as much as possible. They have a very hard job to do. It requires a lot of patience. It is sometimes dangerous. On the occasions where a police officer would do something bad and the facts were there to prove it, I'd write about it, but always suggest this was just one bad apple in the barrel. Only if a police department got way out of hand would I wander further off from that position.

But what do you do when a police department has an officer who keeps getting himself kidnapped, vandalized, and thrown into the town dump? Once he even had an arm ripped out of its socket. I know that is hard to believe.

This was an officer who sometimes worked twenty-four-hour shifts sitting by the side of the road in a police car waiting for perpetrators. He worked in blistering heat and in bitter cold. He never complained. He was never late for work. He never went off AWOL to get a donut. He never got paid overtime. In fact, he never got paid. Manny Quinn was a store mannequin dressed up as a police officer.

I don't think anyone has ever written a complete appreciation of Manny Quinn. So I might as well now.

Manny was originally built as a young, male store-window mannequin. Bought soon after his birth by Saks Fifth Avenue, he worked his way up the chain until he was featured in the front display window of the Saks store on the corner of Main Street and Hampton Road in Southampton. There he caught the eye of the wife of the East Hampton Town chief of police, Todd Sarris, who was shopping there, and who suggested to her husband that the force buy it and use it as a police dummy. This was in 1988.

MANNY QUINN
(Drawing by Mickey Paraskevas)

Manny was taken to East Hampton, where the chief ordered him to be dressed up in a police uniform and police cap and sat him in the front seat of a police car parked by the side of a busy road facing traffic. People would drive along, round a corner, and see what looked to them to be an officer monitoring their speed, then slow down and creep past, glad not to be pulled over. Manny, of course, would just sit there, facing straight ahead.

As it was the 1980s, and the force wanted to disguise the mannequin, he was given sideburns and a moustache. His hair was allowed to stick out a bit from beneath his police cap. He looked like Burt Reynolds in *Smokey and the Bandit.*

No one knows how many accidents Manny prevented and lives he saved during his six-year tenure with the force. But it was not all good. Once I drove by him and noted that somebody had put a beer can right on the hood of the car in front of the windshield where Manny, sitting behind the steering wheel, could stare at it all day. I removed it, Good Samaritan that I am.

The teenagers in town—it had to be teenagers—after a period of wary surveillance, began to have fun with him, always careful to see that there were no other officers nearby. They'd come over and rock his car until he fell forward onto his steering wheel. Fell asleep, this cop did. Then they'd run away. Then they got bolder.

One day when the police came to pick him up at the end of a long, hard day's work, they found him missing altogether. The next morning, an arm appeared on the front steps of police headquarters. A note attached said that more pieces of Manny would follow if the police department did not meet their demands.

I wrote about this story for the paper. There were no demands. And the next morning, at 8 a.m., Manny was found naked, and now with two arms, sitting on the hood of one of the police cars parked behind the police station. Where had that other arm come from?

A full-scale investigation followed. The note was dusted for fingerprints. Interviews were conducted, leads followed, people of interest rounded up.

Astonishingly, the police were so upset by this that they actually conducted a sting. The chief ordered that a *real* police officer sit perfectly still in a police car on the shoulder of Long Lane by the high school, disguised as Manny. He was given a moustache and chops. He appeared there one day at 3 p.m. as school was letting out and, according to reports, the sting *worked*. A car full of teenage boys pulled off the road in front of the police car, the boys got out and then, as they approached, the police officer went BOO! and they ran off. He couldn't help himself, he later told the chief.

One day, in the fall of 1992, I had an encounter with Manny Quinn myself. I woke up in the morning with a cold and decided it might be a good day to take the day off. I'd stay home, build a fire, and write a story on my laptop in the living room.

As I built a fire and settled in about ten, I noticed that the police car I had seen parked on the road in front of the house three hours earlier was still there. The officer inside could look down the road toward the oncoming traffic, but he wasn't. He was positioned so he was looking up the hill into my living room. I knew it was Manny, but it was a bit disconcerting.

I walked down the driveway to try to readjust him. He was out there doing his job. I tried the door, but it was locked. I noticed he had medals pinned on his chest, a strange thing. He also had a patch on his shoulder that read EAST HAMPTON JUNIOR POLICE. Apparently there had been a debate about what patch to put on his uniform, and they had decided on this high-school-kid-police-station-tour patch. I had once written about that. The police gave kids tours of the jail, then this patch.

I went back up to the living room, got comfortable in an easy chair by the fire, and started to write a story on my laptop about a new lifelike CPR dummy that the Amagansett Volunteer Ambulance Department had just obtained. This actually was in the news that week.

"The Amagansett Volunteer Ambulance Company has just taken delivery of 'Resusci Anne,'" I wrote. "She is a demonstration dummy that looks like a woman on whom you can perform CPR. She cost four thousand dollars.

"Bake sales and fundraisers have been held to raise the funds to get her. Resusci Anne is officially called a 'computerized cardiopulmonary resuscitation mannequin,' and her job is to lie there on her back and let different people in the community practice CPR on her. Resusci Anne has two different monitors in her chest. One monitor measures the depth and rate of chest compressions and breaths performed on Resusci Anne by whoever is on top. The second monitor can reproduce any heart rhythm and can aid in teaching about heart defibrillation. Whether the applicant is successful or not is right there on a printout. Resusci Anne issues her own report. No instructor is necessary."

I tried to continue my writing, but Manny was out there, still looking up at me. It put me in mind of a girl I dated some years before who had a penthouse apartment in New York City. My affair with her lasted about a month, and one of the things that turned me off her in the end was this sculpture she had in her living room. You'd get out of the elevator, and there it was, a life-sized sculpture of a ballerina in a tutu and leotard, sitting on a stool carefully adjusting her dancing slippers, while watching curiously to see who was getting out of the elevator. No matter how often I went there, this sculpture gave me the creeps.

Well, out the window, Manny was annoying me like that. The cars were going by, slowing down because he was there. But Manny, it seemed, was more interested in *me.*

At noon, a couple in a Mercedes went by, then pulled off the road and began backing up to Manny. When the driver got close enough, he stopped, got out, and then with a roadmap walked over to the police car to ask a question. He came over to Manny's window, pointed at something on the map, looked in for a reply, then jumped back with a yip. Quickly, he walked back to the Mercedes and drove off.

Now, back to my work, I began to think that maybe Manny and Resusci Anne could be gotten together. They could meet. A blind date, perhaps.

"By any measure, it is not going to be easy for Manny to court and win Resusci Anne," I wrote. "For one thing, she is far above his station in life. Manny is a blue-collar worker—quite literally. And there is nothing high tech about him.

"Resusci Anne, on the other hand, is from the world of scientists and graduate schools and computer laboratories. If anything breaks on Resusci Anne it will be an expensive business, believe you me. Will a female with such expensive tastes allow the likes of a Manny Quinn to even come in the door?

"And if she does, will she be able to resist the urge to judge him? Most men are put off by judgmental women. Who likes to be told whether their behavior is acceptable or unacceptable? And yet, that is exactly what Resusci Anne has been programmed to do. Manny can push down on her chest and he can breathe into her mouth and, instead of getting some sort of emotional response from her, he will get, well, a report. It will be written out and it will let him or anyone else who cares to read it see whether he passed or failed in his attempts at making her happy.

"On the other hand, Manny and Resusci Anne might have a lot going for them. If Resusci Anne is judgmental and demanding, Manny is the strong, silent type. He can take it. If he can sit out in all sorts of weather for hours and hours, he surely can put up with the likes of Resusci Anne.

"Also, they are both model handsome. So there should be the physical attraction, although there may be other causes for concern since neither of them is anatomically correct.

"And there are other considerations. There is the question of Resusci Anne's being faithful. Can Manny really trust that all Resusci Anne is doing with all these people in the community, both males and females, is allowing them to get on top of her and perform mouth-to-mouth resuscitation and chest compression? He'll have her word for it. But will that be good enough?

"There is also the question of their work schedules. Manny works long but steady hours. Sometimes, especially in the summertime, he works eighteen and twenty hours a day. So he won't be around so much. Resusci Anne on the other hand, works on demand. She is a person on call, so to speak, and it is possible that Manny could come home at the end of a twenty-hour stint sitting along the side of the Highway Behind the Lots, and he could kick his shoes off and put his feet up on the sofa, looking forward to a nice evening of watching television with his honey, when suddenly the phone will ring and Resusci Anne will be off to the firehouse to get herself revived by half a dozen members of the local Ladies Auxiliary. This could be hard on them.

"In the end, there is one overriding factor that can almost guarantee there will be wedding bells in the future for these two. In all of East Hampton, Manny Quinn and Resusci Anne are the only two of their kind. With all the other living creatures in our community—dogs and cats, deer and seagulls, sharks and pheasants—there simply is nobody else around that either of them could snuggle up close to, to shake away those nighttime blues.

"Hooray for Manny Quinn and Resusci Anne!"

In 1994, in broad daylight, somebody stole Manny again, this time by smashing the passenger window of the police car. He was gone a week, and then he turned up again at the town dump, this time with his clothes all torn and ripped.

At this point, a majority of the officers of the East Hampton Town Police Department signed a petition demanding that the chief get rid of Manny Quinn. They felt that the bad publicity from these encounters with people up to no good was giving the force a black eye. But Chief Sarris held his ground. The good Manny was doing was outweighing the bad. He'd stay.

I interviewed the chief in his office at this time. Turned out he was deeply affected by the petition, in spite of himself.

"The way I think about this now," he said, "is that if Manny gets stolen one more time, we won't replace him. Leave it up to the fates."

"So he is just like anybody else? He could live to be a ripe old age, or he could be struck down with a heart attack tomorrow?"

"Yup."

That, of course, finally did happen, in 1995. There he was, back in the dump again. They left him there. Presumably, sometime later, he got crushed by the dump bulldozer.

I think about Manny sometimes. Now that the Hamptons have become a glittering summer resort for the rich and famous, maybe we ought to bring him back. I think the likes of him might bring some much needed levity into our little world.

Also, on the occasions I walk by any fashionable store in these parts, I look at that fellow in a fine tennis shirt and shorts standing motionless in the window and think—Manny is that you?

The Little People

~~~~~~

In 1976, twenty years after my dad bought the drug store in Montauk, he collapsed in the prescription room. He was not alone at the time. There were two other pharmacists there. Also in the store, along with some other customers, was one of my dad's best friends, Albie Shapiro, shopping for a bathing suit. Dr. Shapiro had a summer house on Westlake Drive and was a prominent Manhattan internist. Responding to the cries of the pharmacists, he ran to the back of the store, leaped up the two steps into the prescription room, and immediately began artificial respiration. There was no heartbeat for a while. So he beat on his chest with his fists. And Dad came around. The ambulance came and the first I heard about it, at my newspaper office in Bridgehampton, was that he was on his way at high speed to the hospital in Southampton. To this day, I am haunted by the vision of the ambulance in my rearview mirror, its siren wailing and with my dad inside, catching up to me in my car and passing me to arrive at the front entrance of the hospital before me.

When I arrived, a few minutes later, I saw Dad, strapped to a metal gurney, being wheeled by two attendants from the ambulance to the emergency room. And he saw me. He did look all terrible and green. But he raised his right arm at the elbow and made the "V for Victory" sign as the automatic doors opened and he was led inside.

He survived this experience. And so did I. But it had changed things. Soon after, in 1978, he sold the store and began a wonderful and lengthy retirement with my mother in a big house that they built high on a hill in Montauk. They lived there in the summertime, and in a condominium in Pompano Beach, Florida, in the wintertime.

Often during this long retirement, particularly as I began to raise a family, I would go out to Montauk from my home in East Hampton to visit my mom and dad. We'd sit outside and look down from the top of the hill to the great arc of Fort Pond Bay and Amagansett beyond. At the farthest point that we could see there was a brick chimney, rising about thirty feet above this low landscape of sand dunes and beach grass on the bay.

I knew the remarkable history of that chimney and the terrible smell that had emanated from it. But what I did not know was that I was about to embark on my own particular adventure with it, one that would involve one of the biggest lies you could ever tell your own children. At the time, Maya was twelve, Adam was nine, David was three, and Gabriel was one-and-a-half. This was in 1984.

The idea was presented by my new wife, a woman who had a mischievous streak. It was brilliant.

It was a summer evening, about 7 p.m., and the sun was beginning to set. We had spent a wonderful afternoon with my parents in Montauk walking around by the docks at the fishing village—a day off for me—and then we had gone back to their house for an early dinner of cold cuts. Now it was, particularly for the little ones, near to bedtime. We had to go home. And so we packed up, and Grammy and Cappy, as they were now called, said their goodbyes at the front door. We walked down the slate steps toward the car.

"How would you kids like to go see the Little People?" my wife asked the kids conspiratorially.

I was carrying a crib and a box of diapers. I stopped. "Little People?" I said.

"Yeah, the Little People," she said to me. "Trust me," she whispered.

Whatever it was, the kids were all for it. They were jumping up and down. Little People. Little People.

We climbed into the Volkswagen camper bus and started on our way. I was at the wheel. "Where are we going?" I whispered.

A whisper. "Follow my directions." Then, to the kids. "They're like elves. And they live in these little tiny houses. See that chimney out there?"

"Yeah! Yeah!"

"Well, they're special. And they only come out from their little tiny houses after sunset."

"Like trolls?" asked Adam, age nine.

"Just like trolls. Only they're not trolls."

"Why do they have a chimney?"

"Nobody really knows."

We chugged along and my wife directed me out through town and out to the long six-mile stretch known as Napeague, heading toward Amagansett. And I knew exactly where we were going. We were going to the old shacks at Promised Land that the Portuguese employees of the fish factories built and that fishermen now lived in.

"I got it," I grinned.

We rumbled along through the Napeague Stretch, the ten-mile-long barrier beach that separates the westerly hills of Montauk from the easterly hills of Amagansett. With the hills at each end, the winds often funnel across this narrow peninsula with great velocity, and today the vast Napeague Pond and Napeague Bay have become a favorite spot for windsurfers, kite fliers, hang gliders, and kayakers.

I made a right off the Montauk Highway, halfway down Napeague toward Amagansett, onto Cranberry Hole Road, and headed toward the big brick smokestack. Soon, we turned onto Promised Land Road, and there they were.

"I see one," said David, age three.

"Shhh," I said.

I had slowed down.

"I saw him too," whispered Adam. "Right behind the house over there."

"There was nobody there," Maya, the pragmatist, said. She was twelve.

"Yes there was."

These little patchwork houses, some no more than nine feet high, were covered with ship's buoys or lobster floats for

MAYA AND ADAM AT THE HOME OF ONE OF THE LITTLE PEOPLE
(Photo by the author)

decoration and had little tiny brick chimneys and windows. There wasn't a soul around.

"Shall we stop for a while?" my wife asked. "I don't think it's dark enough yet."

I slowed down.

"Speed up, speed up," Adam wailed. "Let's get out of here." And we did.

During the rest of that summer, sometimes we'd leave Grammy and Cappy's for the long drive home to East Hampton and we would go straight home, with the kids looking longingly out at the chimney for the trip to the Little People.

And sometimes we'd go up that narrow Cranberry Hole Road to the turnoff at Promised Land, moving slowly, whispering, and looking for the Little People through the lowering dusk.

Block Island Scam

~~~~~~

Ten years after I started *Dan's Papers* in Montauk, I started a completely separate newspaper on Block Island, Rhode Island. It had come about simply because of looking at a map. I published my newspaper all through the eastern end of Long Island. But there, ten miles offshore, was this island. I hadn't thought anything of it for the longest time, even though you could see it out there. That was because no ferries went to it from Montauk. Ferries traveled to it from Connecticut and Rhode Island. And, as part of Rhode Island, it was practically a foreign country. It was a blank wall. It had nothing to do with the Hamptons.

But then, someone had told me about it. He raved about it. And he said I should put a newspaper on it. It's only ten minutes away by plane. They have a small airstrip. Just go. And so, I did.

I found an island that was just drop-dead gorgeous. Rolling hills and valleys extend six miles across one way and nine miles the other. From a cliff you could look down to a rocky beach and lighthouse at one end and a pristine curving five-mile-long beach at the other called Scotch Beach. Because

BLOCK ISLAND
(Photo by NASA)

there are no trees, a stiff, salty breeze blows almost all the time. And since the sea and a variety of bays and ponds are visible from almost everywhere, you feel as if you are on a ship. The overriding feeling, therefore, is exhilaration. It is a glorious pleasure to be on this lightly populated place.

There was a little downtown. It had been built naturally along a five-block-long Main Street opposite where the ferries from the mainland docked. There were a few stores, restaurants, and hotels on this strip. And that, other than a few marinas, was it for commerce on the entire island.

Well, I thought, I could put a newspaper on this island. Certainly not in the wintertime, when nearly all the stores would be closed. But I could do it in the summertime, for ten weeks, when the population swelled to about two thousand.

I hired an editor. We came out with our first issue on July 1, 1970, and it was an immediate success, welcomed with open arms by the townspeople. They made it their business to help it out anyway that they could. I called it the *Block Island Times*, and it was the only paper on the island. Still is.

In July of 1984, when the paper was in its fourteenth summer, I took my wife and our two youngest children, ages three and one, for our annual weekend pilgrimage to the island, staying in a guest room at the home of the editors I had hired, Peter and Shirley Wood.

About 2 p.m. that Sunday we were strolling down Main Street when we came upon a toy store. We stopped to look in the window. And there we were confronted by a well-dressed young man of about twenty with a clipboard under his arm.

"Are you visiting the island?" he asked.

"Yes," I said.

"Well I'm here to tell you about a remarkable deal being offered on this island by myself and two of my compatriots." He waved an arm at two other young men with clipboards who I could see just down the block. "Have you heard of the Island Sea Resort?" he asked.

"No."

"That's because you know it as the Block Island Motel. It is being converted into a timeshare. And we're here to offer a free lobster dinner for two to anyone who might be interested enough to hear what we have to say about this."

"Where are you from?"

"We work for the owner, but we're from Fort Lauderdale, here just for the month."

Normally, I did not write for the *Block Island Times*. But this intrigued me. Not because I wanted to buy a timeshare, but because there were these three young men on Main Street accosting people who were just normally going about their business.

"A lobster dinner, huh?"

"Yes, sir. All you have to do is hear us out."

My wife and I exchanged glances. She could see I wanted to write this story. Indeed, I thought, this was a terrible intrusion on this quiet and peaceful little main street of Block Island. I sniffed the air. This might be a scam. Did the Woods know about it?

"Honey," I said, "you want to do a little shopping for a while?"

"Sure," she said.

"Come with me," the young man said.

I kissed my wife and the kids goodbye. And then the young man led me along Main Street to where an older man sat with a ledger book on a table in front of him. He took down my name and address. And noted the exact time.

Then we walked to the property in question, a rather ratty two-story motel just a block behind Main Street, on a side street. There, the young man sat with me on a bench until one of the salesmen was free. When one finally came over, the young man introduced me and then walked away.

"These are selling like hotcakes," the salesman said. And he walked me over to a series of booths where other salespeople were sitting across from tourists and talking to them. It was quite an operation.

I listened to this for about fifteen minutes, occasionally answering questions with a yes or a no, as required. Finally, the salesman popped the question. And the answer was, of course, no, I would not care to buy a timeshare.

"Are you sure?"

"Pretty sure. But maybe you can tell me a little more about it. I'm wavering."

"No," the salesman said, looking at his watch. "This interview is over. Sorry."

"Have I listened enough to get the lobster dinner for two?"

"Sure," he said, getting up. Back at the booth, however, the old man told me I hadn't stayed long enough.

"You were only there for twenty minutes," he said, noting the time he had written in his ledger. "You don't qualify. You're ten minutes short."

"What?"

"You have to stay a half an hour."

"You never said anything about that," I said.

I turned to leave, and as I got to the door I considered turning and revealing myself. I will be writing an article about this bait-and-switch, is what I might have said. But I didn't. He would soon see.

That night, back at Peter and Shirley's, I found that they had no idea that this was going on. They absolutely agreed with me that something should be done.

The article I wrote was headlined SELLING TIMESHARES ON THE STREET, and it ran front-page on the next issue of the *Block Island Times* a week later. I described in straightforward terms exactly what had happened with us on Main Street and how this might have appeared to a tourist visiting the island. "Do we really want this kind of thing, accosting people on Main Street, going on, on Block Island?" is how the article ended.

The day the paper was to go to the printer, Peter flew to Bridgehampton to edit it at our office, as he always did. He had been happy to have me do this story. After he left, the article was seen to continue on another page. What we do when an article continues on another page, known as the jump page, is write a single word to indicate that this is the continuation of the article. It's usually a word from the article. It might have been "timeshare."

Three days later, this issue of the *Block Island Times* was out on the street. Flipping through it, I noticed that the word used for the jump was the word "Scam," and a shiver went through me. I had not used this word in either the headline or the body of the article. I had just told of my experience on the island from end to end as I have described it here. How had the word "scam" gotten in there? I knew the moment I saw it. Back in those days, when you typed a story on a computer, you could use only a maximum of four letters to name the file when you saved it. I had, a bit recklessly, because I knew it would never get into the story, used the word "scam." My production manager had not gone to the trouble to read either the story or the headline, and at the jump page, in need of a word, she had typed in "scam."

I was upset at this. It was an error. But perhaps no one would notice. But then, four weeks later, right after Labor Day, a process server appeared at my office with a thick packet of papers for me that said I was being sued for four million dollars by the owner of the Block Island Motel.

I read it carefully. The owner, a Mr. McPhail, had, prior to my story, been an announced candidate for the office of selectman on the island. After the article came out, he lost. He blamed the article for his loss, and he estimated the loss of business he had suffered as a result of this article at four million dollars. The basis for the lawsuit was my use of the word "scam."

Well, I did have libel insurance. But would it cover a four-million-dollar settlement? I called my broker and told him what happened.

"Your policy is for one million," he said. "And it includes a thousand-dollar deductible. So you're pretty well covered."

"Except for three million," I said.

"Come on," the broker said. "I've read it over. You want to settle this?"

"No. Put me in touch with a lawyer."

This turned out to be a very roundabout business. My insurance company was Sterling Insurance, but Sterling was now a subsidiary of Worldwide Assurance, based in London. I wound up calling a man in Bermuda who was in charge of North America who gave me the name of the "Colonel" in Washington who took care of America. The Colonel, in a southern drawl, asked me where this was filed, and when I told him Rhode Island, he told me to call Edwards and Angel in Providence.

"A fine firm," he said. "You have Joe Kavanaugh. Good people."

To this day, I vividly remember my first trip to Providence to meet up with Kavanaugh. Bill Bendokas, the owner of Block Island Airlines, flew me into Providence Airport aboard one of his twin-engine Beechcrafts.

"Wherever you need to go to defend yourself, I'm taking you there, no charge," he had said when he learned of the lawsuit.

On the drive by taxicab toward Providence from the airport, I was able to see, off in the distance, the skyscrapers of the city. There were in fact only four of them. Three smaller ones and a tall one. I gave the cabbie the address I had written down on a piece of paper and asked him if he knew the way. He pointed to the tall one.

"That's it," he said. It was about fifty stories tall. Then he handed the piece of paper back to me.

Joe Kavanaugh was about thirty-five years old, had shiny black hair he combed straight back, was funny, animated, and had pictures of hockey players on the walls of his office. One of them was him ten years earlier when he had played for a farm team of the Boston Bruins. He also had the corner office on the top floor of this building. Can you beat that! The corner office on the top floor of the tallest building in Providence, Rhode Island! My lawyer! The King!

Ten minutes later, after I explained everything, right down to the four-letter word for the computer file, he swung around in his chair to look at that panoramic view for a moment and then he swung back.

"It's opinion," he said. "Even if it got into the paper by accident. And you are entitled to your opinion that this was a scam. It *was* a scam. You are going to win this case."

The wheels of justice turned very slowly. I made four trips to Providence over the next year and a half, the second and third for depositions in Kavanaugh's office, and the fourth for the trial itself.

On the first day of the trial at the courthouse, Kavanaugh led me into the courtroom and motioned for me to sit in a chair next to him at a table. I glanced at the jury. It was a six-man jury. And I looked down at the chair.

"Is this where murderers sit?" I asked.

"Yes," he whispered. "Shut up."

"Everybody please rise," said the bailiff.

And so the judge, a distinguished-looking man in black robes, strode in and sat down high up at the big desk in front of us. He looked down inquisitively. I wasn't afraid. I felt excited. I was on trial! It was for something completely ridiculous. Except for a thousand dollars, it was all paid for. And I had the best lawyer in Providence!

The morning of the first day was taken up with the testimony of the owner of the motel, a glum-looking fellow who described how he had fallen in with this big timeshare firm with projects in Newport, Palm Beach, and Miami Beach, how he had lost the election, and how the timeshare project got stopped in its tracks when my article came out. He did admit, however, that much later it started up again and had eventually sold out.

The next witness was a professor from Providence College who was an expert in linguistics. He tried to describe the definition of the word "scam," but now that he was under oath, he had to admit, under Kavanaugh's cross-examination, there might be other definitions in the dictionary than the bad one he was confining himself to. One of them indeed might be an opinion.

The third witness called was me. The motel owner's lawyer tried again and again to get me to modify my story about the accidental nature of the publication of the word, but there was no other story. He also asked me if I was saying that this was an actual fact that this was a scam, and, as instructed by Kavanaugh, I told him no. "It was my opinion. And though it wasn't intended to be in the paper, to this day, in my opinion, I think this was a scam. There were no lobster dinners."

The day ended with me still on the stand. They would continue with me in the morning. I spent the night in Providence, by myself, at the Marriott, the tab paid for by the insurance company. I felt spooky and frightened being all alone, and in the darkness of that room watched a lot of television until I finally fell asleep.

The grilling continued in the morning, but the fire appeared to have gone out of it. At ten thirty, after just an hour and a half, the defense rested.

Kavanaugh got up. "I move that this entire case be dismissed," Kavanaugh said. "The prosecution has failed to prove their case."

The judge said he would take it under advisement and he called for a thirty-minute recess. Kavanaugh, his assistant, and I walked to a small conference room to talk.

"We have this whole defense prepared," I said. "Why did you ask the judge to throw the whole thing out?"

"It was just a routine thing. The defense always does that. It's never honored."

"Could we finish our defense today," I asked.

"I doubt it."

So this might mean staying a second night.

We talked about our defense. And then, after just five minutes, someone opened the door a bit and asked Kavanaugh to come out. He did, and, very soon, he was back.

"They want to settle," he said. "They'll settle for thirty thousand dollars. You want to do that? You pay the thirty thousand and we all go home."

"Do you think I should do this?"

"It's up to you."

"Well, this is the insurance company's money."

"It's still up to you."

"Don't settle."

"You sure?"

"Let's go back there and finish this up."

When we got back in the courtroom and all sat down at our proper places, the judge came in, sat down, and then shocked everybody.

"I am dismissing this case," he said. "This case is completely frivolous. It should never have been filed, but it was. But, before we all go home, I want to speak for a moment to the jury. You have spent nearly a day and a half listening to this case, and I want to tell you how much I appreciate that. I particularly want to tell you why I am dismissing this case, because I think you deserve that. You deserve to know the law.

"The prosecution has to show that the defendant libeled the plaintiff in his newspaper. The definition of libel is writing something inaccurate that holds a person up to ridicule among his peers. If the person is just an ordinary person, that is all he has to do. If that person is a public figure, the prosecution has to show that the ridicule was of malicious intent. It is a higher bar.

"Mr. McPhail was running for selectman. He is a public figure on Block Island. As for being malicious, it was not. It was a mistake.

"But even if Mr. McPhail was *not* a public figure, Mr. Rattiner was entitled to his opinion. And as the defense expert testified, the word 'scam' can be an opinion. So this *was* an opinion.

"Finally, if Mr. McPhail *did* win this case, he would have to show financial damages to collect anything. Sort of as a bill, tallying things up. They presented no damages. There is no case.

"And so, again, I thank you. I am sorry we have wasted your time. You have served the justice system for the people of Rhode Island well, and you are hereby dismissed. You may all go home."

This was about the most wonderful speech I ever heard in a courtroom. I loved it.

Six months later, the prosecution appealed. They lost that, too.

About a year later, with my two little kids now four and two, I decided to take us all on a one-week vacation to the island of Bermuda. Bermuda is at its best in the spring and fall. This was October. We'd have a great time on the beach there.

"One thing we could do," I said, "is visit the insurance agent who paid all this money to hire the lawyer that won this case."

No one jumped up and down at this idea.

But I did go. Alone. I went into a low, one-story white stucco building with a shiny red roof in the center of town one afternoon, and I spoke to this Englishman, Charles C. Walker, in his office. His office consisted of a telephone, a desk, and one single filing cabinet. He was not, it turned out, only a representative of Worldwide Insurance. He represented a dozen different insurance companies, taking in the work for North America and sending it out to wherever it had to go. Twice the phone rang and he had to excuse himself to talk. Other than that, he listened to my enthusiasm about my case—and this surprised me—with what seemed annoyance. I wanted to talk about the phone call we had three years before. I wanted to tell him why I had been sued and how the case turned out. I wanted to tell him about *Dan's Papers*.

"I'm really busy today," he said. "I hope you'll excuse me. I must get back to work."

Leaving the building, going out into the sunshine, it suddenly occurred to me that the cost of this trip to Bermuda could, as a result of this visit to Mr. Walker, be considered as a tax-deductible business expense.

Then I thought, naah. And I walked out past the white-coated policemen standing at attention directing traffic in the center of town by waving their white sticks.

Lillywhite's

∼∼

Late in the afternoon on a bright, bitter-cold December day in 1986, I was driving my family slowly home from Bridgehampton in a big old Volkswagen camper bus with a Christmas tree on the roof. A huge snowstorm had come through the day before, and although the streets had now been plowed, there were great dunes of snow on both sides of the highway remaining, glittering in the sun.

We entered East Hampton from the west, driving down Woods Lane under the great arch of the snow-covered elm trees, and where the road made the sharp turn to the left to get onto Main Street, I came to a complete stop. Just to the right was Town Pond, all iced over. Out the window I could see hundreds of children and parents, all bundled up in brightly colored snowsuits and hats, either walking awkwardly or gliding along on ice skates. Everyone was talking and chattering happily.

"Daddy, Daddy stop the car!"

"I know! I know! That's why we're here!" I said.

And of course, this was the next thing on my plan for the day. We'd stay there skating, and then, at sunset, walk across the street to the Maidstone Arms and attend the annual tree lighting and Christmas caroling on the inn's snowy front lawn.

Cars were parked every which way by the side of the road.

"There's a spot," my wife said.

The kids weren't even going to wait for us. Grabbing their skates, they tumbled out of the car as soon as it came to a stop and were off crunching through the snow to immediately disappear into the mass of people on the ice.

"They're fine," my wife said. And now she was off, too.

About an hour went by. The sun began to set. I spent some of the time skating and some of the time sitting in the van with the heat on, such as it was. I was forty-five years old and now discovering physical limitations. I needed the breaks.

In those days, Volkswagen heating systems consisted of metal flaps that opened up as you drove along, so the wind could flow over the heated engine and into the cockpit. Parking with the engine on for heat was really just a symbolic activity.

I watched from the car at dusk, and as the spotlights mounted up in the elms around the pond came on there was something new happening on the ice. It was a full-bore hockey game, led by some of the bigger kids. A frozen outfall pipe, defined by two concrete walls at one end of the pond, served as a goal. A thirteen-year-old, crouching in front of it with his stick ready, prowled from side to side, guarding it.

For a while, this hockey game mixed dangerously with the little kids still on the ice. The puck flew here and there.

The big kids chased it, carefully picking their way through the little kids. But then, the little kids, at the urging of their parents, were beginning to leave. Meanwhile, across the street, the carolers, dressed in their elf costumes, had begun setting up for the tree lighting. Plates of cookies and punch were now on folding tables by the tree. And though the elves weren't fully ready, the little kids and their parents were coming over anyway. It was a bit of a confused situation.

From inside the van, I saw my wife wave to me that she was leaving the ice to take our kids to the tree lighting. I waved back okay.

Meanwhile, I could see that the hockey game was getting rougher by the minute. These were junior high school kids for the most part. My skates were still on. I felt primitive urges.

I leaped out, and I bounded onto the ice. I had to be part of this.

But I didn't have a hockey stick. This was frustrating. The kids went whizzing by. The puck flew this way and that. I had to find a hockey stick. Maybe there was a hockey stick not being used on the shore. I looked. There wasn't.

After a while, I saw one of the smaller kids dawdling along near to me, not doing anything. His face was red, he was breathing heavily, and puffs of white smoke appeared at his mouth. He had his stick under his arm.

"Can I borrow that?" I asked, pointing to it.

He looked up. "No," he said.

"Just for a minute. For one minute."

He handed it over. The puck rolled by—actually rolling like a little wheel—and I looked at it in fascination and then got run over by teenagers. Flat on the ground, I struggled to my knees and then got up. I wasn't going to put up with this. And suddenly I was in the middle of the melee, whacking away at the puck with the best of them, finally getting one shot down the length of the pond before getting sent sprawling again. And then that was it.

I lay there on my back. The little kid I had borrowed the stick from came over slowly and stared down at me. The spotlights in the trees gave him an angelic look. He didn't say anything. But I got the idea and held up the stick to him. He took it.

I turned my head. Across the way, the caroling was beginning, even though it wasn't completely dark. They were starting anyway.

"Dan?"

It was my wife calling. I got up wincing. All my bones hurt. But I felt wonderful.

The next morning, after a breakfast of pancakes and bacon and eggs, I built a fire in the fireplace and started to read the newspaper. The kids were building something with Legos on the rug, next to the tree. It was a happy time. After a while, I nonchalantly began to ease into a conversation that I had been quietly planning all morning.

"Everybody okay?" I asked.

My wife looked at me quizzically.

"I was thinking of going into town," I said. "Anybody need anything?"

"Oh sure," she said. And thereupon I got a list that included milk, yogurt, more Legos, wrapping paper, and toothpaste. I am sure the kids thought I was going out to do some Christmas shopping. Well, I was. Sort of.

I bounded out of the house happily. And in moments, I was in the camper bus, out on the street, tootling smartly down toward town.

Don't push it, I said to myself, as I felt a little skid. Easy.

There were two toy stores in East Hampton, and both were open, so I tried both of them. No hockey stick. As a matter of fact, both shopkeepers told me to try Lillywhite's, on Jobs Lane in Southampton, twelve miles away. If there was any place that had a hockey stick it would be Lillywhite's, they said, that would be my best bet.

I didn't like this advice because of the time it would involve. I looked at my list and I looked at my watch. Twelve miles through the snow, twenty-four miles round trip, would add probably forty-five minutes or more to my excursion. I would be missed.

I went to Bridgehampton, halfway between East Hampton and Southampton, to another toy store. No hockey stick there either.

"Try Lillywhite's," I was told again.

Lillywhite's Toy Store was in a little white wooden building at the foot of Jobs Lane, a fashionable street filled with the shops frequented by the WASP set in Southampton. Here at Christmastime, of course, practically all the WASPS had flown south to Palm Beach, so all their stores were closed, or almost all their stores. For two weeks before Christmas, unlike the clothier Shep Miller or the department store Elizabeth Arden, Lillywhite's was open. They were a toy store. And if the WASPS weren't there, there would be others who would buy. Two years earlier, when old Mr. Lillywhite had handed off the keys to the store to his kids, the kids began to keep it open for Christmas, although they did not advertise this in *Dan's Papers*. We were not a publication that appealed to "our crowd" is what they told me for each of the fifteen years I went there with my sales kit.

I parked on the lane. There was plenty of parking there, with all the stores closed up except for Lillywhite's. I went in.

A bell over the front door went ding-a-ling as I pushed the door open. Inside, I found myself behind two very well dressed women talking to a young salesgirl and taking their sweet time about it. I waited. I hoped they wouldn't take very long.

And then, Mr. Lillywhite himself, having seen there was a second customer, appeared from behind a curtain. He was a tall, slender, gloomy old man with a checkered work shirt. And he looked right at me, raising an eyebrow. He did know who I was, after all. I had been turned down by him for each and every one of those years before he handed over the keys.

"May I help you?"

"Yes, you can," I said. "Do you have a hockey stick?"

"No, I don't," he said. My face fell.

"No, wait," he said. He appeared to be deep in thought. "I think I do have one," he said. "Let me think about it for a minute."

And with that, he turned and began looking around. I looked with him.

Lillywhite's, unlike all the other toy stores, had almost no displays or arrangements of any of the toys. It was just a big mess of them, piles of soldiers, Lincoln Logs, a row of Lionel trains on one shelf, and on another shelf Monopoly, Scrabble, Chinese Checkers, Clue, and every imaginable popular game that had been a big seller up until about ten years before, all piled in there.

The other toy stores had all the new games that had just come out, which is pretty much why everyone I knew usually went to all the other toy stores, not Lillywhite's. It would be another few years before Lillywhite's would get the new stuff, and by then it would be old stuff.

But then Mr. Lillywhite smiled.

"Follow me," he said.

And so he led me around the ladies and the sales clerk, through a doorway into a second room full of toys—I had no idea there was a second room—and then through another doorway into a third room, and finally down a flight of stairs into a dimly lit musty basement. Of course I had never been down in this basement before. It had, along one wall, some boxes of model airplanes to assemble. And, leaning on some shelves on the other wall, some hula hoops, which had been wildly popular about fifteen years earlier.

But Mr. Lillywhite didn't even slow down. Making his way from one end of this basement room to the other, we entered a second basement, more dimly lit than the first, and then into a third basement room that didn't appear to have a light in it at all. But near one wall, Mr. Lillywhite found a pull chain and gave it a yank. The dimmest of lights went on.

"I think it's over here," he said, pointing to the left. We walked that way and stopped.

And then, with his left hand, he rolled up the sleeve of his right arm, reached into a shelf about shoulder high and, in a moment, pulled out from behind a bunch of boxes a long, thin, wooden stick. A hockey stick. And then he handed it to me.

"I think this is what you are looking for," he said.

When we went back upstairs and returned to the cash register behind the counter near the front door, I was finally able to have a good look at this object. It was magnificent. Unlike regular hockey sticks, which were just a single cut-out piece of wood, this hockey stick had six plies of wood carefully bonded together and then beautifully shellacked. It reminded me of an old wooden tennis racket made that way. They hadn't made tennis rackets like that in twenty years. And obviously they hadn't made hockey sticks like that in twenty years.

There was a little white sticker on it, brown at the edges and with a price written on it by some long-ago clerk, in ink: ".69."

I handed it to Mr. Lillywhite and he looked at it for the longest time. Then, he looked up at me. There was a twinkle in his eye.

"That'll be sixty-nine cents," he said. He waved an arm. "And we'll just forget about the tax this one time."

Driving back home through the snow, with the rest of the errands completed, I began to think about what Mr. Lillywhite had just done. I loved that he had done that. And I thought he did too.

I could hardly wait for nightfall. And indeed, at six o'clock, with everybody cozied up in front of the television, I told everyone what I had done that day and that I wanted to go out for a while and play a little hockey. I was sure the other kids would be out there.

"You'll have a heart attack," my wife said.

"No, I won't."

"Then go knock yourself out."

"I doubt if I'll last more than about twenty minutes."

And so, I raced down to Town Pond, leaped out of the car, and joined the melee of the game already underway. And indeed, I lasted just about the twenty minutes I said I would. In the course of things, I got knocked down two or three times. I fired two shots—it was basically everybody fighting for the puck against the one goalie—and he blocked both of them. Then I left.

The next morning, I woke up with every bone in my body aching. A week later, as the pain subsided and I thought I might be ready again to play, I found that the temperature had risen to well over freezing and the police were out there shooing everybody away. The pond, with the ice melting, was deemed no longer safe.

And there was also a news item in the local paper. In East Hampton, the mayor had decided that the kids and the hockey players would have to share the pond. The little kids would have it all day every day until 7 p.m. The hockey players could have it from 7 p.m. on, but then only until 10 p.m. During that time, a police officer would be assigned there to keep order and to look out to see nobody got hurt.

But none of this mattered. Because, for the rest of the winter, there was no further freeze to turn the pond to ice. Ice skating was over. And soon enough winter was at an end.

Interestingly, that spring, when I went around selling my advertising in Southampton, I actually sold an ad to Lillywhite's. As it happened, the day I went in, Mr. Lillywhite Sr. was behind the counter.

"I'll take an ad just this once," he said, pointing to the smallest ad for sale. "And just for the Fourth of July. So how much will that be?"

I couldn't resist. "I'm running a special this spring. That size ad will be just sixty-nine cents."

Mort Zuckerman

~~~~~~

Every year, I stand directly behind Mort Zuckerman, the billionaire publisher and real estate developer, for an hour. It's the only time I get to see him. Sometimes he turns around and talks to me. Sometimes I issue him encouragement. Sometimes we have momentary disagreements. I have been having this relationship with Mort Zuckerman once a year every year for twenty-two years. And though I don't think he knows too much about me, I know a great deal about him. As a billionaire, he is in the news quite a lot.

This annual encounter takes place on a sandlot baseball field directly behind the Waldbaum's Supermarket in East Hampton on the second Saturday in August between 3 and 5 p.m. At that time, we both participate in the Annual Artists & Writers Charity Softball Game held on that field, he as the perennial pitcher for the writers, I as the chief umpire standing directly behind him, peering over his shoulder to call balls and strikes. In a typical year, movie stars, politicians, and models will play in this game. You might find Paul Simon, Alec Baldwin, or Chevy Chase on the field.

MORT ZUCKERMAN AND THE AUTHOR
(Photo courtesy of *Dan's Papers*)

Christie Brinkley might come up for the artists. She swings and misses. "Strike one," I say. Zuckerman, who is in t-shirt and shorts, turns toward me and grins deliciously.

"Lob them in softer," I say. I'm thinking, everybody wants to see Christie run down toward first base after hitting one. She swings and misses again. "Strike two."

I give Christie five strikes to hit it, but it's no use. She's a classic beauty in the classic All-American-Girl model. She swings, as we used to say, like a girl. Hopeless.

At the start of the game, after the introductions made by the mayor, the toss of the coin, and the playing of "The Star Spangled Banner," I walk out onto the mound and raise both arms and shout, "Play Ball." And so the game begins.

Zuckerman looks exactly the same as he did twenty-two years ago when he first joined the game. He's slender and athletic, curly haired and very self-contained. He talks, but it's kind of poker-player talking. You never know what he's thinking.

"Hey," he says, pounding a softball into his glove.

"Good to see you," say I. "Another year."

I get to decide whether I want to congratulate him about something I read about him or just leave the thing alone. One year, he came strolling out to the mound after putting money down to purchase the southwest corner of Columbus Circle, in Manhattan, where, at the time, there stood the shabby and outdated New York Coliseum. He would build a sixty-eight-story skyscraper there, he had told the mayor. He had put down a deposit of tens of millions of dollars. I congratulated him on that.

After that game (the writers lost), and after the summer was over, the bottom fell out of the real estate market and Zuckerman was left holding the bag on an approved $800-million skyscraper that, if built, would be worth maybe a quarter of that. Fortunately, no shovel had broken ground on the project yet. He still had some wiggle room. I had nothing to say to him about that.

I met Zuckerman in 1986 when he called me on the phone at *Dan's Papers* asking me to help him out with something.

It was the damndest thing. Earlier on, I had met and become friends with another tycoon, a man named Frazer Dougherty, who had built a public television studio in East Hampton. It was a one-of-a-kind structure, a great gift for the community and a feather in Mr. Dougherty's cap. I had, from time to time, visited Frazer at his home, which was an oceanfront mansion he shared with his wife Margaret, an heir to the A&P fortune.

I could not help but notice, during one of these visits, that the person who owned the oceanfront mansion next door had built, just fifty yards from Dougherty's house, a three-stories-tall satellite dish. It loomed there and partially blocked Dougherty's view. What an inconsiderate thing to do.

"What are you going to do?" I asked.

"I've tried to talking to him," Dougherty said. "But he says it's his property and he'll do what he wants. And he says it's the only spot where he gets good reception from New York City. It has to be angled toward me that way."

"Who is it?" I asked.

"Mort Zuckerman. He owns *US News and World Report*, *The Atlantic Monthly*, and he's a builder of Manhattan skyscrapers."

This was in the days when satellite dishes were *satellite dishes*.

About a month later, Dougherty called me and insisted I come over to see something. He was very excited. And he sounded triumphant.

I went over. Dougherty had commissioned a local sculptor, Bill King, to construct a cartoon sculpture of steel pipes welded together that were unmistakably Don Quixote on a horse. The sculpture was taller than the satellite dish. Quixote had been placed facing the satellite dish with his lance aimed right at its heart. It was just about fifty feet from it, on Dougherty's other side of the property line.

I wrote about this. And a week later, the satellite dish came down. Then I got a call from Mort Zuckerman asking for a favor.

"I want you to get me in to play in the Artists and Writers softball game," Zuckerman said. I'd been umpiring the event for ten years by that time. It was logical that he would think to call me about getting him in, although, in fact, I was not the boss of the game. An artist named Leif Hope was the boss.

I told him that, but he persisted.

"You have the influence. Look. Every Saturday I play in the softball game held in Sag Harbor. I'm a good player. A lot of the guys there play in the Artists and Writers game. And in spite of what happened with Frazer, I'm not such a bad guy. Really."

Indeed, there was great pressure from people to get into this game. It was the world series of softball games in the Hamptons. Still is. It sometimes gets national media attention.

And so I got him in.

In the first game he was in, Mort pitched. He'd talked Leif Hope, who was also the manager of the artists, into letting him pitch. And so there he was. There was really no need to prevent this very rich man, clearly a really good athlete, from playing amid the abstract expressionists, celebrities, millionaires, and novelists. He was soon accepted as one of us. Honestly, he was a very good ballplayer.

During the years I have known him, Zuckerman got married, had a child, got divorced, bought the *Daily News*, got skunked out of buying *New York Magazine* by billionaire

Bruce Wasserstein, and built skyscraper after skyscraper. Also during this time, I got divorced and remarried and then divorced again. But on the mound, we never talked about any of it. Nor did we ever talk about the fact that the mayor of New York essentially had let Zuckerman off the hook for that huge commitment he had made for Columbus Circle, which didn't pan out.

I visited him in his oceanfront house early one evening a few years after I met him. This was a twenty-room, one-hundred-year-old mansion built in the summer-cottage manner right smack at the top of a sand dune overlooking the ocean. He lived there alone. But he did have friends and, of course, a staff. He invited me into his library and we sat there in this dark gloomy room with the spray from the sea just outside the window, and we went over a business proposition I hoped he would be interested in. I wanted to expand *Dan's Papers* to resort locations all around the world—and in fact, already had begun to do so with my venture out to Block Island. I needed financing. But he declined.

As I was about to leave, his girlfriend, Gloria Steinem, came bounding down the grand staircase from upstairs. They were going out and she was all dressed up for the evening. Mort introduced her to me and we shook hands, and she told me she was a fan of the paper. Then I left and, I presume, shortly thereafter, they did too.

Zuckerman loved the game in those early years, without letting himself get caught up in the details. It really was just a pleasant, fun game for charity, after all. One year—it was in 1988, I think—Zuckerman had gone off to Morocco to be part of that famous weeklong birthday party for Malcolm Forbes, who was the publisher of *Fortune*. Every wealthy man in the world had been jetted to Morocco by Forbes, Zuckerman among them. But Zuckerman left early and flew back so he could be at the Artists & Writers game. Leif told me this story.

But then, now that he was "in" at the game, Zuckerman's attitude began to change. It started first as just this fierce will to win, which many of the players had. He'd snag a line drive, and then double somebody off first.

"Yes," he'd say, pumping his fist in the air.

On occasion, he would disagree with me about some call I'd made. If I called a strike a ball, he'd turn and briefly glare at me.

"You were right," I'd whisper. "I owe you one." And the next close pitch would go his way.

At other times, I'd try to settle him down after a long period of either bad pitches or consecutive hits that sent opposing players scurrying around the bases.

"Come on, Mort," I'd say.

On more important calls, however, especially when people would run out on the field to have a shouting match about it—usually for the benefit of the crowd—he'd be right there, and if at first it seemed in fun, as the years went by, it seemed to me he was getting very serious. He'd get red in the face. A vein would become visible on the side of his neck. I don't think I'd like to be on the other side of the table in an important matter, is what went through my mind.

On one particular call—and this was around 1999, eleven years into his tenure at the game—Mort, in my view, went over the edge about a call I made. Mike Lupica, who was the lead sportswriter for the *New York Daily News* (which Mort had just bought), slid into home and I called him out.

Mort raced out onto the field.

"ARE YOU OUT OF YOUR MIND? ARE YOU OUT OF YOUR MIND?"

I tried walking away from him. But he followed me.

"THAT WAS THE WORST CALL IN THE HISTORY OF THIS GAME," he continued. "THE TAG WAS LATE! YOU WERE LOOKING RIGHT AT IT!"

I was looking right at it. There had been a tag. But it had not been late.

"YOU'RE A TERRIBLE UMPIRE. YOU SHOULDN'T BE UMPIRING THIS GAME."

What I should have done at this point was declare the play over and "batter up," but I was so intimidated by this man I could not speak. He followed me around, yelling. I thought he might hit me. Finally, others came out and restrained him. Another umpire, Ed Bleier of CBS, minding the calls at first base and seeing what was going on, came over and shouted back at Mort where I had not been able to.

"The umpire has made the call," Bleier said. "He was out. I saw it too. That's *it*. No more. Next batter."

And so things settled down.

The next year, however, I discovered that as far as Mort was concerned, the battle was still going on.

I went out to the mound after "The Star Spangled Banner," prepared to do what I always do. There was a big crowd. Leif Hope strolled out.

"Mort has brought Rudy Giuliani to be the guest umpire this year," he said.

There was nothing new about our having a guest umpire. We'd had Bill Clinton one year. I'd ump three innings and then the guest umpire would come out and ump the next three. Then I'd return and close the game.

"Mort says that he doesn't want you to umpire at all. He wants Rudy to start as umpire. You should umpire third base."

"That's ridiculous," I said. "You're running the game."

"You're right," he said. And he handed me the ball.

I umpired the first inning, grimly at first, but then, when Carl Ichan came up and I called him out with the bat on his shoulder when he failed to swing at a ball right down the middle, I began to settle in. I finished the first inning. Mort had said not one word to me.

Before the start of the second inning, however, Leif came out to me again.

"Mort says he is going to take his team out in protest if you umpire the second inning," he said.

I thought, this man is playing hardball.

"What are you going to do?" I asked.

"I think I have to move you over to third."

"Whatever you think best," I sighed. And I handed the ball back to Hope and he handed it to Giuliani, who was now strolling out onto the field. He smiled. I smiled. We shook hands.

Miserable, I nevertheless umpired at third. And I became so paranoid out there that when a line drive came sizzling down toward me, I imagined that it had been aimed at me. There were a number of them after that. Then I thought I was going crazy and banished that thought.

I finished that game umpiring at third. And the next year, the same thing happened. Again I umpired at third base.

All through the winter of 2000–2001, I wondered if I would be umpiring the Artists & Writers game behind the pitcher's mound again. Had that call really been out? I really was about out of my mind with this. And I had no answers. Checkmate.

Feeling bad about what seemed to be a third upcoming humiliation, I arranged my life so I was almost late for the game, which begins exactly at three o'clock every year. I walked onto the field at five to three, shuffled out, really. And suddenly, there was Leif Hope, rushing out to me, all in a lather.

"Dan! Dan! Where have you been? We can't start the game without you!"

I wanted to hug Leif for saying that. And then he handed me the ball. Zuckerman came out to stand right in front of me, ready to pitch. He said not a word to me for two innings. Then, in the third inning, I called a pitch that might have been over the plate a ball. And he went nuts again. But just for one minute. He took a deep breath. Then he settled back in.

During this twenty-two-year period, every year, the pitcher for the artists was another great athlete, the actor Roy Scheider. Scheider was just as slender and quick as Zuckerman, but it was a whole different thing. He was warm and friendly. He asked me about my life. I asked him about his life. Sometimes, we'd meet up after the game and have a drink. Sometimes I'd go over to his house, or he to mine. It was, unlike my relationship with Zuckerman, a friendship. With Zuckerman, it had become some kind of poker game that had exploded into a power struggle. I had no idea why.

Well, I once said to myself, that is why Zuckerman is a billionaire and I am not. Then I thought about Don Quixote and the satellite dish and I thought yeah, but he *owes* me. Why doesn't he see that?

And so, Zuckerman and I and the game soldiered on. The next year it was more of the same. Leif came out to tell me that Mort had brought somebody new to the game. "I've had it with Mort Zuckerman," I blurted out, then I saw Zuckerman on the sidelines not far away. He had to have heard it.

Somehow, after that single sentence, everything changed. We got along famously for that game, and if I thought it was a fluke, it was the same at the next game, when he was out there with his arm around my shoulder and a smile on his face. You'd have thought he was an entirely different fellow.

But there it was.

I have simply never been able to figure this guy out.

Frank Perdue

~~~~~~

I have never met Frank Perdue, but I did speak to him over the phone once. It was about ten o'clock on a Wednesday morning, Eastern Standard Time, which means that he had returned to his office just three hours after personally raising the American flag up the pole in front of Perdue Poultry corporate headquarters in Salisbury, Maryland. He did this rain or shine. He was, after all, just a chicken farmer who'd made good. His routine was well known around the country because his PR people saw to it. The flag got raised at 7 a.m.

During the 1980s and 1990s, Frank Perdue was one of the most famous men in America. He was a short, ugly fellow with a long face and thin dark hair that fell over his forehead, and he was the last person in America who you'd think would become famous. All he did was go on television asking you to consider buying his chickens. He even looked like a chicken. Maybe even talked like one if you thought about it. And he spoke directly into your living room with great sincerity, as if he were your friend. He had his own special way of raising chickens, he'd say. It was a secret and he wouldn't tell you any more about it.

FRANK PERDUE

"My chickens are the best in the world," he'd say. He made a fortune.

My call to Frank Perdue, and his return call to me, came about because of a ridiculous promotional event I dreamed up one day, which I intended to pull off on Main Street, in Southampton. I put my call in to my friend Frank because I wanted him to attend.

One of the things that was a very big deal during that era in the Hamptons was late Friday afternoon art gallery openings. There would usually be a dozen of them, if you counted every town in the Hamptons. All would take place at exactly the same time of day, which would be between 5 and 7 p.m. Gallery-goers by the hundreds would gallery-hop to two or three of them, drinking wine, eating cheese and crackers, meeting the artists and the gallery owners, walking around amid all the beautiful paintings, and talking to their friends. Sometimes a painting would get sold. That could be quite a big deal. Paintings were often the work of Roy Lichtenstein, Andy Warhol, Larry Rivers, Willem de Kooning, or Fairfield Porter, all of whom either lived or had lived in the Hamptons. But mostly it was a social occasion.

In the paper, we'd publish art gallery listings, and we'd review one or another of the artists showing. There were sometimes ads from the galleries accompanying this information. It was a lively business.

One day in 1986 I was in the Marisol Gallery on Main Street in Southampton, talking to Claudia Lang, the owner. She was one of our largest advertisers that year.

"You ought to do a story about my gallery," Lang said.

"We don't do that. We review the openings. We run the listings."

"I'm your biggest gallery advertiser. Tell you what. What if we had a showing of *your* work? You draw cartoons in the paper sometimes. You'd write about that, wouldn't you?"

She had me there.

A week later, it all came to me. A big lightbulb went off. And I started drawing.

I drew a whole lot of happy girl chickens all in a row, their wings around the girls on either side, kicking up a storm, cancan style.

I captioned it "Chicken Croquettes."

Then I drew a bunch of scowling male turkeys carrying rifles, wearing helmets, combat boots, and belts of ammunition across their chests.

I captioned it "The Turkish Army."

It went on and on. I drew Moby Duck. I drew Attila the Hen. I drew a safe-quacker. Pretty soon I had over twenty cartoons involving geese, ducks, chickens, hens, turkeys, and wordplay. People told me they thought it one of the funniest and stupidest things I had ever done. This, I thought, would be my art show at the Marisol.

I called Lang and tried to describe it to her.

"Bring it over," she said.

The opening was planned for Friday, the kick-off of the Fourth of July weekend. We'd serve the obligatory wine and cheese. We'd get a fiddle player to wear farmer's clothes and play hoedowns and square dance music, sitting on a stool off in a corner. We'd have a poster of Frank Perdue—you could, for a few bucks, buy a poster of this ugly man at that time—and put it up on the wall by the entrance to the gallery. Inside would be the twenty-six poultry cartoons, smartly matted and lined up in rows, all along the walls. Then, at seven, it would be over and everybody would be out just in time to have a quick dinner and then go off to the Town Fireworks in East Hampton, which would begin at nine thirty. What a plan!

A month before the opening, we began running the listing about the upcoming gallery show in *Dan's Papers*, and through the use of a uniquely disguised and fictional Manhattan marketing company—because our newspaper competitors might "fail" to notice my opening otherwise—we told the world about the show in a series of very breathless press releases. FOR IMMEDIATE RELEASE each one said in big letters across the top.

Two weeks before the big day, all the material relating to my art show was piled up in a conference room just across from my office on the second floor of *Dan's Papers*. Often, I would pass the poster of Frank Purdue. He was indeed a very disturbing looking fellow. But he got me thinking.

Why not ask him to come? I thought. Wouldn't that be something? All he could do was say no.

I found his number—he sometimes ran it right on the television screen so if you weren't satisfied you could call him—and I called. I figured I'd get a secretary. I'd try to talk my way through to Frank. Amazingly, I did.

"You don't know me," I began when I got to him, "but we are having an art show about chickens here in the Hamptons a week from this coming Friday afternoon and we would like to invite you to come."

"A chicken art show?" It was him, all right.

"You know the Hamptons?" He didn't know the Hamptons. I told him it was this exclusive resort on the tip of Long Island where the rich lived. I told him he could stay at my house if he came. I'd show him around.

And then I told him about the chicken drawings. Our artist, me, had at one time sold cartoons to *Esquire*, *Saturday Review*, *Playboy*, and the Canadian magazine *McLeans*—this was all true—and now I was unveiling drawings of not only a whole series of chickens, but also turkeys and ducks. I let him in on the joke. The Turkish Army. Chicken Croquettes. We would very much appreciate it if he could come. It would be great publicity.

"It sounds wonderful!" He had this high squeaky voice, almost a soprano voice like a girl. "I think I'd like to go. I have a plane. Let me look at my schedule and I'll call you back."

I was ecstatic. I wrote up a new press release as if he *were* coming, so I would be ready. But what if he wasn't coming? He said he was coming.

He wasn't coming. He called back the next day. "I have to wish you the best of luck," he said, "but I just can't fit this in. I really thank you for thinking of me. It does sound like fun and I love fun."

"We will have a poster of you at the entrance. We will make do with that," I said. "And thanks for considering this. You made my day just doing *that*."

"I wish you the best."

So, no Frank Purdue. But would the poster be enough? I did not think so. So I had that Manhattan firm send out another press release.

"Frank Perdue, the chicken impresario, has been invited to attend the POULTRY CARTOON show, but unfortunately called back to say he could not fit us into his schedule. On the other hand . . ."

At five o'clock on Friday, July 4, 1986, we opened the doors to officially welcome guests to THE POULTRY CAR-TOONS OF DAN RATTINER. Almost everything was in its place. On a table pushed against a wall were wine and glasses on one side and cheese and crackers on the other side, but in the middle was an empty space because what was supposed to be featured in that spot had not yet arrived. A few people came in and wandered around. I looked at my watch.

At ten after five, the front door banged open and in came Ralph Carpentier, a widely respected landscape painter who lived not far down the road from me in Springs. His wife Horty was accompanying him and between them they were hefting in a large wooden tray, about two and a half feet across, covered in aluminum foil. They brought it over to the table and set it down in the middle.

"Sorry I'm late. I had some finishing touches to do on it," Ralph said.

"You're just in time," I said.

Horty slowly peeled off the tinfoil to reveal what her husband had done. He had carefully carved a life-size bust of Frank Perdue, made out of chopped liver, just as I had ordered. And there was an embellishment: the whole thing was bordered by flowered radishes.

"It's perfect," I said.

People came over to stare at it. It was a perfect likeness. Then I saw a woman going for a cracker in anticipation of dipping in, and I asked her to hold off for a moment. I got a camera and took its picture.

"Now, it's okay," I said.

It was a great opening, even though I did not sell a single cartoon. Maybe the price was too high. They were marked at eighty dollars. Or maybe the price was too low.

In the last few years, the art scene here in the Hamptons has begun to take serious note of my drawings. I don't know why. They've always been real good in my opinion. But that year, the owner of the Tower Gallery in Southampton, which in prior years had shown the work of Fairfield Porter and Larry Rivers, called me up and offered me a show. I framed eighty-two of my drawings and we had them up on all three floors of that space. It was a great financial success and we sold about a dozen for between eight hundred and fifteen hundred dollars each.

I had two cartoon shows in 2009, one at the Wintergreen Gallery in Sag Harbor and the other in the hallways and conference rooms of the Southampton Inn in Southampton.

In the winter of 2009–2010, the new owners of Southampton College—it was now part of the State University system—invited me to hang my cartoons in the lobby of their newly completed college library. The paintings were not there for sale, but for decoration. Nevertheless, my wife and I went to the college and held an "opening" anyway on a freezing cold Friday evening in January 2010. A snowstorm was in progress and only four people came between 5 and 7 p.m. So we just sat around with the few guests amid all the food and Pellegrino water and alcohol-free champagne—we couldn't have alcohol in a student library—and we talked and talked, quietly of course because this was a library, and I told them about the great Poultry Cartoon Show and Frank Perdue not being there, but being there instead in chopped liver, and it was a lot of fun.

Behind us, on the other side of a glass door, the students were studying away at the tables in the main reading room, the snow falling beautifully in great flakes just outside the windows.

It was a scene that would have made any decent landscape artist proud.

THE TURKISH ARMY

Alastair Gordon

~~~~~~

In 1989, there was talk at town hall that they should build a new terminal out at the old airport field. The existing one was not much on charm. It was two 12 x 24–foot cedar shingle bungalows, each one-story high but distinctly different one from the other, attached together alongside the single runway where the planes flew in and out. It had been there like that since my family had first moved here in the 1950s.

I figured there might be a story about how these two buildings became the airport terminal. Charles Lindbergh took off from Roosevelt Field on Long Island when he flew the *Spirit of St. Louis* to Paris in 1927. Maybe this makeshift arrangement had been put together around that time. So one day I drove the six miles down to Daniel's Hole Road and parked by the split-rail fence that kept you from walking out onto the runway and into the aircraft.

There were actually three structures that made up the airport terminal. There were the two pushed-together shacks— one where the public waited and the other where the airport manager worked—and then there was a narrow two-story rectangular cedar-shingle tower alongside, which I had never seen anybody use. Inside the shacks there were seats along the interior walls of the small main room, as well as a soda machine and a candy vending machine. Nobody was there.

A narrow door led into a tiny, decrepit bathroom with a light on a pull chain. But you had to step over a part of the floor that was sagging to get to it. This had something to do with the toilet repeatedly overflowing. It smelled funky.

Conversation was coming from behind a larger closed door. I knocked. Someone said come in. Inside, I found two guys in their sixties sitting on squeaky metal office chairs, facing a microphone and radio equipment. The guys looked up. I introduced myself and told them why I had come. Did this place have any historic value? Any interesting stories to it?

What I learned from these two men, who it turned out were the airport manager and his assistant, was really depressing. As there were no planes coming in and out at that particular moment, they were happy to tell me the whole history.

The two buildings were an oversize chicken coop trucked in by a farmer around 1925 and an abandoned World War I army barracks, trucked over from Yaphank, Long Island, around 1930. The tower was built in 1950 but did not have heat or electricity, which was why nobody ever used it. Also, the windows on the second floor did not open.

"It's broiling up there in the summer and freezing in the winter," the manager told me. "At least down here we have heaters."

"The last few years we've been catching mice," the assistant told me. "The place is full of holes. Maybe that's a story."

The manager put his hands behind his head, leaned back in his chair, and sighed.

There was a squawk over the radio, and both men leaned forward. A plane was coming.

"Gotta get back to work," the manager said. "Hope we've been of help."

Back at my office, I wrote what I had learned. This was not much of a history. And yeah, they'd have to do something to replace the terminal, but it seemed to me it needn't be anything fancy.

"Maybe it could be like a shingled barn with a snack bar in it," I wrote. "They have an airport terminal like that on Nantucket and also on Martha's Vineyard. It's a gateway to the community after all. It's what visitors first see."

I wrote about our old colonial downtowns, our beautiful wooden English windmills, our beaches, and our saltbox houses. They should build an airline terminal in keeping with all the rest of the town.

Tony Bullock was the town supervisor at that time. He was a nice guy. I figured he'd come up with something and I'd hear about it. I didn't have long to wait, but it wasn't what I expected.

"Did you see this?" my friend Elaine Benson asked one afternoon, coming into the office to attend our weekly editorial meeting. She owned a nearby art gallery. She held up a copy of the local East Hampton newspaper, the *East Hampton Star*, our competitor.

"It's wonderful news," she said. "The town is going to have an architectural competition for the new airport terminal, and they've chosen Alastair Gordon to judge it."

AN ENTRY IN THE AIRPORT COMPETITION
(Courtesy of *Dan's Papers*)

Alastair was the architectural critic for the *East Hampton Star*. I'd never met him, but I'd seen him around. He was a slender, very dramatic, animated member of the art community, full of himself, very handsome, and, in my opinion, someone who thought he was at least two notches above just about everybody else as far as architectural criticism went.

He had been an architectural critic for several newspapers and magazines and had reported excitedly on some of the modern homes that were now being built in the potato fields for some of the city people. He was sure madly in love with modern architecture. As for me, I saw modern architecture as something completely alien to our 350-year-old historic towns. I not only didn't like Alastair's opinions, I didn't like his attitude. Elaine, on the other hand, owned an art gallery down the street. Many people came to our editorial meetings from the outside, and she was one of them.

I had a look at the *Star*. The contest, authorized by Supervisor Bullock, would be open to architectural firms all over the world. The new building would be four thousand square feet in size—about eight times the mess we had up there now—and after its design was selected it would be built right on the site, with the airport people working out of a mobile trailer while they built it. It would consist of a waiting area, café, luggage area, observation deck, and airport manager's office. There would also be several bays where airline companies could have booths if they so desired. The competition would last six months and would be, at Mr. Gordon's suggestion, called "Beaux Arch 89."

"I think Mr. Gordon is the wrong person to have put together this competition," I wrote. I also don't like the French title of the competition. This is not France."

Elaine told me later that Alastair had taken exception to what I wrote.

"He wants you to stay out of this," she said.

"I'm not staying out of this," I said.

"You know," Elaine said, "this could really put East Hampton on the map. This could turn into one of those really important international art competitions."

"That's what I'm afraid of," I said.

"Dan, you write really interesting stories, but you really don't know anything about art and architecture. Leave it to the experts."

"I went to architectural school."

"Yeah. And you flunked out."

"It was Harvard. And I was there three years."

"And then you flunked out."

"I know what I like. Modern architecture for a home is one thing. Modern architecture for a gateway into our community is another."

I called Tony Bullock. I told him what I was worried about and that I thought Alastair Gordon shouldn't be chairing this effort.

"We have numerous gateways here," I said. "Look at our nineteenth-century railroad stations."

"I'm way ahead of you on this," he said. "There will be a panel of judges—very prominent internationally known architects. Gordon won't be one of them. Also, we've put into the rules of the competition that if we don't like the winner, we could take the runner-up, or number three, or number four."

"Okay," I said.

Six months went by, and the competition was held. During those six months, I wrote in my paper my thoughts about how the terminal ought to be in keeping with the historic nature of the town. I published photos of the Victorian gingerbread on the East Hampton Railroad Station, of the seashells embedded in the stucco on the exterior walls of the Southampton Railroad station. Gordon wrote in the *Star* about how many modern glass-and-steel entries they were getting for the airport competition.

"It looks like we will have more than a hundred," he enthused. "This is incredible."

He was interviewed by the *New York Times*.

"Every potential rich client walks through the airport," he said. "I expected a lot more shingle style, but not one was up to the jury's standards. The jury went for oomph and a sense of scale."

I went down to a warehouse in East Hampton where scale models of all the entries were on display. One was designed like a Quonset hut, another featured a building that looked, from the air, like intersecting runways. Another looked like a suburban house with a six-car garage.

You would not have believed what people wrote about their entries.

"Excitement, fear, happiness, some anxiety or sense of transitions between two worlds and two scales," wrote Barbara Marks. "I was thinking of Sakkara in Egypt."

"The resolution of differences between magnetic north and grid north is explored in this proposal," wrote entrant Uwe Drost.

"Two mono-pitched buildings facing opposite directions intersect while addressing the terminal's primary functions of arrivals and departure," wrote Solveig Fernlund of the firm Solveig Fernlund & Neil Logan.

I asked to speak to Gordon and was told he was not there. I should come back another day, or make an appointment. I decided I would not.

Finally, July came and the winners were announced—in Alastair's column in the *East Hampton Star.*

I thought of calling Tony Bullock about this. But then I thought not. He didn't need to get in the middle of any newspaper wars. Besides, though we had a free circulation almost five times the size of their paid circulation, they were the official newspaper of record.

Fourth prize was an entry from Germany, which was in the shape of a giant wooden propeller. Third place, from an Argentinean firm, was a glass-and-stainless-steel box. Second prize went to something from Spain in the shape of an airplane wing, and first prize was an angular building with glass sliders and a flat roof with louvered windows reminiscent of something that might be built in a Moroccan desert.

I was just stunned. The winning entry would be featured in *Architectural Digest* next month. The drawing of the plans and an artist's rendering of what it might look like accompanied the story. This was a disaster, I thought.

That afternoon, I went down to the East Hampton Main Bathing Beach pavilion and made a sketch of it. It was a grand building, nearly one hundred feet long, built in the 1920s in the sort of cedar-shingle summer-resort style you'd see on Nantucket or Martha's Vineyard. Taking the drawings home, I got out my old angles and t-square, and that night in my living room carefully made plans and elevations of an airport terminal modified from my drawing of the bathing pavilion. The centerpiece of my drawing was a two-story wooden rotunda.

"This rotunda would look like the housing of a merry-go-round carousel," I wrote. "The Hamptons are supposed to be fun. Carousels are fun. Also, keep in mind that one of New York City's first airport terminals has a rotunda—the Marine Terminal at LaGuardia Airport, built for the International Seaplanes flown by Pan Am Airlines in the 1930s. It is still in use today. The head of Pan Am, Juan Trippe, had a home in East Hampton."

I published these drawings on the front page of the next edition of *Dan's Papers*. I also tried entering my plans in the competition, even though the competition was over. I left them off at the warehouse where the entries were on display. They were returned to me unopened.

This is war, I thought. So I wrote about being turned away at the door.

Four days later, two architects from Sag Harbor appeared at my door and offered to make official detailed plans out of my drawings for me.

"Just tell us exactly what you want," one of them asked. "We will turn it around in four days. We completely agree with you."

"I flunked out of architectural school," I told them. "Just save the town."

The architects, good as their word, had the plans and elevations in my office four days later. I put them on the front page of the next edition. I also mailed a copy of the plans to Tony Bullock.

Alastair Gordon and some of his supporters were now firing back every week with all guns. The winning bid would be built. There was the contract. East Hampton would never again host any competition of international renown if this winning entry was not built. East Hampton would be a disgrace to the international art world if this entry was not built.

Through it all, Elaine Benson sided with Alastair Gordon. She was one of my best friends and she did so with respect, but nevertheless, we disagreed.

"You are wrong about this," she said.

As for Tony Bullock, he told me he could say nothing to me on the record.

"But off the record," he said when I went to his office, "just turn around. There's the set of plans your architects designed on the wall of my office. I look at it every day."

At this point, the two newspapers were at war with one another about what should be done, and there were letters to the editors of both papers. Here were some written to *Dan's Papers*:

"Please, please, can we just let it be," wrote Mary Buckley of Amagansett. "Do all places here have to be raped and ruined?"

"A new terminal should be in keeping with the style of the old and consistent with the charm and character of the Village," wrote Camille Romita of East Hampton.

"Nothing denotes 'Arrival' as much as an airport," wrote Tina Fredericks of East Hampton. "You immediately get the flavor and feel of a place—and subliminally it builds an attitude. . . . Certainly what has been described as one of America's Most Beautiful Villages deserves an airport building that conveys a sense of place—New England heritage, colonial roots, definitely the shingle style that works so well in seaside architecture."

"They are proposing to build a pretentious Taj Mahal over there," wrote Edith Davis of Bridgehampton.

On the other hand, there was Kerry-Elisabeth Heerlein of Wainscott, who opposed my efforts while writing wonderfully about what a dump the current airport terminal was.

"Lighten up and get with the program," she wrote. "The old terminal, a combination World War I Army Barracks from Yaphank and local farm chicken coop should be nuked . . . as soon as humanly possible. They are infested with rodents. I can't even count the number of times the men at the airport scared me with dead mice. I am glad I quit that job. The place is just about to rot into the ground. If we don't do something about it now, it's going to blow away during the next big storm. What kind of image does that project on our town? I am embarrassed by this 'airport terminal.'"

The town board could not ignore this. Time passed. The winning entry was not given the okay. They were now looking at entries two, three, and four. An announcement would be made soon. But none was.

I called Tony. "What are you going to do?" I asked.

"I don't know. Off the record, two of the town board members are completely opposed to building any of these four. With me that makes three out of five. But we are bound by our contract."

Eventually, the board made a very Solomonesque decision. All four of the winning entries exceeded the number of square feet called for in the rules. Thus, they all could legally be disqualified. But the board felt that the townspeople should make the final decision, because there would very likely be lawsuits filed by the winners, which could tie up things for years. Meanwhile, we'd have to continue with what we had now—and that was not pretty—plus we'd have lots of legal fees to pay.

The model of the Moroccan entry that had won the competition was then put on display in the window of Bernie Kombach's Village Hardware Store on Newtown Lane. It would be left on display there for thirty days. The whole town was invited to look it over. After that, in November, an item on the ballot would ask people to vote yay or nay. And that would be the decision.

Seven years later, I attended the dedication of the newly built East Hampton Town airline terminal. The town had overwhelmingly voted no. The winner sued. And it had taken five years and many generations of mice to make its way through the courts where, finally, the town prevailed, then two more years to design and get a new terminal built.

Tony Bullock was no longer the town supervisor in 1995, but I stood with him in the center of the rotunda as speeches were made and a ribbon was cut. The rotunda does look like it might have once held a children's carousel, and, to tell you the truth, although the local architect who finally designed it did make improvements and take some liberties with what I had submitted, it did capture pretty much the spirit of what I had hoped. Well, what did I know about architecture. Nothing.

In 2009, I attended what was to have been a panel discussion with three nationally known architects and one prominent art critic, all of whom have homes in the Hamptons. Attending were Paul Goldberger, the architectural critic of *The New Yorker* and former architectural critic of the *New York Times*, as well as architects Richard Meier and Robert

A. M. Stern. Charles Gwathmey, another legendary architect, was also supposed to attend, but was too ill to make it to the John Drew Theater in town, where all this took place.

Alastair Gordon was in the audience, but as usual, if he did see me, he took no notice of me. I saw him and pretended to take no notice of him either.

The topic was, essentially, a discussion about the rise and fall of modern architecture in the Hamptons, which had its heyday from about 1950 to 1980, when it all ended to be replaced by the giant reproductions of old mansions—called McMansions—that put an end to the modern era. Many modern masterpieces are now surrounded by foliage and are out of view. Others are falling into ruin for lack of proper maintenance. Turns out that boxy modern residential architecture does not stand up well in damp weather.

"Modern architecture does look grand in open fields," Stern said. "But all closed in with foliage as they are now, they are not so grand."

After the discussion ended, while everybody else was leaving the theater, I made my way up to the stage to ask a question. Robert A. M. Stern was closest to me.

"Do you recall the battle for the design of the East Hampton Airport terminal?" I asked.

"I do."

"Do you recall the winning entry?"

"I remember it well."

"What did you think of it?"

"Not much. A poor design. Glad they never built it."

THE AIRPORT TODAY
(Photo by the author)

I fairly skipped up the aisle and out onto Main Street toward home.

Odeda Rosenthal

~~~~~~

The house was on a little side street in East Hampton. There was a sign out front. I went up and rang the bell. My mother, who had gotten wind of the fact that my wife and I were planning a trip to New Zealand for the month of January, had called me and said I should meet this woman named Odeda Rosenthal. This was in the autumn of 1992.

"She runs a rooming house in East Hampton," she had told me. "She wrote a book about New Zealand. You have to go see her. I told her you would stop by."

"You said I would stop by?"

"It's called *The Jews of New Zealand*. She's written a whole book about it. It just came out. And it's a big success. I met her at services. She's very excited to meet you. She is going to give you a copy of it."

"Why would I want to read a book called *The Jews of New Zealand*?" I asked. "New Zealand was settled by Scots."

"Because there are Jews in New Zealand."

Whenever we went away for the winter, which we did because business was slow at that time of year and we thought it would be exciting to see interesting places in the world, before we left, in every case, my mother would butt in. Usually it was about Jews.

I put off going to visit Odeda Rosenthal for a while. But, since the rooming house was quite near my home, I couldn't put it off forever.

Mrs. Rosenthal answered the front door. She was a small woman of about sixty with a heavy Yiddish accent who talked loud because, as she said, she was hard of hearing.

"Come on in," she said, after I told her who I was.

"I can, just for a minute," I said.

"Oh, you can stay more than a minute," she said. "Everybody's out for the day."

Mrs. Rosenthal brought me into the living room and offered me some apple juice and pastries. I cannot resist Jewish pastries. Then she gave me a copy of her book, *Not Strictly Kosher: Pioneer Jews in New Zealand.* My mother had come close.

"It just came out last year. I went on a tour of New Zealand when the book came out. You would be amazed at how influential the Jews were in New Zealand. Mention my name when you get there. Everybody will remember me. New Zealanders were almost carrying me around on their shoulders."

I had read a lot about New Zealand after we decided to go there for a month. This book, though, I put on a shelf. Just because my mother had recommended it, I wouldn't read it. So much for the Jews of New Zealand, I thought.

Here's a Jewish joke. My mother told me her father had told it to her.

ODEDA'S BOOK

"A plane crashes on a mountaintop in Peru, and they tell this old man about it. When they finish he thinks for a minute and then says, 'Is that good for the Jews or bad for the Jews?'"

So much for my mother.

New Zealand is one of the most beautiful places in the world. It was summer there. There are mountains and lakes and miles and miles of ranch lands filled with sheep. But no Jews. I think there was one synagogue in the country, in Auckland, but we didn't go there.

What we did do on that visit was to take the equivalent of a bed-and-breakfast tour of the country, driving a car we rented at the airport from town to town. In New Zealand, however, they don't have bed and breakfasts. They have what are called farm stays. You arrive at a farm at 5 p.m., and at six you sit down with the family for dinner. You spend the night. After breakfast the next morning, you either hang around the farm helping out and stay another night, or you just leave after breakfast for the next farm a hundred or so miles away. Having dinner with a farm family, I have to say, is a great way to meet people. We loved it.

One day, after the first night of a two-day stay at a farm near Queensland, we drove to what we were told was a small resort village called Arrowtown. It was in the middle of the country, with a Main Street bordering a shallow river. We had an amazing adventure there.

First of all, we found that it was not much of a resort town. It had been a gold-mining town in the 1850s, and it got built up a bit. Now, there was a single main street alongside the river with a mix of nineteenth-century retail stores, now 130 years old and still standing, side by side on both sides of the street. Tourists walked up and down a wooden sidewalk, shopping for Outback hats, postcards, and wool sweaters. Though it was summer in New Zealand—our winter—it was a bit of a cool day.

There didn't seem much else to do there, which puzzled me. In one store, I asked somebody about that.

"You can drive golf balls," a clerk said.

This turned out to be a small rise at one end of town with a man holding a golf club by the side of the road. We parked near him and got out of our car, and found ourselves looking down on the Arrowtown School. To the right of the school was a pasture, to the right of that, woods. You paid a dollar and this man gave you a golf club, ten golf balls in a bucket, and told you that you could hit them toward the pasture to the right of the school from this little doormat they had set up there. Just be careful.

I still remember this experience. Some of the balls went into the woods to the right since I was fearful of hitting the school. "No worries, mate," the man said. Other shots went into the field. There were two children, each about ten years old, who watched as you did this, then when I finished, ran off to find the balls.

"They're my retrievers," the man said as I handed him back the club, a driver.

I asked if there were anything else to do in Arrowtown. And he told me that we ought to visit the Chinese Camp. I asked him where that was. We were up for anything.

"Just go down that path into the woods. It's about a ten-minute walk. You'll find it. It's a little village where the Chinese laborers lived during the gold rush. The houses are a bit falling down, but the government is finally restoring the place." He paused. "It's free admission until they get it restored."

What we found were eight tiny stone-and-thatch cottages no bigger than dog houses. The workmen slept in them, a government sign said, either curled up or with their feet sticking out. The buildings were less than five feet high at the rooftops. Up a path not far away, there was Ah Lum's Store. This was the only building in the community big enough to walk into. It consisted of three rooms with doorways so low you had to duck down to get through. There was a front retail area with a counter, a storeroom in the back, and way in the back a small area that appeared to be an indoor jail with barred windows but, the sign said, was the store's office. It was very cool and damp in Ah Lum's.

Nothing was in this place. It had been swept broom-clean, ready for restoration, which, apparently, was underway. A government sign in there said not to touch anything. We had no intention of doing so.

As we were about to leave, however, I noticed that in the storeroom, on a wall just above where it met the floor, some rotten wood had been pulled away to reveal—did my eyes deceive me?—pages of a very old newspaper between the studs. I walked over to it and squatted down. The newspaper had some sort of shellac on it so it would stay waterproof. In the Hamptons, I had seen seaweed in the walls of the old houses used for insulation. Apparently, here in Ah Lum's Store, they used newspaper.

"Are we going to go?" my wife asked.

"Just a minute. I have to read this. I can't leave a news-paper like this without reading it."

The pages of the newspaper were pasted on top of one another very haphazardly. But at one point there was a date, November 14, 1861. And the name of the paper was there, along with the volume number. The *Otago Daily Times.* Volume 1, Number 1.

There was an article entitled THE ROUTE TO THE DIGGINGS ON ETIERI ROAD, there were lists of arrivals and departures, and a main article that described the arrival of "The Escort," either a steam train or a stagecoach pulled by horses, which had come in from the mines with 35,100 ounces and seven prisoners.

Then there was what appeared to be an editorial. It was headlined MESSAGE TO READERS. It was an announcement by the publisher about this first edition of his new newspaper. This, I decided, I would write down. I took out paper and pen. I had to save this before new paneling got put back up. Here is what it said.

And now let us make an appeal partaking of a rather egotistical character. One which we trust we will never again have occasion to make.

The cost and expenses of bringing out a daily paper are enormous, far more than people generally suppose. The benefits arising from a daily paper are not to be exaggerated—independent of the opportunity it affords to the community of making its wants felt and its wishes known to the outside world, and so asserting its dignity and advancing its importance, the moral, social and commercial influences of a daily journal are strongly marked.

It brings the members of the community into closer unity; brings bonds of fellowship between them not lightly severed; facilitates business, advances the value of property and in short mixes itself up so intimately with the daily events of life that once having experienced its benefits, its absence is nothing short of a public calamity.

To the community as a whole, then, we appeal
to assist us in carrying out what to themselves we
hope will be beneficial. We do not fear for the result
commercially when the paper is once started but a
beginning is very difficult. The French wisely say *ce
n'est que le premier pas que qui coute,* and we feel sure
after once obtaining a start, the rest will be plain sail-
ing. Let the public foster the first days of the young
bantling, not only with copious supplies of advertisements, but with assistance in enlarging in every way
the circulation, and we promise on our part that the
infant shall advance to rapid development, and shall
become a journal calculated to reflect credit on those
who aided its earlier days.

What a find! Rarely has the role of a newspaper in a
community been spelled out so magnificently. It read like
something Winston Churchill would write. Who could have
imagined that a man so eloquent would have been in a small
mining community in New Zealand a hundred and forty-five
years ago?

We walked back up the path and out into the sunlight
toward town. I wondered about this strange and very moving editorial. Who was this man? And how long had this
newspaper—the *Otago Daily Times*—lasted? I imagined that
when the gold rush ended, so did the newspaper. And why
Otago? What a strange name!

When we arrived back on Main Street to our rented car,
I opened the door to see the local daily newspaper I had

bought when we had come into town that morning sitting on the dashboard where I had left it. It was the *Otago Daily Times.* I was in shock.

What the heck was Otago?

As we headed out of town, we passed a policeman directing traffic at an intersection. I pulled over and rolled down the window.

"Why do they call this place Otago?" I asked.

He shrugged. "This is the Otago district," he said.

And that was that.

About a week later, we arrived for dinner at the next farm on our list, a farm south of Nelson in the village of Thorpe, about eighty miles from Arrowtown. It was run by a couple named Joan and Robert Panzer. Over dinner, which was not lamb—nobody served us lamb the entire month in New Zealand because they thought everybody else served us lamb—Mrs. Panzer asked about what we did in the United States and my wife said she was a psychologist and I said I edited a weekly newspaper in New York.

"We have another newspaper editor staying with us. His name is Byron James. He and his wife stay here every year when he takes a two-week vacation. Perhaps you'd like to meet him."

"I would."

"They went out for the evening. But tomorrow morning, they are going to help us round up sheep in the north pasture. We're moving them. Perhaps you could join us."

"I'd like that very much. What do you mean 'round up sheep'?"

"Well, there's a way out that we want to block. People all hold hands and make a chain to block it off and the sheep go down where we want them to."

I looked at my wife.

"Sounds good to me," she said.

And so it was that the following morning, while five hundred sheep rumbled and baaaaahed their way by, we met Byron James and his wife Elizabeth. James was about ten years older than me and looked very much the editor in a leather vest and jeans. He smoked a pipe.

"I hear you're a journalist too," I said. I was holding hands with him. "What's your paper?"

"*Otago Daily Times*," he said. "I'm the editor."

Before the sheep had been fully rounded up I had told him of my find. He was quite amazed.

"We're the regional daily paper covering the South Island," he said. "We had a huge celebration on the occasion of the paper's hundredth anniversary, thirty years ago. I was a reporter then and I remember it well. Among other things, we published excerpts from that first edition. Except we could not find the first edition. So we published excerpts from the second, third, and fourth editions and called them the first edition. Nobody knew."

"Well now you know where the first edition is," I said. "It's in the storeroom wall of Ah Lum's Store in the Chinese Camp outside of Arrowtown."

"This is great."

"Who wrote that editorial? It wasn't signed, but it's wonderful."

"The paper was founded by a man who subsequently went on to become the prime minister of New Zealand. His name was Julius Vogel. And he got knighted. He was Sir Julius Vogel when he retired. To tell you the truth he was not a very good prime minister."

"Well, he was a good publisher. I write stories about my travels in my paper," I said. "I will definitely write this story."

"Send it to us after you publish it. We'll publish it too. And we'll pay you."

Byron James and I and our wives spent the day together. And when we got back to the farm, I found that in a little office in a barn they had a copier and I made him a copy of what I had transcribed from the wall longhand.

For many years after that, we corresponded back and forth. My wife and I pledged to come back. But we never did. It's just so damned far, nineteen hours on an airplane. Soon our correspondence petered out.

When we got home from that trip three weeks later, I wrote this story up for *Dan's Papers* and sent a copy of it to Byron James. The very next day after the paper appeared, the receptionist at the office asked if I wanted to see a woman named Odeda Rosenthal, because she was downstairs. I said I would be right down.

We sat together at the round table just inside the front door.

"I just wanted to tell you one thing," she said.

"What."

"Sir Julius Vogel was a Jew."

"I didn't know that. Isn't this an amazing coincidence," I said. "I met the editor of the paper he founded down there. Apparently, he was good at publishing his newspaper, but he wasn't a very good prime minister. He only served one term."

"He had the gout," Mrs. Rosenthal said. "It can be very painful. And it put him in a very bad mood. Well, I just wanted to stop in."

Six months later, I got a letter with the return address of the *Otago Daily Times* main headquarters in Dunedin. I thought it might be from Byron James, although in his previous letters, he had always written me on his personal stationery.

Inside was a check for $42.00 in New Zealand dollars. I took it to my bank, turned it in, and a week later, got an amount back in American dollars, which, after deduction for fees, came to $26.12. This was the best $26.12 I ever made.

Colin Powell

~~~~~~

On August 1, 1994, a sunny day on the East End, my wife and five of my friends joined me in heading out to the Indian Field Ranch in Montauk for Rusty Leaver's annual "Back at the Ranch" concert. What would be just a just a five-minute drive on other days would on this day take more than an hour. Tens of thousands of people were coming to this concert to hear Paul Simon, a resident of Montauk, sing two sets from a giant stage in a pasture to all these screaming fans sitting on hay bales.

We drove along. Some of the people in the other cars wore caps with stuffed parrots on them. Others had tiny palm trees on their shoulders. It made no sense. We parked, went in, and sat down on the hay bales in the media section. I think we expected another mediocre warm-up band again, like the one that had accompanied Simon the year before. But that is not what we got.

Out came Paul Simon. He waved to the cheering crowd, walked over to the microphone, and, looking offstage, smiled broadly and invited the crowd to welcome the music of Jimmy

Buffett. And there he was! He came out leading a steel band and five Caribbean female dancers dressed in enough spangles and feathers to win a prize at Mardi Gras, and quickly launched into his classic hit "Margaritaville." Immediately, the entire crowd got to its feet, went nuts, and sang along too.

And then I saw what I had seen in the cars waiting on those long lines. Maybe five thousand of the thirty thousand people were wearing parrots on their heads. And they swayed with them back and forth as they sang.

"Fruitcakes in the kitchen. Fruitcakes on the street."

"What is that?" I whispered into the ear of one of my friends next to me.

"Parrotheads," came the reply. "He has a following of parrotheads. Didn't you know?"

"I guess he does," I said.

Buffett had only had one huge smash hit during his career, but boy did he have a following. A song would end, and he'd launch into another. The band would thump along, the girls in the feathers would sing and sway, the stuffed tropical birds would bob around, and out in the crowd, beach balls would be punched from one person to another overhead.

And then, slowly at first, but then absolutely amazingly it seemed to me, an entire billboard of a volcano rose up at the back of the stage—a hundred feet long and ultimately fifty feet high—and it began puffing white smoke as it kept time to the music. If the crowd had been crazy, this made them even crazier.

At that moment, I saw him. He was standing in the VIP section, a big smile on his face, a stuffed parrot on his head,

COLIN POWELL
(Photo by US State Department)

pumping his fist in the air and singing as loudly as he could. It was General Colin Powell.

At first, I didn't believe I was looking at Colin Powell. I nudged my pumping, singing wife next to me to no effect, so I nudged harder and she turned irritably as if to say WHAT? And I motioned to the general, across a yellow rope just twenty feet away. Her eyes widened and she smiled and nodded yup to the music and then turned to watch what Buffett and the girls on stage were going to do next.

I don't know. Maybe it was just me. I thought it was very remarkable that this general of the United States Army, this former chairman of the Joint Chiefs of Staff, who had vanquished the Iraqi army in the Gulf War just a few years before, was standing here in Montauk with a parrot on his head, pumping his arms and singing. And he was not in uniform. Of *course* he would not be in uniform. As a matter of fact, he was probably hoping he would not be noticed. There was talk about drafting him to run for president in 1996. He could not be seen to be in full parrothead mode.

When the event ended, *Dan's Papers*, along with several other newspapers, published several pages of pictures of people who had attended or performed at the concert. They included Edward Albee, Christie Brinkley, Billy Joel, and many others, but no Colin Powell.

Had I really seen him?

Yup, Colin Powell was a parrothead. And seven years later, having declined to make a run for the presidency, he was serving as secretary of state under President George Bush.

One day in 1992, we got a call at the newspaper office that someone was driving a tank through a potato field.

"That's very odd," I said.

I dispatched a reporter to go down into Wainscott, three miles away from our office, where this potato field was located, to see what was going on. He came back with a photograph of Colin Powell, in uniform, standing up through the hatch atop the tank, grinning at the camera. The gun was pointed forward, but slightly upward.

"It's not a regular tank," the reporter said. "It's a World War I tank. An antique."

I looked closely at the picture. That's what it was, all right. And there was General Colin Powell with his row of medals. And there was this tank being driven toward the camera parallel to the rows of potatoes.

"What is Colin Powell doing driving an eighty-year-old tank?" I asked.

"I have no idea," the reporter said.

I made some phone calls. And what I came to learn was that Colin Powell was vacationing at the home of Ronald Lauder, the president of Estée Lauder, who had bought the 120-acre Osborne potato farm about ten years before. The deal was that the Osbornes could continue to raise potatoes on their farm for the rest of their lives. Lauder and his family would live in one of the farmhouses, a small clapboard affair on Wainscott's Main Street, surrounded by a mowed lawn bordered by a white picket fence and the potato farm all around. And when Powell came out to visit, he asked if it would be okay if he came with a tank. He wanted to drive it around on the farm just for fun, just to see how it worked.

Where he had got the tank and whether he had used taxpayers' money to get it hauled out here—it would not have come out under its own power—I have no idea, because at that point, I was asked not to write this story by a member of the Osborne family, who were now tenant farmers of Ronald Lauder. It might embarrass Lauder. And it might embarrass Powell. I wouldn't want to do that would I? Of course not, I said. And so, this story and photograph never made it into print.

Eleven months later, Secretary of State Colin Powell, at the behest of President Bush, addressed the United Nations Security Council and, in a giant PowerPoint presentation, projected photos taken from spy planes that clearly showed the buildings where Saddam Hussein was supposedly manufacturing his weapons of mass destruction.

"This photo was taken on March 23, and you can see all these trucks lined up making a delivery along one side," he said. "Now we come to March 28, the day before the weapons inspectors were scheduled to come, and you can see that the trucks are gone."

He was wearing a dark blue suit and was seated at his place in the Security Council, behind a placard that read UNITED STATES. Mostly, it was just him talking, but occasionally there were shots of other delegates, and whenever there was a slide, they showed it on the screen. I sat in my living room watching him.

And I thought—you can't be serious.

Paul Sidney

~~~~~~

In 1994, several sports-car racing enthusiasts in the Hamptons decided they wanted to organize an antique-car race through the streets of Bridgehampton in the summertime. This was a pretty extraordinary thing to do. Around 1920, when the Hamptons was all farming and fishing, some other race-car enthusiasts—they would have been called "motor-car enthusiasts" at that time—had done just that. They had laid out a seven-mile course on dirt roads through the potato fields of Bridgehampton, and about forty motor-car enthusiasts had brought cars with nameplates that said HUPMOBILE and STANLEY and PACKARD. They had torn up the place at speeds of up to one hundred miles an hour until finally, as you might have expected, one of the local citizens sitting on a hay bale by the side of the road watching the race got killed.

This event was revived in 1994, put together by several local residents who owned some of these now antique cars, and of course they weren't going to crank them up to a hundred, but they would be parading them around the old course one at a time at a stately pace through modern traffic,

PAUL SIDNEY AND LISA DABROWSKI
(Photo courtesy of *Dan's Papers*)

with the owners sitting in the open cockpits wearing ancient leather helmets and goggles and waving at all the passersby. The event would finish right where it started, on the grounds of the Bridgehampton Historical Society on a side street just off Main Street, one hundred miles and five hours later.

I thought that, as an event, it would be neat as hell. I was happy to give it advance publicity in the paper. And I absolutely intended to show up and take pictures and write about it.

The day came. I went with a camera around my neck and pad and pencil in hand. At ten o'clock, there were fifty antique cars lined up on the lawn, with their proud owners standing around shining them up with rags and happily answering questions of the hundred or so tourists attending.

At eleven, they'd begin heading out, one at a time, onto the regular highways and byways at five-minute intervals.

If this was just about the most fun you could imagine for a Saturday morning in July, the effect was considerably heightened by the presence of a man named Paul Sidney, a radio announcer with a puffy face, a big circus-like grin, and an urgent, nasal voice that spoke to you over loudspeakers atop the WLNG news wagon parked behind him.

That he would be there was the stamp of approval for any event. It meant he had personally chosen to cover it. And since he and his news wagon had been doing this every day, through snow, rain, sleet, and sunshine for thirty-five years somewhere in the Hamptons, it meant a lot. There he was, holding his microphone and sitting in a folding chair on the sidewalk alongside his news wagon. He sat in a shady spot, on the sidewalk under a maple tree in front of the historical society. His voice, a circus barker's voice, booming, demanding, and upbeat, wafted out over the crowd.

He had seen me.

"Hey Dan!" he shouted into his microphone. There were two empty folding chairs next to him. He motioned me over to one of them.

What the hell. Everybody loved WLNG. Half the East End listened to it every day. I ambled over.

"Now we've got Dan Rattiner of *Dan's Papers* over here for a bit. Dan, what do you think of all these antique cars?" he asked.

"Beautiful, beautiful," I said into the microphone, getting into the rhythm. "It's quite an event. I had no idea there were so many antique cars in the Hamptons."

"Think they'll get tickets out on the road?"

"No, they won't, Paul. Unless they break down and block traffic. They'll look pretty weird, people will wonder what's going on, but it will be quite a good time."

Right in front of us, a couple with two kids, tourists who had been walking along, stopped. Here were these two middle-aged men sitting in lawn chairs, and behind them, a big mobile home with gold trim, lightning bolts, paintings of microphones, and WLNG, THE VOICE OF THE EAST END, in great big letters on the side. It was just part of the scene.

A radio interview with Paul never lasted more than three minutes per person, and in this case, at the three-minute mark he started looking over my shoulder.

"Hey, there's our town supervisor, George Stavropoulos," he said. "Hey George?" George walked over.

"Let's get our supe in here for a minute to join us, okay?" he said. "Oh wait," he said, cupping a hand over his ear. He was wearing a wire. "Now we've got to break for a commercial. But we'll be right back, with Dan Rattiner and George Stavropoulos."

Coming out over the loudspeakers now was the recorded ten-second sing-song signature of the radio station, some girl quartet, in harmony, singing the call letters of the station they had probably recorded thirty years before. WLNG plays it a hundred times a day. Still does. A band was in the background. It ended as suddenly as it started, with the sound of a chime.

Then, over the loudspeaker, Paul Sidney's recorded voice was interviewing the recorded voice of Ben Hull, the longtime owner of Hull Chevrolet, about the line of cars available at the dealership.

Stavropoulos had sat himself down in the third lawn chair for the Paul Sidney treatment.

"So how is everything, George?" Paul asked. It was my cue to leave, and I did.

I had first met Paul Sidney shortly after I started my newspaper, in 1960, and of course, it was at an event. We both were in our twenties, then, and we sort of hit it off. I could hardly not hit it off with him. He played rock-and-roll music and in between rang cowbells and shouted and otherwise made a lot of noise. I loved all that.

A month or two after getting to know him, I was walking up Main Street in Sag Harbor and saw him sitting alone on a park bench. I joined him. We were both single, but while I was looking for a good woman, he was not looking for anything. He had already found it. It was the radio station.

It was always kind of eerie talking to him privately. There on the park bench, he was not shouting. He was offstage. It was like meeting an actor in his dressing room with the performance behind him, resting up. I thought to make an interview out of this, asked him if it would be all right, and then asked him how he had gotten into radio.

"Radio is my life," he told me. "My first broadcast was when I was ten. It was over a ham radio set my dad got me. Then when Mr. King, who started the radio station, said he was looking for a disc jockey, I fit the bill. I've never looked back."

Now, at the antique car event, I got up and wandered over to a large white tent that had been erected alongside the historical society building. Inside, there was a registration table, coffee and donuts, and people selling racing books and other paraphernalia. A few hundred spectators milled around. You could tell the drivers and navigators by their driving goggles, leather helmets, and other racing gear.

On a side lawn, racing legend Jackie Stewart, also with a microphone, had now begun talking to the crowd. He was dashing and handsome in a racing suit, but he would not be racing in any car. Instead, he was now interviewing the antique car drivers at the starting line just moments before they would be heading out, one at a time, onto the "race course."

I walked over.

Mr. Stewart and these drivers were on a platform about four feet up. Ramps led up to it on one side and down from it on the other. Stewart stood with a microphone in his hand, leaning over, talking to a driver sitting in the antique car with the motor running, ready to go. The car engine thundered, smoke belched out the back, and it was quite a racket. Behind him, partway up the ramp, was the next car, and then after that the next. But Stewart, the legend, was the star, pacing back and forth, laughing, parrying one comment or another, telling a bit about his many achievements in his perfect Scottish brogue. He had won fourteen major races in his driving years.

The interview ended just as a timer with a checkered flag, on the lawn in front of the car, began to count backwards from ten.

"Five, four, three . . ." the flag would come out, "one, ZERO!" And the car, banging and belching, would be off the ramp and away. What a great day!

I wrote extensively about the day in the paper the following week. And the week after that, sitting in my office, I got a call from Peter Mole, the chairman of the event.

"The committee would like you to be master of ceremonies at next year's event," he said. "Would you do that?"

I was so surprised.

"Are you *sure* you want *me* to do this?" I asked.

"We are."

"But I'm no racing legend."

"We know. But we would still like you to do it."

I said I would be happy to emcee.

"What do I ask the drivers?" I asked.

"Just ask them about their cars. It's easy. They'll tell you. One after another. Forty or fifty cars and drivers."

I know this is going to sound crazy, but all that winter and into the next spring, I thought about the fun I'd have standing there with the microphone being Mr. Personality and getting laughs from the crowd. I thought this was terrific.

It was, by this time, a fact that for years and years, I was already the master of ceremonies at a variety of events. I would start them. I would run them, talking about them with a microphone before a large crowd, year after year, and I just couldn't imagine myself *not* doing it.

As a matter of fact, as I write this today, we have just concluded, for the thirty-second year in a row, a running race called the *Dan's Papers* Potatohampton Minithon. And for the thirty-first year the *Dan's Papers* Kite Fly out on the Sagaponack Beach. I am seventy-one years old. I am wondering how I am ever going to get out of this.

In any case, that spring of 1994 turned into summer and I just couldn't wait to get out there and be the master of ceremonies of the Bridgehampton Grand Prix.

On Grand Prix morning I woke up at eight at my house in East Hampton and had an immediate brainstorm. I was no Jackie Stewart, but I sure could wear a tuxedo with a red tie, cummerbund, and shiny black shoes to make myself look special. The grand prix would join the long line of other events I had adopted over the years. They asked me once. They got me. I'm their guy, for every grand prix coming up in the future. Count on it.

And boy, was I terrific. We had sixty cars, and even more people attending than the year before. And I was the star of the show—just me out on the front lawn on the platform talking to the drivers on the microphone with as much exuberance and enthusiasm as I could muster, and over by the curb Paul Sidney yakking away on his radio station.

After all the cars were off, I walked across the lawn and did my obligatory interview with Paul Sidney, and as I was leaving to go home, walking under the maple trees, Peter Mole ran over to me.

"Please do this again next year!" he said.

"You liked it?"

"Oh yes."

I was so happy. "Well then, I will."

On the appointed day the following year, I once again dressed myself in my tuxedo. I ate breakfast at nine and headed out. It was another beautiful day.

I parked across the street, in front of the Candy Kitchen, and walked past Paul Sidney in his lawn chair talking to Christie Brinkley and over to the platform to check myself in with Peter Mole. The pennants were flying. The cars, even more than the year before, were lined up in the back, getting ready to move out into the line.

I couldn't find Peter at first. I went into the tent. But I did see Jackie Stewart, off to one side, signing autographs. So he was here. This time, he would watch *me*.

People looked at me in amusement—a man in a tuxedo at nine thirty on a Saturday morning. They would soon see.

At that moment, Peter Mole ran up to me. He was out of breath.

"What are you doing here?" he asked.

"Why, I'm master of ceremonies. Like you said."

"No, that was last year."

"You asked me after the event last year for this year."

"Jackie Stewart is back again to do it this year."

"You might have called," I said. I could feel the heat rising. I was getting angry. "I got all dressed up."

"That was a year ago I asked you," Mole said. "You should have checked back with me."

And then he was gone.

I look like a fool, I thought. I *am* a fool. The crowd was swirling around. I'm not staying for this. The hell with this. And so I turned and, snaking myself through the crowd, went out toward the street and my car across the street and then I stopped.

Between me and my car there was Sidney, sitting in a lawn chair, in my way. Christie had left. He hadn't seen me yet. But he soon would. At that moment, he was bantering on about the big crowd, about the oompah band, about how everybody should all come on down to enjoy this wonderful event and contribute to the charity, which was the Bridgehampton Race Track Defense fund at that time. And he was scanning the crowd, looking, looking . . .

I zipped behind a maple tree. Made myself thin and tall. He shouldn't see me.

I was a wreck. Humiliated, angry, a fool. I was in no condition for this. I peeked out. Sidney was looking to his left, up the street, away from me. And so I zipped to the next maple tree and again made myself thin and tall.

I'm a goddamn Roadrunner cartoon, is what I thought. But I'll be damned if I'll let myself be interviewed by Paul Sidney. I'll blab to the whole East End about what they had just done to me, I'm so damn angry.

He turned, reached down to the grass, and picked up a cup of coffee in a cardboard cup. I zipped to the next maple tree.

And thus it was that I picked my way from tree to tree until, finally, I was able to race out into traffic and across the street to my car, unnoticed by Mr. Sidney. I would drive off. Safe. A man who had safely avoided being interviewed by Paul Sidney.

As I settled myself in the driver's seat, I could hear Paul interviewing a couple from Larchmont. The husband was a car buff. Had a 1964 Pontiac Firebird. Yes, he'd come out here specifically for this event.

I'm outta here.

Kim Cattrall and Mark Levinson

~~~~~~

Gerard Drive in East Hampton is a narrow, two-lane road that runs down a long peninsula for three and a half miles before coming to an end at the entrance to Accabonac Harbor. On one side along its length is Gardiner's Bay. On the other is the harbor. In some places, Gerard Drive is only a few feet wider than the road itself, while at others it is as much as fifty yards wide. Along the way are old fishermen's shacks, perhaps fifty of them, built in the 1940s or 1950s by determined fishermen who loved the isolation of this place. Today they are owned by a wide variety of people, from retirees and locals who can no longer afford to live in a larger sized house in this community to young people roughing it and anyone who prefers ambience to luxury. Certainly there is plenty of ambience. The sun rises over the bay and it sets over the harbor. There's the smell of salt and decaying sea life. Drinking the water is iffy. The whole thing is sand. And the cars crawl by just a few yards from your front door.

KIM CATTRALL

(www.flickr.com/thehearttruth)

In this unlikely setting, in 1995, two people of an intellectual bent, each of whom owned a house on Gerard Drive, met, discovered they were just two doors down from one another, and fell in love.

They were, and are, Mark Levinson, an audio and sound genius, and Kim Cattrall, the actress. They courted for just three months. Then they married and set up housekeeping in both homes, moving from one to the other as they desired, and maybe or maybe not dreaming of the day they could buy the two houses in the middle.

At that time, *Sex and the City* had not yet debuted on HBO. And Kim Cattrall, originally from England but now, after many acting and voice classes, bereft of her British accent, was appearing in B movies and soaps in New York City.

As for Mark Levinson, he spent many of his days working in the city on his audio inventions. Ten years earlier, he had stunned the industry with a new development in sound that dramatically increased the quality of music reproduction. When I met him, which had been a few years after this development, I found a slender, curly-haired man of about forty who was one of the most focused, likeable, and clueless individuals I had ever met. We became friends. I found him fascinating. But he always seemed broke. Businessmen would invest in him, he told me. A Mark Levinson stereo was one of the most desired systems in the world. Yet he was hardly earning a penny from it.

"I don't own my name anymore," he said at one point. "And I don't know quite how that happened."

Six years later, in 2001 (Kim was a household name by this time), I thought I ought to remodel a bedroom in my house into a flat-screen-TV home theater with stereo wrap-around sound. I went on eBay in search of rows of movie theater seats. I called Mark for advice about the electronic components, and he asked if he could come over the next day and see the room.

"Sure," I said.

"Could I come over for lunch?" he asked.

"Sure," I said again.

At noon the next day, he was over—he drove a battered old 1954 Rolls Royce—loaded with the sound equipment he felt he would need for my job.

"I'll just charge you what I paid for it," he said. "I do get it cheap."

"This is *great*," I said.

A half an hour later, when I went to tell him lunch was ready, I found him on the floor, flat on his back behind a stereo table, messing with a whole lot of colorful wires. It occurred to me at this time, because it was true, that this was the man who had just developed the sound system you could upgrade into your new Jaguar. It was called "The Mark Levinson." It's extra, but worth it.

"Want to ask a favor of you," Mark said.

"Anything."

"Kim and I are coming out with a sex book," he said. "With pictures. We're going to have a press conference about it in the city next week. Could you be there? Could you write something up about it?"

"Sure," I said.

When he finished, we sat at the kitchen table. I had prepared tuna fish sandwiches, chips, bread-and-butter pickles, and Coke. The stereo system, which had rattled the windows with the Rolling Stones just a few minutes earlier from the other end of the house, was now reset down to a whisper.

"We originally had a deal with Simon and Schuster," he said between bites. "But it didn't work out. We told them we wanted to publish a 'how to' book that would be anatomically correct, an instruction manual if you will. They said they wanted juicy tidbits about *Sex and the City*. We said that was not the book we wanted to do. They said do that one, and then we'll do the one you want."

"How can I help?"

"The press conference is to announce the inking of a deal with Warner Books. It's what we want. We think. With your help, if you give it press and support our idea, it'll make a big difference."

"Sure."

But I wasn't so sure I wanted to see anatomically correct photographs of Kim Cattrall, or those of the wife of anybody else I knew for that matter.

"Err . . ."

"What?"

"Nothing. I'll be there."

The press conference took place upstairs above a fashionable restaurant in midtown Manhattan. Everybody wanted to take pictures of Kim. She was happy to oblige.

Kim spoke. "I wanted to do this book because after living inside the skin of Samantha Jones for several years, I really wanted to better understand the mechanics of sexual satisfaction. How does it happen? What is the nature of desire? Of orgasm? Personally, I had not understood the nature of this until very recently. You know, I'm not Samantha. I'm a very proper girl from England actually. Don't mistake me for her. And I think there are a lot of girls out there like me who would like a book like this." She smiled at Mark.

"And we think a lot of people will pay attention to this book because of *Sex and the City*," Mark said.

Afterwards, Kim gave me a hug and thanked me for coming. Mark thanked me too. I wrote it up exactly as instructed. It was easy. I believed in the project.

The book, entitled *Satisfaction: The Art of the Female Orgasm,* became a best seller, with drawings by a Japanese illustrator of people in sexual positions. It was really an instruction manual, and it would be a big stretch to say there was anything erotic about it.

The following year, Mark and Kim bought a fifty-five-foot yacht, which, in fact, was really just a shined up lobster boat that Mark had motored down from Nova Scotia. Nobody would mistake it for a big luxury craft. On one occasion, we went out on it because it was my birthday. Kim served hors d'oeuvres that she cooked on the stove and Mark served the drinks. It was up to me to pack the place with guests, which I did. I think there were twenty-five, among whom were my best friend at the time, financier Wilbur Ross, with his wife, Betsy McCaughey Ross, the lieutenant governor of New York State.

As sometimes happens with these things, however, the marriage of Kim and Mark collapsed after eight years. As I had come into this with Mark, I got gifted to Mark in the dividing up.

Mark soon sold the lobster boat. But he took in four bobcat kittens, which he kept at his Gerard Drive shack and which, he said, were both trainable and cute.

"Can you housebreak them?" I asked.

"No," he said.

The bobcats grew, and one of them scatted out of there, to turn up elsewhere on Gerard Drive, where the neighbor reported it to the authorities.

"They don't understand bobcats," Mark said.

The last time I was at Mark's place, it was surrounded by an eight-foot fence with barbed wire on the top. We had a dinner, which he cooked. One bobcat slinked around. But another slept. I gently scratched one. It purred.

"Another one got out," Mark said. "So I had to put up the barbed wire." He seemed frustrated about the cats and apologetic about the barbed wire. "There's some kind of wild animal license I have to get. I might have to give them away."

He was opening a software audio business and he had named the main product "The Bobcat." "You won't believe the sound you get with this," he said. "It mimics analog so closely you can't tell it from old vinyl sound."

I didn't see Kim for a number of years after that, but at a Saturday afternoon at Bridgehampton Polo, she came up to me and gave me a hug again. Paparazzi cameras clicked and flashed.

"I miss you," she said.

"I miss you, too," I said.

Peter Jennings

~~~~~~

One day, in the spring of 1992, I got a call at the office from Peter Jennings, the longtime anchor of the *CBS Evening News*, asking if he could fire the starting gun of that year's Dan's Papers Potatohampton Minithon. In each of the prior eighteen years, other celebrities had done this to help raise money for Southampton Hospital. Jennings would do it, he said, if we'd agree to give the money this year to a different charity. The Bridgehampton Child Care and Recreational Center. I said sure.

"Just come down to the starting line on the day of the race at nine thirty in the morning. Race starts at ten. You know where it is?" He said he did.

I then put an article in the paper saying he would be coming.

Peter arrived that morning a half hour before race time with his wife Katie Marten and several of his small children. Tall and movie-star handsome, he was quite reserved and gracious, just as he always was on TV, and he shook my hand hello.

"Just let me know what you want me to do," he said.

MR. G. WITH PETER JENNINGS AT THE RACE
(Photo by the author)

"Wander around. When you see everybody begin to gather near the starting line, just come over to where I am. I have a bullhorn. I'll introduce you."

"Quite a nice turnout," he said, looking around at the hundreds of people. Two guys dressed as French fries hopped by.

The time came, he took the bullhorn from me and said a few words about the child care center, then waited for the appropriate time and fired the runners off. He hung around afterwards. An hour later, during the trophy presentation ceremonies on the front steps beneath the portico of the Community House, I thanked him again for coming.

I thought it was very nice he did this. On TV, he always seemed formal and stiff, not the sort of person who would take to having unbridled fun of this sort easily. But he got through it.

That November, I received in the mail a beautiful Christmas card from him. With it was an invitation to attend a Christmas carol sing and party at his house on the Saturday evening before Christmas. He lived on Loper's Path, Bridgehampton, a road that I remembered as dirt, potholed, and at the edge of a woods. Also included, on a separate sheet, were the printed lyrics, including all the choruses, of the Christmas carol "Good King Wenceslas," just in case we had forgotten it. He was apparently hoping we would rehearse for the big event. Of course we would go.

Snow blanketed the community on the Saturday before Christmas that year. I hadn't told my wife of the exact address, of course, but I knew something that she did not. During the two years of our courtship just before we were married, we often went up to this bumpy dirt road along the edge of the woods on a warm summer's evening to make out. We'd bring a blanket, champagne, a portable radio, a flashlight, incense, and candles, and we'd stay out alongside this dirt road overlooking the farmland on the downhill side way into the early dawn enjoying the most sensual of pleasures. No cars ever went out there at night. That was Loper's Path.

"Uh-oh," she smiled, as we turned onto it.

We saw now that a short stretch of it had been paved, and new homes had been built along it. Beyond that stretch, however, it was the same bumpy dirt road we knew. Soon there was a dirt driveway to the right marked by balloons that went up a steep hill through the woods to the base of one of the most magnificent modern steel-and-glass homes I have ever seen. It sort of leaped out through the trees up there, a two-story affair above some stone garages on the first floor for the cars. It was fabulous place, and on this occasion all decked out in Christmas tree lights. Men with flashlights showed us where to park and where to walk up a steep path that circled behind the house to enter from the back on a top floor.

At the door, Peter and his wife Katie greeted us warmly. They wore red Santa hats. Behind them, a fire roared in a fireplace, and beyond that, a roof like a bird's wing soared above magnificent living-room sliders to this fabulous view of the farmland beyond and the town and ocean beyond that.

Peter shook my hand firmly. "Dan," he said, "good to see you." There were already fifty people or so there. Soon there would be fifty more. Never has there been a Christmas party in the Hamptons like this one, is what I thought.

I also thought—how long has this house been here high in the woods? Had it been here ten years ago when we had parked secretly down on the road below?

Everyone milled around for an hour having drinks and snacks, then everybody gathered in the living room, with some people on sofas, some standing in the back, and others standing in an adjacent family room or dining room and looking in. Peter stood with his back to the view, in front of the window, with his wife and dogs alongside, and it was from there that he would lead this crowd in singing the selected Christmas carols.

The fire crackled in the fireplace. Nearby, sitting at a grand piano next to a Christmas tree, was the legendary restaurant owner Bobby Van, an accomplished pianist, waiting for Peter to begin.

Practically everybody who was anybody was at that party. There were TV stars and starlets, great novelists, playwrights, painters, Broadway actors and producers. I recall George Plimpton there, and Kurt Vonnegut, Christie Brinkley, Joe Heller, Lauren Bacall, Billy Joel, and many more.

Peter spoke in this comforting, wonderful baritone that was the trademark of his news reporting. He seemed so delighted that everyone was there, and he conducted the caroling as if he were a minister at a church service.

"You all have your song sheets," he said. "Please turn to page five where we will begin with the singing of 'Silent Night.'"

We sang all the verses. Every one. It was wonderful getting us all singing.

"For our next carol," Peter said as we finished that, "turn to page six, where we will have a special treat. Jesse Norman from the Metropolitan Opera, would you please come forward to lead us in this?"

And so we sang "It Came Upon a Midnight Clear." And after that and a few more, dinner was served, buffet style.

There was a time after that when, finally, it became clear it was time to go home. We thanked Peter and Katie profusely. He shook hands again.

Leaving the house, we walked down the path toward the street with Joe Heller, the author of *Catch-22*, and his wife, Valerie.

"Peter Jennings is so, well, *nice*," I said.

Heller thought about it. "He's Canadian," he finally said, as if that explained everything.

The following year, the second year of his Christmas carol parties, was a sad affair. Peter hosted as usual and his kids and dogs were besides him, but Katie Marten was not. She and he, as everyone knew, were beginning a divorce action.

That whole evening, Peter never once mentioned anything about his wife, but there was a sadness in his eyes. On the other hand, he was soldiering on. I felt bad for him. His friends, all one hundred of them, rallied to his side, in song. I thought it was an amazing display of character.

As the years went by—the Christmas party was almost exactly the same every year—Peter Jennings's financial support for the Bridgehampton Child Care and Recreational Center grew. Now there was a second annual event. It was called "Jazz at Jennings" and it was also held at his home, but in the summertime. Attendees paid $1,000 a couple to listen to great musicians perform in the yard behind his house. Attending were major celebrities such as Tom Wolfe, Ken Auletta, Percy Heath, Dina Merrill, and Steve Kroft. All the proceeds, about $100,000 per event, went to the child care center.

Dan's Papers was, by this time, regularly sending photographers to take pictures of those attending fundraising events. But there would be no photographers at the home of Peter Jennings and his new and very stunning young wife Kayce for this event, just as there were none allowed at the Christmas party.

After the fourth party—there were to be six in all—I felt my presence at these parties was longstanding enough to find a club chair in the living room when Peter called us all in to begin with the caroling. I had never been in one of the club chairs before. And so I sat. When I did, a man came over and, as an usher would in a theater, leaned over and asked me politely to get up and go stand in the back. I guess not, is what I thought.

After that, I attended the two final parties being much more careful about where I stood and sat. Now it was I who was feeling stiff and formal. But these Christmas parties were still among the most enjoyable of the year, only coming to an end when Peter Jennings became ill, went into seclusion, and then, much too young, died.

The world mourned him.

The I Survived
the Winter Party

~~~~~~

At 5 p.m., the snowstorm was still raging. And I thought, well, this is a fine thing to have to get all dressed up for a party. Well, what can you do? It was my party, sort of.

I went to my closet and pulled out my tuxedo, something I had not worn since Labor Day weekend seven months earlier, and I carefully put it on. Then I put on my black shoes. Then I called my wife, who had said she was sorry she couldn't go to this party because she had to be at one in New York City that night, a longstanding commitment at work. She had left that morning, before the snowstorm had started. Now she answered the phone.

"Do you know where my party is?" I asked her.

"You don't know?"

"Linda Shapiro, the fundraiser lady, agreed to run it for me this year."

"Well call her."

"I tried. But she doesn't answer the phone." This was before cell phones.

"I think it's at the Harborside," she said. "At least that's what you told me."

I hung up. Maybe I should call the Harborside. The owner of the place, Ed Burke, a local lawyer, answered the phone.

"Hi Eddie, this is Dan Rattiner. Is the big bash going on as scheduled tonight?" I asked.

"Sure is. These things go on rain or shine."

"Okay," I said. The Harborside was this restaurant and catering hall at the end of Long Beach in Sag Harbor. On normal days, it had a spectacular view of Peconic Bay. It was about ten miles from the house: an easy drive if I took it slow. I also imagined that, well, not too many people were going to come this year. And that's a shame, because we'd sure gone all out for this affair. I headed down Three Mile Harbor Road. It was a quarter after seven now and dark. Winter might be almost over, I thought to myself, but this is a hell of a way to end it.

The event, an annual winter affair called the Dan's Papers I Survived the Winter Party, was something I had concocted five years earlier, in 1988. In that first year, when the party was held in the last week of March, which, as I think you know, comes in like a lion and goes out like a lamb, it was a huge hit. Three hundred people came. In the second year, over five hundred people came.

The idea had come to me because of this distinct lack of sophisticated human contact that occurs after October every winter in the Hamptons. During the summer, the city people come out weekends. Their numbers would slowly taper off in the fall, and then after Thanksgiving they would hardly come out at all. Those of us who remained all winter, us locals, would face the blizzards and snowstorms and ice and sleet and freezing weather alone. After which, we were supposed to have smiles on our faces to greet all the summer people when they would begin to come back in April and May.

And so, came the I Survived the Winter Party. It would be an annual event held on the last Saturday night in March to celebrate this magnificent accomplishment.

I found a big warehouse on Long Wharf in which to hold it. A disco had been there for ten years, but now that was gone and the place was vacant. I cajoled the landlord into letting us use it. "Maybe somebody will come and rent the place because of this," I said. I really figured that I could pull off this entire party on free donations.

The warehouse was in serious disrepair, with the fixtures pulled out of the walls and the disco floor pulled up. I thought this was a plus. The party would be down and dirty. I'd have a chili contest, I'd have a talent contest on the disco stage with dancing and singing, a dance contest, a beauty contest (Miss Local Person), and a band. I'd ask restaurants for food. And I'd even lean on some bars to come up with the booze to donate. I'd also try to get a celebrity to judge a beard-growing contest. Everyone who paid the thirty-dollar fee to get in would get a free t-shirt.

In subsequent years, the event went through changes, although it was still the I Survived the Winter Party and it still was held on the last Saturday night in March.

After the second year on Long Wharf, the big old disco got sold to three partners, who opened a live performance

INTRODUCING A TAP DANCER
(Photo courtesy of *Dan's Papers*)

arts theater they called Bay Street, and so we held the party the third year at another former nightspot, now abandoned, at the end of Hampton Road and County Road 39 in Southampton, next to the Princess Diner. Here, it developed a more child-friendly theme. The year-rounders were family people after all.

We asked people to wear bathing suits and Hawaiian t-shirts if they had them. We had a slide into a huge plastic indoor pool alongside the dance floor, we had a bar serving piña coladas, we had food from six different restaurants, we had a place where people could dress up in padded sumo wrestler outfits and do two-falls-out-of-three sumo wrestling with one another on a big mat. We had human bowling, people stuffed into rubber beach balls and sent down an alley to giant Styrofoam bowling pins, we had a band doing Beach Boys impersonations, calypso dancers, beach volleyball (on sand we brought in), and in a kiddie-friendly area an inflatable castle with piles of ping pong balls inside, a trampoline, and several nannies to keep track of it all. We were also supposed to have a Velcro wall, but it never arrived. I learned later it got in an accident on the expressway, coming out. Food came from Barristers, Basilico, Village Cheese, Driver's Seat, Paul's Pizza, Gristede's, Le Chef, and Tate's Bake Shop. And at this third event, as with the earlier ones, all the money that came in (after paying for the t-shirts) went to Southampton Hospital "to help the emergency room deal with frostbite."

I personally put out posters all over town, and we had 255 paid and another 150 who snuck in the back free. We also got raided and shut down by the police for making too much noise after 10 p.m.

And so it was that on the appointed day in the fifth year of this event I headed out that snowy March evening to yet another new venue—the Harborside—where the party was to transform itself once again.

This time I asked everybody to dress up as formally as possible. It would emulate a fundraiser under a tent, as if it was summer. There would be no tent, however. Instead, it would take place inside this banquet hall in Sag Harbor. I drove along. The snowstorm was getting worse.

I suppose at this point it would be fair to answer the question—how come I didn't know where my own party was? And the answer is that this woman, Linda Shapiro, a friend of mine who had recently gone through a divorce, had, at my suggestion, closed down her exercise studios in town, and begun a career as an event fundraiser. For this event, she said, she would take care of all the details for free if I would give her some publicity in the paper.

She got the venue. "All you have to do is show up," she said. I really liked that. Leave it to her. It would be at the Harborside, or the Harbor View, or the Harbor Café, all three of them advertisers, all in Sag Harbor. One of those.

Even the windshield wipers were not clearing the snow off the windshield very well. What a disappointment this was going to be after all the work Linda must have put into it.

I pulled into the Harborside, and immediately realized that in spite of all my fears, this party was another big smash. The parking lot was full of cars and I had trouble finding a parking spot. Finally, I did find one at the far end and, with my heavy coat over my tux, walked through the storm to the main entrance. Eddie Burke was standing there, in a suit and tie with no overcoat.

"Welcome, welcome," he said.

The place was packed. Apparently, I had not even gotten the time right. I had thought it was at eight. But this looked like it had been going on for at least an hour before I got there.

Eddie indicated where the coatroom was and I gave my coat to the hatcheck girl and headed inside.

As I expected, everyone was dressed to the nines. What an affair. Linda had obtained the services of a six-piece orchestra to play dance music from the forties. There were people dancing and standing around with drinks in their hands. I thought I ought to find her and congratulate her. I began looking for her, but at least at that time, she wasn't there.

Everywhere I went, though, people came over to me and shook my hand. It was a great party, they said. Don't you think? I didn't recognize any of them, but that didn't seem so unusual to me. This was a huge crowd. I was sure I would come upon people I knew soon.

Then I saw the food. Lobster, steak, fish. The buffet was open and there were people lined up. Waiters scurried around, carrying drinks to the people sitting at the tables. I still didn't recognize anybody. But I got a plate and waited, and after a while I was sitting at a table next to two couples. I introduced myself. We all shook hands. Then they went back talking to each other.

After about a half hour, the band stopped. And a man in a tuxedo got up and went over to the microphone and, to a drum roll—I will never forget this for as long as I live—said this.

"Now we are going to have the cutting-of-the-cake ceremony by the bride."

These words went through me like a shot. And I found this very hard to believe.

I got up and went to a bartender standing by a table of bottles and glasses nearby.

"I, uh, think I am at the wrong event," I whispered.

"This is a wedding," he said.

"I'm supposed to be at the I Survived the Winter Party," I said. "I'm the host."

The waiter looked at me blankly. Then he went off to talk to somebody else.

I have to find a pay phone, I thought. I ran back out to the lobby—I certainly didn't want to see Eddie Burke—to where my coat had been checked. The hatcheck girl looked at me inquisitively.

"You know where there's a pay phone?" I asked.

She nodded, turned around, and pulled some coats to one side. There it was, way in the back, on the back wall of this little coat-check room. She motioned for me to come in and so in I dove.

Amid these wet furs and overcoats, it at first occurred to me I had no idea who I could call. But then it came to me. I'll call my son David, who is home. The coats kept closing in on me and I would push them away. It was hard to keep my balance. But I got the quarter in.

"David?"

"Hi dad," he said. He was eleven years old.

"I want to ask a favor of you. Is there a copy of the current issue of *Dan's Papers* in the living room? I think I saw one on the coffee table before I left."

The band had started up again. I put my finger in my other ear so I could hear.

"Why do you want me to get that?"

"Could you just do it? Bring it to the phone and flip through it. I need you to look for an advertisement for the 'I Survived the Winter Party.' I think it's a half page, near the front."

"Okay."

He brought it to the phone and I could hear him flipping through it.

"I found it," he finally said.

"Tell me where it says where the I Survived the Winter Party is being held."

"Okay." There was a pause. "It doesn't say."

"It has to say."

"Well it doesn't."

"Does it say *when* it is? The date and time?"

Another pause. "No it doesn't say that either."

"Really?"

"Dad, I'm not kidding. I'm looking at the ad. They left it out."

"Impossible."

"They did. Honest."

"Could you read it to me?"

He sighed, and then he did read it to me, from top to bottom. It said there was the party, it said it was formal or suit and tie, it said it was a fundraiser, it said the food was being supplied by 75 Main, by Citron, Basilico, Great Gatherings, Le Chef, Santa Fe, Harbor Rose, the Seafood Shop, Southampton Public House, Alison by the Beach, Crazy Dog Diner, Bay Street Café, Nick and Toni's, Bridgehampton Café, the Crow's Nest, and Sapore di Mare—I kept popping nickels and dimes into the phone—and it didn't say where it was or when. These were hard things to believe. My production department had left all this out. Amazing. How dumb can you get?

"You okay in there?"

It was the hatcheck lady.

"I'm fine. Thanks for looking, David. What are you doing back there?"

"Watching *Seinfeld*," he said.

What do I do now? I thought. I felt miserable. I was wet, suffocated, in hiding, and embarrassed. And in that moment, I got a brainstorm. These restaurants all had to have, earlier on, been delivering food to wherever this was.

Brilliant, I thought.

I popped in another quarter, dialed 411, and asked for the number for Sapore di Mare. Another quarter went into the phone.

"This is Sapore di Mare. May I help you?"

"Hi, this is Dan Rattiner from *Dan's Papers*. I was just checking. With the snowstorm and all. Just want to make sure you delivered the food to the right place for the 'I Survived the Winter Party.' Where was it you sent it?"

"Harbor Cove Café. Didn't they get it?"

"Of course they did. Just checking up on the people running it this year. You know, this year I have other people running it. Just checking."

"Ha, ha."

"Ha, ha."

The Harbor Cove Café was in downtown Sag Harbor on Bay Street, facing the frozen boat docks. It was only five minutes away.

There were maybe thirty cars out front. That was it. I parked near the front door, and I strode inside. It was five after nine.

Linda, the marketing lady, was there, together with about fifty people in formal dress. It was not such a big success. She looked at me. "Where have you been?" she asked. "People are asking for you."

"Oh, you know." I motioned at the snowflakes outside one of the windows. "Well, I'm here now."

"I need you to make a little speech," she said.

Leon Uris

~~~~~~

As both the Hamptons and *Dan's Papers* got busier and busier during the late 1990s, I began to yearn for the old days, when everything was quiet and you could sit around and talk endlessly with people before having to go off somewhere to do something.

I knew a couple who lived in East Hampton and who rented their house out for the entire month of July—the busiest month of the year—to go to Nova Scotia, where they owned a cottage. I never went to visit them because I couldn't get away. But I imagined them up there, without a phone, reading novels and visiting neighbors—at least until August, when the mosquitoes start to get really bad there.

As a result of this thinking, I occasionally took my wife to this very peaceful little island called Shelter Island that sat between the two peninsulas of eastern Long Island, the Hamptons on the south and the North Fork on the north. It measured about four miles by five, and was only accessible by ferryboat. You could take your car with you on the ferryboat if you wanted to and the ferries went back every ten minutes, but the ferries only carried about ten cars at a time.

LEON URIS

How many automobiles could get to the island in the course of a day? Not many. Shelter Island, with maybe two hundred local people living there year-round, was very reminiscent of the 1940s when I was a small boy. You'd walk or bike places. There were woods and fields and little beaches—in that sheltered island just little bay beaches—and there was an ice cream parlor and a school and a luncheonette. You could get to know everybody.

We'd stay, usually for a two-day mini-vacation, at the Deering Harbor Inn or the Chequit Hotel. But our favorite place was the Belle Crest, a large Victorian bed and breakfast on the main road that was open only in the summertime. It was run by the Loining family, which included George, who spoke with a jovial German accent; his wife, Yvonne, from the Deep South; and their daughter, Amy, who was, at that time, about ten. They'd make a wonderful breakfast for the people staying in the five bedrooms upstairs in their house, and in the morning, Yvonne was out front as the hostess, George was in the kitchen cooking sausages and eggs, and their daughter Amy acted as waitress. After breakfast, of course, you were free for the day.

Nothing much happened on Shelter Island. There were tennis courts and golf courses, two of them, but they were exclusively for the fifty families who came, many of them from the Midwest, to their mansions in the exclusive summer community called Shelter Island Heights on the north shore of the island. I'd see them playing golf. They all looked like General Motors executives, or at least I imagined that. We delivered stacks of *Dan's Papers* to each of the eight retail establishments on the island. Everybody read them.

One day, back at my office in the Hamptons, I learned that the great novelist Leon Uris was now living on Shelter Island. He'd written *Exodus*, the story of the birth of the State of Israel, back in 1948. It was the bestselling book of that year, and my mother had read it, all eight hundred pages of it, and it brought her to tears. Leon Uris, she told me, was a god. And now, because of him, all America knew the truth about the new State of Israel.

I thought I'd like to meet Leon Uris if I could, perhaps to interview him for the paper, but when I tried to contact him I found him unlisted.

A week later, on the island at our little hideaway Victorian bed and breakfast, I asked Yvonne and George if they knew him and if, perhaps, they knew where he lived.

Yvonne steered me to one of the large living-room windows and pointed through a sparse woods at a house down a hill that sat on a pond. It had skylights on the roof. And there was a little dock in the pond for a boat.

"*That's* where he lives," she said.

It was maybe three hundred yards away. To get to it, all you had to do was go down a long dirt driveway, which started right next to the Belle Crest.

"Have you ever met him?"

"Oh no," she said. "Nobody's met him. He's sort of a recluse. And so everybody just leaves him be. I think he's writing a new book."

"He comes out summers?"

"He lives here year-round," she said.

For the rest of that weekend, and over the next three years that we frequented the Belle Crest, I imagined him down there, writing away on an old Remington typewriter, enjoying the view of the water and perhaps sometimes going out in his little boat. If you walked along the shore of the pond for about a hundred yards from his house, you came to where the main road curved around and there were five stores. He'd buy his groceries there, I thought. And all he wanted was just to be left alone.

The following week, I looked him up on the Internet. He was about seventy years old at that time. His books were vast in scope, sometimes six hundred or seven hundred pages. They included *Battle Cry*, one of the three or four greatest World War II novels ever written, and he'd written *Terrible Beauty*, about Ireland, and *QB VII*, about English royalty. All of them were best sellers and most of them had become epic movies. And then, of course, there was *Exodus*, his masterpiece.

In June of 1999, Senator Bill Bradley of New Jersey, in the thick of the race for the Democratic presidential nomination, came to eastern Long Island for a fundraiser.

The centerpiece of his visit, it turned out, would be at the seven-acre waterfront estate of Bob Oehl, on Shelter Island, where Bradley would give a rousing stump speech about his candidacy. Always curious to hear what a presidential candidate would say, I arranged press tickets and, along with my wife, went.

We arrived at a white wooden gate where a picnic table had been set up so Bradley's aides could check us in. Then we walked up a long gravel driveway to a magnificent white-shingled Victorian home with a wraparound porch and a broad lawn where perhaps five hundred people were mingling. White-gloved waiters served champagne and hors d'oeuvres. It was a beautiful day. Bradley, who was a former New York Knicks basketball star and six foot six, soon came out of the house and made a stirring and patriotic speech about his candidacy for about thirty minutes.

After the extended applause at the end, he walked through the crowd shaking hands, and my wife and I tried to get to our car for the trip home. But the lawn was so packed with people that it appeared the best way out would be to walk up onto the porch of the house and around it to the front lawn and the cars. As we made a turn on the porch, we came upon an elderly, slightly heavyset but pleasant-looking man with a cane, sitting on a bench by a railing. He had been watching the goings-on from there.

The man was accompanied by a young woman of perhaps nineteen.

"You write that newspaper?" he asked, referring to *Dan's Papers*.

"I do."

"I recognize you from your hat. I like your stuff." He mentioned something that I had written the week before, and so we stopped, me and my wife, and talked to them a while.

It was Leon Uris.

"So what are you going to write about this?" he asked, indicating the crowd on the lawn.

"It's always the same," I said. "Every one of these I come to, I come in skeptical, listen to their resounding speech, and end up believing that they would make the best president in the history of the country. So yes, I'm going to endorse him."

Some of the crowd, still leaving, began passing us. As a result, my wife and I sat down, me next to Mr. Uris, my wife next to the girl. I told Mr. Uris my mother cried when she read *Exodus* and I was really glad to meet him. I told him it was a crime we couldn't elect Bill Clinton for a third term, and he agreed with that.

Soon we were the only people on the porch, and after a while, the host, Bob Oehl, came over wearing a New York Knicks hat. He was a great Knicks fan, he said. Always was, always would be.

And so I helped Uris up to his feet and we walked down the front lawn. He really didn't make much use of the cane.

"I'd like to see you again," I said. He told me he'd call me and we'd get together. He knew how to reach me.

As we drove home, I was ecstatic to find that a great novelist was a fan of my paper, and that we might see each other again.

"Who was the girl?" I asked. "His granddaughter?"

"His girlfriend," my wife said. "I think. Or else she's somebody he hired to take care of him. It wasn't all that clear."

I saw Leon Uris several times after that, but he never did invite me to his house. He came unannounced to a party we held under a tent behind our Bridgehampton office to celebrate my fortieth year publishing *Dan's Papers*, and he seemed very pleased with himself for having come. I spent time with him. And got to know the girl he was with, who was different from the first girl.

"I'm his masseuse," the young woman said. "I answered an ad in the paper. I'm organizing his life for him right now. I might stay for another year."

My wife, meanwhile, had talked to Leon for a while. And she said he was very flirtatious with her.

"He likes the ladies," she said. "I asked him if he attracts girls. He said it's a hard sell."

"What did he mean by that?"

"He meant he's not much of a catch physically anymore," she said.

"Was he after you?" I asked.

"I think he was. But it was all playful."

What had brought him to Shelter Island? Did he have a wife? Kids? Why would he live a life all alone? Just to write?

In February of 2003, Leon Uris was found dead in the living room of his house on Shelter Island by the twenty-year-old girl he employed to cook him his breakfast and take care of his house for the day. A few days before, he'd had a small day bed brought down from upstairs so he could sleep in the living room. He was seventy-nine, and he died of renal failure. He was widely mourned around the world, but his passing was of little notice here on the East End.

Three years later, I became friends with Isabel Sepulveda de Scanlon, a woman of about forty who had become an important power broker for the Hispanic community in the Hamptons. She's served on the boards of nonprofits, mostly notably on the board of the Bridgehampton Child Care and Recreational Center, where I am also on the board. She also ran a weekly bilingual newspaper in the Hamptons.

One day, we got to talking about a plan for a drug rehab that somebody wanted to build on Shelter Island, and I mentioned that Leon Uris had loved the place for its peace and quiet.

"Leon Uris was the first person I worked for when I came here fifteen years ago," she said. "I was his cook. And I worked for him for twelve years."

I had a ton of questions for her, and so I asked them. Here are the answers.

He had two children, who are twenty-three and twenty-five now and who were nine and eleven when she came to work for him. She has kept in touch with them. Mr. Uris had been divorced. His wife had gotten this big house in Aspen and was raising the kids there. But now she had sold the house to billionaire Mort Zuckerman and had moved back to New York City to be with another man. The kids stayed with Leon for the summer, and they all got along.

"And he had a boat," she said. "It was a speedboat, and he had a captain for it, a young man from Shelter Island, for years."

"Sounds like a nice man," I said.

"I really miss him. He loved being with his kids. He and I would sometimes get into great political discussions. I loved his mind."

"Did he have friends on the island?"

"Very few. There'd be people from New York who would come to see him."

"What brought him to Shelter Island?"

"He'd been a world traveler. He'd lived in Hollywood. He'd lived the high life as a famous author. Sometimes he'd tell me about his experiences with one or another girlfriend in the south of France or somewhere. But then this New York City producer wanted to make his book *Trinity* into a Broadway show. The producer had a house on Shelter Island. Leon came and fell in love with the place. So he moved here. I think after all that excitement in his life he just wanted the peace and quiet of the island."

Isabel worked for him every day from 7 a.m. until 2 p.m. He'd be up when she'd arrive, and she'd prepare either bagels and lox or eggs and matzoh for him. And he followed a routine. After breakfast he'd read the *New York Times* from cover to cover, and he'd watch CNN. Then he'd have lunch, take a nap, and then go to work.

"He had a little writing room up on the third floor, overlooking the pond," she said.

And the kids who came out in the summer? Oh, they loved him and had great times with him.

Sometimes the most extraordinary things come from very ordinary circumstances, it turns out.

Tate King and the
Survivor Chicken

~~~~~~

Late in the afternoon on a warm day in June of 2001, I drove north of the Montauk Highway in Southampton, up North Sea Road, into an area far from the wealthy enclave of homes down near the ocean. I was visiting a dairyman named Tate King, who owned North Sea Farms. Tate King had become involved in some sort of top-secret project involving the television show *Survivor*, and I thought there might be a story there.

I had never met this man before. But I had often passed his farm heading up North Sea Road on my way to somewhere else. It consisted of about fifty acres of rolling hills with several barns and outbuildings nearby to an old farmhouse with a sagging porch. It was the kind of place, far from where any New York developer might want to put in a housing development, that had probably been there for centuries, handed down from father to son to son to son. I suspect it will probably be there a hundred years from now, the same way. There's a sign out front that reads NORTH SEA FARMS—A LITTLE BIT OF THIS AND A LITTLE BIT OF THAT.

TATE KING
(Photo by the author)

Bumping up the dirt road that served as a long driveway, I passed a pen of pigs and a small field containing goats. Off to the left, there were chicken coops and a pasture of black-and-white cows. From time to time I'd bought containers of milk that read NORTH SEA FARMS on them. Yup, I thought. A little bit of this and a little bit of that.

A more bucolic and wonderful scene, with the afternoon sun casting long shadows over the fields and buildings, would be hard to imagine. Where was Mr. King? I had called ahead and spoken to him. He said come on up. He said he'd be happy to tell me the story about the special chickens.

The farmhouse, I thought, would be a good place to start, so I pulled up and parked. As I got out of the car, a heavyset man of about sixty wearing boots and suspenders over a sweatshirt walked over from behind an outbuilding. A baseball cap covered a broad face. Hair fell over his forehead. He smiled and held out his hand and we introduced ourselves, and there, alongside my car, we talked. His daughter Kathleen had told me he had these special chickens. I wanted to hear about them. Maybe write a story about them for the paper, I told him.

"About six months ago, I got a call from the son of the man who owns the Sip 'n Soda Luncheonette," he said, referring to the place where everybody in that town has breakfast. "He's a big-time lawyer for CBS, this young man. And they had these two chickens they wanted to bring out to the country and give them a new home where they could be pampered for the rest of their lives."

The chickens had been brought out in a cage in the back of a black limousine. Two men in suits accompanied them. Tate had signed a receipt for them. Then the limousine drove away.

Tate raised the chickens as he said he would. He kept these two separate from the others on another part of the farm.

"Why was that?" I asked.

"They didn't want them mixing up with my regular chickens. That was the deal."

"Did they pay you?"

"No. I did this as a favor to Pete."

Pete owns the Sip 'n Soda.

"But they did leave me with this very nice steel crate. And I had a friend who needed one, so I sold it to him, so

I guess yes, you could say they paid me what I made from selling the crate."

We said nothing for a while.

"You know," King said, "I asked them why don't you just wring their necks and be done with it? They said they had their reasons."

"Can I see the chickens?" I asked.

"You could see one," he said. "The other had a crooked beak. He died. But I have to tell you, this chicken looks like any of the other chickens."

He motioned to a path that led over a hill. The sun was heading down toward sunset. I didn't take him up on it.

I asked Tate to fill in the missing pieces of the story about the chickens. Here it is.

About eight months before, there was an episode of *Survivor* filmed by CBS on a remote island off the coast of Australia. As part of that episode, the contestants kill a pig. It was not a local pig on that island. There are no pigs on the island. It was a pig flown over by CBS from New York, purchased from a shop in Harlem. The pig had to go through an audition to make sure he would look okay before he died. The pig arrived on the remote island and was used in a scene where it was caught by one the contestants, who stabbed it to death, then butchered it and cooked it. Then some of the contestants ate it.

Nothing unusual happened while this part of the episode was being shot, but the next day, one of the contestants, a woman from Chicago who is a vegetarian, said she was very upset by what happened and felt it should not have taken

place without first some kind of warning so she could prepare. She said she was considering telling some animal rights
group what happened.

This information made its way back to the lawyers at
CBS in New York City, and, fearful of a lawsuit or something, they got all in a lather and talked to the woman. After
a bit of negotiation they got her to sign a release that she
wouldn't sue them for pain and suffering, and she wouldn't
tell anybody about her concerns. Then the show proceeded
on with the filming of the next week's episode.

As it happened, in the next round of voting, this woman
(Tate did not know her name) got voted off the island. And
that, it seemed, was that.

But then, the suits at CBS suddenly learned they had
another potential problem. Two chickens had now been purchased in Harlem, vetted by the producers, and were about
to be shipped to the island—cargo planes were going back
and forth—where they, too, were supposed to be rounded up
and stabbed to death and eaten.

Indeed, to their horror, the suits now found out the
chickens were already on the island. What if the woman who
complained about the pig learned about *this* from some of
the other contestants? They had a release for the pig, but no
release about the chickens.

The word went out: Stop the chickens. Do not put them
near the contestants. Get ready to send them back on the
next plane.

And it was at that time that one of the CBS lawyers, Pete's
son, called the Sip 'n Soda and asked his father if he knew of

any farm nearby where they could send these chickens, keep them from harm, and give them first-rate care for the rest of their lives. They wanted to be able to tell anybody who asked that this was the fate of the chickens that had been on this island just a few days earlier. In exchange for the trauma of the flight to the island, they'd have this lifetime vacation in the Hamptons.

"Clean water. Fresh air. No questions asked," Tate said.

"How come your daughter says you can tell me this story now?"

"Because the episode ran. I don't watch *Survivor*, you know, but that's what they said. It's all taped ahead of time, so you can't say nothin'. Now you can."

The sun was beginning to set. Tate had been talking about this for nearly a half hour.

"The one that didn't die," he said, "I almost gave away last month."

"I thought you weren't supposed to do that," I said.

"This came from CBS. One of the people there had a girlfriend who lived on a farm in Watkins Glen and wanted a chicken as a pet. I said sure. The one we have is fine. I've got a new shipment of pullets coming in May, so it's no problem. He said she would give me a call. But she never did." He paused.

"How long do chickens live?" I asked.

"Well, these are meat chickens, not laying chickens. Laying chickens last about fourteen months, then you replace them. With meat chickens, they can live up to two years, though the meat gets kind of tough after about six months."

"Did you tell them that?"

"Yeah. But they didn't care. You know, I once gave away a rooster to a friend like that. He had a girlfriend who worked as a bartender in Rockville Center and loved roosters. She had rooster potholders, rooster trivets, rooster napkin holders. It was her birthday. He asked if I could come and bring a rooster on a leash for her. I told him roosters don't go on leashes but I could bring one in a cage. And I did. It did make her real happy. I went back to pick up the rooster, but the man told me everybody liked him so much they wanted to keep him. They named him Tate. So now I have a rooster named after me."

It was getting dark. I looked at my watch.

"Could I buy a couple of quarts of milk?" I asked.

"Well, no, actually, we closed the store for the day." He motioned to a small building up by the road. "But if you wait here, I could get you a couple of dozen eggs."

"Okay."

Tate went up onto the porch and into the house. In a few minutes, he was back out. He held out two egg cartons.

"How much are they?" I asked.

"Oh, it's a gift. Tell you the truth, I just enjoyed telling the story again." He grinned. "It really is something."

"Then thanks very much."

We shook hands again, I put the eggs on the passenger seat of my car and then left.

"Whipped Until Bloodied"

~~~~~~

"Now here's an interesting story," said Justin DeMarco. "The Sagaponack School wants to jackhammer up the sidewalk that leads down to the general store."

"Why would they want to do that?" I asked.

DeMarco turned the pages of the *Sag Harbor Express* newspaper to read the rest of the story.

"They don't want to make it easy for the kids to go to the store."

We were sitting, Justin DeMarco and I and six other editors and writers, in the first floor conference room at *Dan's Papers* in Bridgehampton, having our weekly editorial meeting. Part of the meeting consisted of reading each of the latest editions of our competitors to see what stories they had covered. From the street, if you looked through the sliding doors along our front wall, you could see all these *Dan's Papers* editors and writers sitting around this big table, reading everybody else.

"That's exactly the case," DeMarco said. "Here's a quote from the teacher. They can be out playing in the yard. And there's the store with the candy bars down the way. And it's across the street. 'When there were just a few cars, this was not a problem,' she says. 'Now it is.'"

That sidewalk, one block long, was the only sidewalk in the whole town. I thought briefly that it might be a story about how the little town had changed, then thought better of it. Probably wasn't worth the effort, this being just about the sidewalk.

"What else we got?" I asked.

At noon, I went out to enjoy one of my favorite ways to have lunch: drive the two miles to the Sagg Store, get a sandwich, and take it out to the beach at Sagg Main where the road ends, a mile further along. The sun was out. It was a beautiful September day. I had a beach chair in the car, and I had my laptop computer in my bag. I'd write a story for the paper before coming back to the office.

In 2003, when all this was taking place, the village of Sagaponack was still just about how it had been for the previous hundred and fifty years. It consisted of twenty square miles of farmland right on the Atlantic Ocean, with about four hundred residents, three hundred of whom were summer residents with vacation homes sprinkled between the farms. There was one main street with two public buildings, about three hundred yards apart. One was the two-room schoolhouse, a cedar-shingle school with about twenty kids. There was a school bell in a tower on the roof. The other was the Sagg Store, which actually occupied only one half of this old wooden clapboard building. The other half was the post office. There was an American flag out front, a few benches.

Driving along, I heard and saw the elementary school kids out back of the school playing. It was recess.

As for the sidewalk, somebody, somehow, long ago, must have thought it would be a good idea to have a sidewalk from one building to the other. At least nobody would be tracking mud into either of them.

I drove slowly along Main Street. Halfway down between the two buildings, where the potato field backs up to the road, there was a sign, a big steel historic marker. I'd seen it before of course. What did it say? I'd forgotten. I pulled over and parked next to the sidewalk and read it.

"On this site during the Revolutionary War stood the Spider Legged Mill to which Major John Andre, the British Spy, was tied and whipped until bloodied by William Russell," it read.

Pretty nasty message for a bunch of nine-year-olds to be reading as they walked along with the teacher's assistant, it seemed to me.

The town never did tear up the sidewalk. Later that year, they voted to put a low fence around the school. It wasn't quite the same, a two-room schoolhouse with a chain-link fence around it. But people would get used to it. It did make me wonder how serious anybody might have been about tearing up that sidewalk, though.

The next spring, however, there was another piece of news presented at our weekly editorial meeting about the situation

THE SIGN ON SAGG MAIN
(Photo by the author)

down on Sagg's Main Street. It was a press release about the
sign from the director of the nearby East Hampton Historical Society. There was no evidence that Major Andre, a well
known British spy in the history books, had ever been in
Bridgehampton or any other Hampton. The sign, as near as
they could tell, was inaccurate.

This, I thought, was a story. Imagine this. Day after day,
the school children walk by a sign near their school touting
a pretty bloody episode in the history of this country right
in their hometown. And it is wrong.

I made a phone call to the people who put up the sign,
the officials at the New York Education Department, and

after wading through a blizzard of secretaries, receptionists, and bureaucrats, got to talk to somebody there who knew about this situation.

"The sign was put up in the 1930s," this man said. "But then in 1975, it got stolen. When it didn't turn up after six months, we decided to redo it and put a new one back up there. But what did it say? We looked around. We couldn't find the paperwork for it. I think we were very embarrassed about this at the time. So instead of making waves, somebody sent some people down to talk to some old-timers. And this is what they said it was. It was this British Major whipped there."

"What does it cost to put up one of these signs?"

"Back then? About three hundred dollars. Today, maybe a thousand."

"You've heard that is not what happened there?"

"Yeah. We're going to redo it again. We're going to fully research it this time."

I wrote about this in the paper. It was almost impossible not to. What a bumbling bunch of morons they had up in Albany that they'd lost all this paperwork and then did this sign based on what somebody said. Dumb, dumb, dumb.

But two years went by, and they had not fixed it. Now it was 2005. And the kids were still walking by a very official looking steel sign, painted dark green with bright yellow raised letters, still wrong. I wondered what the teacher was telling the kids about this. What could you say?

And then a few months later, we had another thing come up at our editorial meeting about a historic marker in the area. This involved the beautiful granite Bridgehampton War Memorial in the middle of the street on a pedestal right in the center of busy downtown Bridgehampton, not far away. Twelve feet tall, it has on the top a beautiful bronze eagle, its wings spread to protect the plaques on the shaft that referred to eight different wars.

The news was that on a Saturday night, a man named Pedro Martinez, driving a 2003 Honda Civic, jumped the pedestal and collided with the monument. It had been two in the morning. The monument had shifted twenty degrees and slid on its pedestal seventeen inches. The Honda was totaled. Martinez was arrested for DWI.

I had always wondered what might happen if somebody hit this monument. Now I knew. The monument won. There were a few chunks chipped out of it and it would need repair. The eagle, however, was fine.

Interestingly, directly across from the monument, in front of a store on the north side of the Montauk Highway, is another New York State historical marker. This reads, "On this site once stood Wick's Inn, the famous Revolutionary War Tavern."

In Sagaponack, two miles away, the Spider Legged Mill is not there anymore. Here on the highway, Wick's Inn is not there anymore. But at least, at both spots, there is something—these historical markers—to tell you that they had been.

Two weeks after this car hit the monument, the state highway department announced it had appropriated $84,000 to repair the monument and shine up the various bronze plaques about the Revolution, the Civil War, the Spanish

American War, World Wars I and II, Korea, Vietnam, and Iraq. And, in addition, while they were at it, they were going to shine up the Wick's Tavern sign, the Spider Legged Mill sign down on Sagaponack Road in front of the school there, and a few others nearby. Might as well, while they had all the tools and steel wool out.

I now had another story. The old inaccurate sign down in Sagaponack was now, at taxpayers' expense, to be shined up so everybody could read it even better. Terrific.

With the first article, I had published a photograph of the old sign filling the entire top of the page. When the time came, I would do it again, this time, showing it all shined up. So six months later, with the monument repaired and the Wick's Tavern sign all shined up, I drove down there with my camera, past the school with the kids inside and the fence around it, and took its picture. Of course I did not read what it said again. Whipped. Bloodied. What an awfully violent thing, all wrong, all wrong. It never came to my attention, as I took this sign's picture, that the names of the participants were changed and now reversed.

Here is what it read in the picture in the paper:

SITE OF THE SPIDER LEGGED MILL

TO WHICH MAJOR COCHRANE TIED

WILLIAM RUSSELL DURING

THE REVOLUTION AND ORDERED

HIM WHIPPED UNTIL BLOODIED

I hadn't noticed there was any difference.

The week after I wrote this second article, I got a friendly letter to the editor from a Joseph R. Sahid of New York City, telling me it was true that the major *did* whip the American patriot, and by publishing that this sign was not accurate, I was taking serious liberties with American history.

I still didn't get it. As far as I was concerned, here was another dolt, just like the old-timer who had the wrong information the state acted on. I certainly wasn't going to publish *this*.

But two weeks later, there was Mr. Sahid with another letter, this time as part of a big packet that included Xeroxes of pages from a history book written in 1890 that described the incident from old newspaper records and the testimonies of the descendants of those who were there. They affirmed that Major Cochrane *did* whip William Russell, and would whip anybody, and his whipping of William Russell was especially brutal, and everybody was afraid of the major and kept clear of him, including some of the other Redcoats, who sometimes said they wished he would just go away, which eventually, of course, he did.

The historical material was real. But I *still* wouldn't believe it. Had the sign that was there for these past thirty years actually been correct? Would the new sign someday going up be incorrect? What if the state did the research and found that indeed this was correct and the old sign just ought to be left? I'd look like a fool if that was the case, after beating them up in the paper twice for doing nothing about all this.

I Googled Major Andre, the spy. He had been arrested in New York City and hung from a makeshift scaffold set up on Wall Street in 1780. There was no mention of his ever being out in the Hamptons.

I made a decision. I took Mr. Sahid's letter and put it on top of the pile of stuff on my desk that is the pile of stuff to be decided upon later. It's a good-sized pile. Usually if something sits there undecided upon for six months, it ceases to be a problem and is ready to be thrown in the round file.

But Mr. Sahid was not giving up. Two weeks later, I got a third letter. And this time, there was nothing friendly about it.

I have now brought you the historical proof that your account in the paper is wrong and that it was Major Cochrane who did the whipping. And you still do not publish it. I spoke to Justin DeMarco in your editorial department. He said he personally put the packet that contained all the proof on your desk. Why do you continue to perpetuate a historic inaccuracy like this?

I was just about to put this, too, into the special pile when I stopped. Major *Cochrane?* What happened to Major *Andre?* A bolt of fear went through me.

All our back issues are bound in black volumes in a conference room next to my upstairs office at the paper. I went in there. And I took out the volume that had the first article I wrote in 2003, and I took out the volume that had the second article I wrote in 2005, set them on the conference table and opened both, side by side to turn to the two photographs of the sign. The signs were different.

Now I knew the truth. The state had come in, put up the new sign, and because they looked almost exactly alike, I hadn't even noticed. It was Major Cochrane who had whipped William Russell, not William Russell whipping Major Andre.

You have to hand it to that Sagaponack old-timer. He remembered it as the famous Major Andre who got hung who got whipped. They must have whipped him just before they hung him.

And I thought, oh, how embarrassing this is.

Sitting there, my hand on my forehead, what came to mind, however, had nothing to do with the sign. I was remembering an editorial meeting that we'd had in our offices twenty years earlier. Same competing newspapers, same round table, different cast of characters.

I had written a story—I had heard about the incident from someone—about a raucous town board meeting at which a farmer's wife, very angry about the fact that taxes were going through the roof, had thrown a plucked chicken at the town supervisor. The farmers would not survive these higher taxes. Repeal them, the farmer's wife had shouted, and to make her point she had thrown the chicken, and then had left the meeting.

At the editorial meeting the following week, one of the reporters for the paper took me to task for writing this article.

"I was at that meeting," she said. "It was not a plucked chicken. It was taxidermy, a stuffed duck on a pedestal, and she had walked it up to the supervisor's desk and placed it in front of him and she said keep this on your desk to remind yourself of what this place is all about." She paused. "You should write a correction."

I took all that in. I considered this and that. Then I said this: "The plucked chicken is a better story. I'm going to leave it alone." And I did.

What, in the end, did I do about the letter from Mr. Sahid? Well, I wrote an explanation and an apology and published that. I also wrote Mr. Sahid a letter personally apologizing to him. The paper muddles along. What a mess.

We subscribe to the Plucked Chicken School of Journalism.

Paul Jeffers

~~~~~~

On a hot afternoon in the summer of 2002, I pulled into the Bridgehampton Carvel for a vanilla ice cream cone with chocolate sprinkles. As I walked back out, happily licking it, a car with four black men inside pulled in next to mine and, as they all climbed out, one of them looked over the hood at me.

"Hey Dan," he shouted. "How'd you like to be on the board of the Bridgehampton Child Care Center?"

The man was someone I had seen around. He was a beefy fellow of about fifty, and he wore around his neck a thick chain with a gold cross dangling at the end. He was, I now remembered, one of the church deacons from the black community on the Sag Harbor Turnpike.

"Who's that?" I asked.

"P. J.," he said. "Paul Jeffers."

I took a lick of ice cream. Joining the board of the child care center wasn't a bad idea at all.

"Sure," I said.

Maybe *Dan's Papers* could do an article about the child care center, or at least run ads to promote their upcoming

PAUL JEFFERS
(Photo by the author)

events. Anyway, with the paper thriving, I had some time on my hands. The place was just down the turnpike from my office. It would be an easy thing to do.

The Bridgehampton Child Care and Recreational Center was a twenty-two-acre former farm in the midst of the black community on the Sag Harbor Turnpike. It was founded in 1955 as a safe haven for the children of black migrant workers up from the South to pick potatoes for the summer.

Now, although there are no more migrant workers coming north anymore, the Bridgehampton Child Care and Recreational Center has continued on—there was day care, summer camp, basketball, baseball, soccer, and learning centers—for the local black and Hispanic children in the area, often helped by contributions and funding from the community at large.

I attended my first meeting of the board of directors of the center in late August. It was not held in the old farmhouse. It was held in one of the classrooms inside the brand-new McCall building, recently constructed near the farmhouse with funding mostly raised largely by television anchorman Peter Jennings a few years earlier. The little kid-sized desks and chairs had been put off to one side. A folding table with stackable grown-up chairs had been set up in their place.

"This is Dan Rattiner from *Dan's Papers*," P. J. said, introducing me to the others around the table. "He said he was joining up to maybe provide us some publicity."

Around the table was the chairman of the board, an attractive young black physician named Dr. Florence Ralston, two older black women, the local deacon of the Baptist Church, Reverend Faison, and another black man who looked to me like a high school coach. He was Ed Barnes, the director of the center.

"Any publicity, any advertising, any press releases, that's what I do," I said.

I soon learned that if I had joined the board a month before, I would have not been the only white person in the room. Before that time, about a half dozen other white people had been on the board. But they had all resigned at once after a terrific fight among themselves about the future of the center.

Furthermore, by this time the center had fallen into terrible financial shape. An annual donation of $100,000 made for years by ABC anchorman Peter Jennings had come to an end when he had fallen ill a year earlier. So the center borrowed $100,000 from a bank to make up for what Jennings was no longer contributing. It was needed so they could continue to operate. Now the loan had come due and they were still further behind.

The fight among the board members who resigned was about a plan to pay off this loan. The town wanted to buy the development rights to twenty of the twenty-two acres of this former farm for $100,000. One group of white board members thought this was a great idea. Another group of white members thought it was the worst. The argument had almost come to blows. After that, all the white board members had simply quit.

"Next meeting we're getting another visit from the bank about our loan," Ed said. We would be meeting once a month. Ed then handed out a blizzard of monthly and annual report paperwork that I found completely incomprehensible. I run a newspaper. I know how spreadsheets look. These were not spreadsheets. What was going on here?

The months went by. The center continued to operate. There were ten employees and about thirty-five school-age children. High school boys played basketball on the courts in the back. The children dug in the playground and climbed on the swings by the McCall building. The controversial fields in the back were still in use. The small summer camp was still in session.

At the next board meeting I found myself thinking, listening to the banker, that $100,000 wasn't very much money for twenty acres in the Hamptons used for recreational purposes by the black community. A million dollars would have been more like. It made me angry. I would have sided with those who didn't want to do it if I had been around at the time.

At the board meeting after that, we had a lecture from Tony Hill, who was the director of the Southampton Town Sports Center ten miles away up in North Sea. He gave us a talk about how to run a center like this one. It sure sounded very organized. Ours was organized, too, but the money was not.

"There doesn't seem to be much in the way of fundraising," I said to P. J. as we walked back out to the cars. "I wish there were some publicity I could do."

I had dinner with P. J. at Bobby Van's Restaurant that evening. An odd thing was that although he had gotten there before I did, I found him standing out front rather than waiting for me inside, seated at a table by a hostess.

It was then it occurred to me, for the first time, that other than the well-to-do blacks from the city, I had never seen a middle-aged black guy with a gold chain and cross around his neck in Bobby Van's unaccompanied. Why had I not noticed this before?

I got to know P. J. He had been one of the children of the migrant workers.

"My daddy came up here from North Carolina in the summertime and then one year decided to stay. He brought me and my mamma up. I was six. I was teased and bullied in the Bridgehampton School by the other kids. It was because I was from the South and had this accent."

The Bridgehampton School was half black and half white at that time. It still is.

"Also, my mamma made me these lunches that the other kids had never seen. The other kids had baloney sandwiches. Mine was strange and different. Grits and beans. They'd steal it, until I learned to hide it."

I drank rum-and-cokes and P. J. drank club soda and grenadine. He had given up alcohol fifteen years earlier, he said.

P. J. had graduated from Bridgehampton High, married, had three kids, and made a living as a handyman, working among other places at the Jewish Center of the Hamptons. He and his wife had been foster parents to numerous kids, raising them at their home.

"I want to set an example," he said. "There's no need to go down the wrong path in this world."

He also loved the ladies. Toward the end of that dinner, our conversation descended into descriptions of various ladies we had known during our lives, without mentioning names, and how we had loved them. We had bonded.

"I'd like to buy you breakfast over at Billy's Deli some morning," P. J. said as we parted. "Just name the day."

Billy's was the busy deli, also along the turnpike, frequented by the black community and now, more and more, the Hispanic community. I took him up on this the following week.

As the meetings of the board of directors of the Bridge-hampton Child Care and Recreational Center extended into the fall and winter, it was becoming alarmingly apparent that the place was falling further and further into huge financial trouble. And now I knew why.

Ed Barnes, the director, simply did not seem to have the will to cut back from the level of spending that had been there earlier when Jennings was making his huge contribution.

That January, at the next board meeting, Dr. Ralston announced that she was resigning. In her place, she said, a wealthy man from Sag Harbor, Wallace Green, would be taking over as board chairman, and he was right there in the next room. She asked him to come in.

A light-skinned black man of about fifty with a cowboy hat on his head now came in and sat down. Introductions were made all around. Ed Barnes squirmed in his seat.

"I've become quite successful promoting rock concerts," he said.

He described grand plans for the center. He would hold a big rock concert on the property in the back two or even three times a year. The place would soon be awash in money.

"First thing, though," he said, "is that we have to revisit the name of this place. Right now it's the Bridgehampton Child Care and Recreational Center. I want us to get out our bylaws and change it to the Bridgehampton Child Care, Music, and Recreational Center."

At the rest of the meeting, the man grilled Ed about where the money had been spent. He became very angry at him. He said the place was leaking money and he would have to step in and shore it up.

Wallace took *me* out to dinner that evening at Bobby Van's. I was initially fascinated by him, but soon saw there was something odd about him. He didn't drive a car, for example, and he didn't want to talk about it. That was his private business. One night, my wife and I had dinner with him and his wife in their Sag Harbor home. It was a nice place but not the kind of flamboyant affair that a wealthy man might own.

"Our new board chairman is having all the locks changed on the center," P. J. told me a week later. "Just thought you ought to know. He's also said he was bringing in some of his own people to look through the books."

"Who's he sending?"

"He mentioned a bookkeeper. But so far nobody's shown."

The next thing I learned was that the man had fired Ed and would be running the place himself. He was chairman of the board, and now he was the director, too. But he had no experience running a child care center.

One week later, at 4 p.m. on Monday afternoon, P. J. called me, hysterical.

"You gotta get over here," he said.

"Where?"

"To the center. All the doors are locked. We're all locked out."

"I'll be right over."

I was in the office when I got this call. In five minutes I was over at the center. The only person there was P. J. He was pacing around in the parking lot.

"The whole place, shut tight," he said.

"What happened?"

"We got a call from a secretary here about an hour and a half ago. The kids for after school were just arriving. She said tell their mothers to pick them up, they're going home. Everybody leave. Everybody was fired. Then this locksmith came and changed all the locks. We're closed."

"He did that? Did you call him?"

"He won't take my calls. Next I called you."

I tried him on the cell phone. All I got was to leave a message.

"Let's see if he calls me back tonight," I said.

P. J. looked at me sadly.

"Just until tonight," I said.

During the rest of the day, I continued to leave messages for our new director. I called his offices in the city. I got a woman who told me he was busy and would get back to me. He did not.

"I've got this locksmith I know," I said to P. J. that evening on the telephone. "You tell everybody to come back to work tomorrow morning. This place is not closing. We can't do that to these kids."

"Who is going to pay them?" P. J. asked.

"I don't know," I said. And I didn't. "And call all the parents. We were closed, but it was just for the night."

The next day, of course, I went to work at the paper and, after getting everyone settled, raced over to the center to see how things were going. It was business as usual. Kids and teachers. Several administrators. I got some worried looks.

"Don't worry," I said.

Late that afternoon, we met in the old two-story farmhouse, which we were using as an office building: me, P. J., and a woman named Sylvia Fredie, a professional bookkeeper who came in for a few hours every week to balance the books.

"Look," I said. "I know how to run a small business. *Dan's Papers* is big now. But it started small. Somebody give me a piece of paper and a pencil. What does it cost to run this place?"

Down the left side, I wrote what I knew. Electric. Telephone. Light. Heat. Petty Cash. Bookkeeping. Director.
Secretary. Teachers.

"Is there a mortgage?" I asked.

Everybody shook their head no. Just the short-term loan.

"Real estate taxes?"

"No. We're a nonprofit."

"Maintenance?"

"Mr. Joe. He has a lawnmower. Comes once a week.
Fixes things up. Paints."

"What do we pay him a week?"

"Eighty dollars a week."

"Okay," I said. "We're going to run this place bare bones.
After school. Basketball. Day care. That's it. Let's figure it out.
P. J., you and I are going to have a meeting with the bankers
at Suffolk County Savings Bank. Give me the phone number
and I'll set it up. I think it has to be tomorrow."

"Are you going to run this place?" P. J. asked.

"No. You are. You're president. I'm making you president.
And chairman of the board. You're the heart and soul of the
place."

"I can't run it."

I turned to Sylvia.

"How about you run it?" I asked.

"I could," she said. "I am a licensed school teacher as well
as bookkeeper. But I couldn't be here full time. I have places
I work part time. But maybe I could be here half time."

"Okay."

"And what are you?" P. J. asked.

"I'm the vice president," I said.

The next day, I rode with P. J. to the regional offices of the Suffolk County Savings Bank in Hampton Bays. We were all excited.

"We just need them to hold off a year," I said. "I can do it. Let's play good guy, bad guy. You be the black guy. I'll be the white guy."

"I'm bad," P. J. grinned.

At the bank, we were introduced to a young branch director in his thirties who led us to a conference room where we were introduced to an older man, who was a regional vice president. I introduced P. J. as president and myself as vice president.

"I don't want to make this too hard on you," the young branch director said, "and I appreciate you coming, but this loan came due eight months ago. You were supposed to be paying it back. You haven't."

"What's the full amount owed?" the vice president asked.

"Nearly $116,000. With the interest and penalties."

"Look," I said. "I just came in. I run a newspaper and I can keep a budget. Here it is. It's easy. Between what we get from the town tax and a little bit we need to raise, we can run the place dead even for a year. All we need is for you to extend this loan for a year."

"Would you guarantee it?" the bank manager asked.

"No."

The vice president had a look at the budget while P. J. talked a bit about how the center had started so long ago and what it did. He mentioned Sylvia Fredie, our new director.

"She's in the budget," I piped up. I pointed to the line.

"Well," the vice president said, looking at the bank manager. "Here's what we're going to do. We're going to make you a new loan. It will begin today and go for a year."

"What about the old loan?" the bank manager asked.

"We'll just end it," the vice president said. "The new loan will replace it." The vice president turned to us. "The new loan will be for one year, interest free. Zero percent. I'll take you for your word on what you have said. We'll draw up the papers."

And we all got up, shook hands and went away. Out at the car, I began to cry.

"I can't believe they just did this," I blubbered. "Banks don't do this. It's amazing." P. J. looked out the window. "Good guy, bad guy," he said.

I kept thinking of the kids. I thought about the sign which is out front of the center.

"That sign we have," I said, "needs repainting. It's all dirty. We need to have it scrubbed up," I said.

"I'll talk to Joe."

"And maybe we ought to think about getting a bigger one. This one has pretty small letters. You could drive right by."

And that's how I became as bonded as I am today with the Bridgehampton Child Care and Recreational Center.

At the next meeting, the board fired Wallace and appointed P. J. as president. He is president to this day.

The following year, dressed as an elf, I attended the Christmas party held at the center. It was well underway when I came through the door at the newly refurbished teen center. P. J. was there, and the new full-time director,

Bonnie Cannon, was there. All the mothers had made potluck dishes—dumplings, sweet potatoes, turkey, ham, barbecue, creamed spinach, corn bread, and a variety of cakes and sweets all sitting on tables everywhere. Twenty or thirty kids were there working with crayons or drinking Orangeade or Coca-Cola. The presents had been opened under the tree, the gift wrap scattered around. It was a happy scene.

But as I stood in the doorway, I became aware that all eyes had turned toward me. I took a few steps inside. What was the matter? I'm the only white boy? Across the way, Mr. Joe, the handyman, motioned me to come over and sit by him.

When I did that, he leaned over toward me. "Your fly is open," he said.

Brenda Siemer

~~~~~~

A lot has been written about Roy Scheider, the late actor who starred in the movie *Jaws* and lived out in the Hamptons for thirty-five years, but very little has been written about his wife, Brenda Siemer. A stunning woman about fifteen years his junior, she kept and still keeps a low profile, busy with her family.

In June of 2004, however, something happened that brought her front and center into the news in a way she had never known before. She had emerged from her yoga class on Main Street in Sag Harbor that day to discover that directly across the street there was a workman up on a ladder in front of the Sag Harbor Theater taking down the first three of the nine giant red neon letters reading SAG HARBOR that are attached to the front of the theater building above the entrance.

These letters marked not only the theater but the very center of downtown Sag Harbor and had been there shining mightily over the town at night for sixty years. Oil paintings had been made of these letters on the front of this theater.

BRENDA SIEMER
(Photo courtesy of *Dan's Papers*)

Postcards presented them all lit up. Sag Harbor residents considered this sign to be the heart and soul of the town.

The three letters already down were BOR, and they were leaning against a wall of the building. What remained up, each letter six feet high, spelled out SAG HAR.

Brenda stopped on the sidewalk, frozen to the spot. There was a pickup truck next to the ladder. In the flatbed in the back were plastic letters, crappy blue ones, about half the size of the big red neon ones.

She ran across the street to the ladder and shouted up to the workman.

"What are you doing?" she shouted.

(Photo courtesy of the author)

"Taking down the sign. It's all rusted out."

"You can't do that."

"Sure I can. I'm putting up these new plastic letters."

"Who told you to do that?"

"Jerry Mallow, the owner."

"You can't do that!" she shouted again.

He ignored her.

Brenda then ran next door and into the Granderson Art Gallery to tell the people there what was going on. They came out onto the street. Then, she ran in and out of every store on Main Street, up and down the lane, shouting the alarm. And more people began coming out. Soon, she had assembled quite a crowd out there, including the village clerk from the village hall.

Cell phones came out.

"Call everybody you know!" she shouted. Then she took her own cell phone out and made some calls of her own. I was in Bridgehampton at my office six miles away at the time. But David Lee, the town jeweler, called me and told me what was going on. I said I would be right there.

"Bring your camera," he shouted.

There was a huge crowd in front of the movie theater when I arrived. Apparently there had been a lot of shouting going on. The workman had climbed down briefly at one point and had gone into the theater to find the owner, Jerry Mallow, but Jerry was not there.

This workman, who was named Carl, had then climbed back up the ladder and from there was negotiating with the crowd.

I pulled up. Carl had now once again begun removing the rest of the neon from the building. He said the sign was rusted out and dangerous. He'd broken bolts to get the first few letters down. Now he'd take the rest down.

But as the voices below continued to rage, he became intimidated. These people were not going to let him get away with this. And so what he decided to do was leave all these old rusty letters leaning against the side of the building, and *not* put the new plastic letters up. Instead, he'd go back to his office, in Bohemia, with the plastic letters. He'd tell his boss that this crowd would not let him put them up. The boss would have to talk further to Jerry Mallow.

I stood in the back. Brenda, whom I had never seen so animated, was shouting back and forth at people to get them to move out of the way. Let him go. Let him go, she shouted. The man got into his truck with the blue plastic letters in the back and off he went, scared as a jackrabbit.

Brenda then stood in front, apparently having decided to take the lead in solving the problem she had just created.

"Anybody got a truck? Can anybody get a truck?" Somebody ran off. It was apparent to me she wanted those neon letters out of there before Jerry Mallow showed up.

"Where do we take them?" someone asked.

"Gerald, is the Whaling Museum open?"

"We've got a shed in the back."

"Does it have a lock?"

"Sure does."

A truck from the Bay Street Theatre down the street, used for carrying scenery around, appeared, and people were quick to carefully load the old letters up into the back. It drove off.

After that, people stood around for a while. There was no neon on the building anymore, nothing to identify the movie theater. And Brenda was telling what happened. "I was just coming out of yoga class," she said. "And I saw *this.*"

After a while, everybody dispersed. Nobody wanted to be around when the owner of the theater arrived. They'd just stolen the most famous sign in the Hamptons!

"I'm sure I can keep the letters in the shed until at least tomorrow," Gerald said. "After that, I don't know."

"We'll figure something out," Brenda said.

The following day, the story of what had happened appeared in *Newsday* and the *New York Times*. The *New York Post* had it on page six. Brenda, in every case, was described as "the wife of the actor Roy Scheider." Also quoted, in *Newsday*, was the mayor of Sag Harbor, Ed Deyermond. He said that Jerry Mallow had a permit to remove the signage on his building, but he didn't have any permit to put any new sign up.

"It's a pre-existing sign," the mayor said. "If you take it down, you have to either put it back up exactly the way it was, or apply to the Zoning Board of Appeals for a sign that would be in keeping with the new ordinances. And he hasn't done that."

In other words, the mayor didn't want anything up but the old sign either. And where was the sign? Nobody was talking.

It's an odd thing when you think about it, that the townspeople of a village founded in 1707 would be so passionate about giant neon letters spelling out the name of their village on the village movie theater. What's odd about it is that Sag Harbor was, for over a hundred and fifty years after its founding, a whaling town. It's just one of four old whaling towns in the country, the other three being the island of Nantucket; New Bedford, Massachusetts; and Lahaina, Hawaii. All celebrate their whaling heritage, including Sag Harbor. But Sag Harbor also celebrates its heritage from the 1940s, when whaling was long gone. What an odd thing!

The reason is that unlike the rest of the villages in the Hamptons, which retained their even older colonial roots while filling their storefronts with Tiffany and Gucci and Polo and Cartier, Sag Harbor fought fiercely to keep such stores out and instead celebrate the mom-and-pop kinds of stores popular in the 1940s. There's a five-and-ten, a locally owned pharmacy, a hardware store, a market where everybody shops that is too small to be called a supermarket, and all sorts of other old-time businesses—the bank, the ice cream store, the art galleries, the pizzeria, the bar, the smoke shop. It's like a trip to prewar America. And that neon sign, typical of the 1940s, is a big part of it.

Brenda Siemer was, of course, a hero in that town in the days that followed, but the job was only beginning. The neon was rusted and squirreled away. The movie theater building was now without a sign. And Jerry Mallow, the owner of the movie theater—they show art films there on weekends year-round—was very, very angry. He told the media that his sign had been stolen from him, taken right off his property. He used the word kidnapped. And he also said those particular letters could never be put back up. The frames were rusted out. A letter could fall down and kill somebody.

My wife and I met with Brenda and Roy at the Candy Kitchen two mornings later. I'd been thinking a great deal about this.

"The neon could be down forever," I said. "After a certain number of years, even with everybody's approval, it could not be put back up. It would lose its grandfather status."

"He's going to have to make an exact replica of that sign," Brenda said, referring to Jerry Mallow.

"You must know Mallow," Roy said. "You've got to. He advertises in your paper."

"I do. I talk to him, or one of our clerks talks to him, every week to get the movie schedule," I said. "I'm going to call him. By the way, is the neon still at the Whaling Museum?"

"You won't tell anybody?" Brenda asked.

"Promise."

"We moved them. Afraid Mallow would find out. They're in one of Pat Malloy's warehouses on Long Wharf, next to the Bay Street Theatre."

Pat Malloy was the richest man in Sag Harbor. He owned half the town. And his 240-foot yacht was the biggest ship docked at the wharf.

I called Jerry Mallow at his home in Lynbrook. He lives in Lynbrook, seventy miles from the Hamptons, and he also has a home in Sag Harbor.

"Nothing happens until those neon letters get returned to me," he told me.

"But they're all rusted out," I said.

"This is my property. I'm going to hire a lawyer and sue the town for this. The mayor was even in on it."

"Well, where were you on Saturday morning?"

"I was in Brooklyn. My son Jamie is making a movie about a prizefighter. They were filming in a gym."

"Jerry, listen to me. There is goodwill to be gotten out of all of this. And maybe even some money to be made. You've just got to play this right. You have to be the good guy."

"I'm listening."

"Would you like a replacement neon sign up?"

"It costs a fortune to redo the neon. I priced it out. I am not spending a small fortune on this. I don't make any money showing films. It's a hobby. I got the plastic signs."

"I think if you agree to let a replica of the neon be put back up, the town will raise the money to pay for it."

"I'm listening."

"Just say you don't care about getting the old rusty neon back. Say you love the sign too."

"Everybody loves that sign."

"Say if the town will raise the money to recreate that sign, you will allow it to be put back up there."

"That's it?"

"Maybe even make a donation."

"A small donation."

"Can I tell them you will do that?"

"You the spokesperson?"

"I can handle it."

There was a long pause. "Yes," he said.

In the next issue of the paper, I wrote all about this idea. The fundraiser was held at the Bay Street Theatre. About two hundred people attended. And the hit of the evening was an "auction." Brought out on stage were the rusty neon letters SAG. Bidders could now commence to bid on them. They were not in good enough shape to be put on the side of a building anymore. But they might make neat artwork for a private home.

Jerry Mallow was there. The bidding was brisk and spirited. SAG was won by model Christie Brinkley and her then-husband, architect Peter Cook, who lived in Bridge-hampton. They vowed, after they won, to give these letters back to Brenda temporarily so they could be brought to a sign maker and measured up for a new neon sign to match the old. Brenda had already found a sign maker to do the job, a man named Clayton Oreck, who lived in Ronkonkoma, sixty miles from Sag Harbor.

All together $17,000 was raised at this fundraiser for the new sign. Brenda was in a happy mood, but onstage, Jerry Mallow asked Brenda if they could use a sign maker that he knew, a guy named Bob O'Brien in Bohemia, who had sold him the original plastic letters, which he had now taken back.

"Sure," Brenda said.

"My son is just finishing up the movie. He produced it and stars in it along with the actor Eddie Jones. It's called *Fighting Tommy Riley* and it's going to be entered in the Hampton Film Festival next October. It will also be shown at my theater. I want the new sign to be back up by then if possible. And everybody come."

The crowd cheered.

The next day, Brenda ordered the nine letters of the sign taken by truck to the workshop of Bob O'Brien in Bohemia, together with the instructions given to Clayton Oreck. It was the opinion of experts that the new sign to match the old should be made of aluminum. It wouldn't last just sixty years. It would last a hundred and sixty years.

Brenda talked with Bob once or twice and mailed him a fifty percent deposit as he requested, but six months later, with just four months to go before the premiere of the movie, nothing had been done. So she and a friend got in a truck and drove to Bohemia, which is an hour away from Sag Harbor.

What she found was that Bob O'Brien was no longer there, but his brother was. And he did not do signs.

"Bob had some personal problems," the brother told her.

Brenda demanded to see the nine letters left off there, and when the brother took her out to Bob's shop in his backyard, six of them were there.

"Where are the other three?" Brenda asked.

"They were farmed out to another sign maker," the brother said. "But I know where they are."

The brother showed Brenda the template that Bob had made before abandoning the project. It was crude and made of the wrong material. Brenda had all the old letters put into the back of the truck she had come in, and, after gathering up the last three, drove with her friend to Clayton Oreck's shop, twenty minutes away.

Oreck took them in. He couldn't promise he'd get the job done in time for the movie opening, but he'd do his best. He also showed Brenda some of the high-quality work that he had done. Brenda, impressed, decided to proceed with Oreck.

On her return, she noted that half the money they had raised was now gone, wasted away. "We'll have to get more funds," she said.

In the end, the movie theater bore no sign when Jerry Mallow's son's film premiered there in October 2005 as part of the film festival. Jerry, very proud, was there with his son Jamie.

Everyone thought the movie was pretty good, though. And, indeed, it found a distributor and had a modest run.

In the end, more money was raised, and the sign was back up on the building in time for the summer of 2006. And everybody lived happily ever after.

Peter Beard

~~~~~~

In late June of 2007, I got an invitation to go to Southampton to see an exhibit of the photographs of Peter Beard. It was held in a private oceanfront home on Meadow Lane owned by the real estate developer Jenna Bullock, someone I did not know. Proceeds would benefit one of our local charities and Peter would be there.

Eleven years before, on one of his frequent safaris in Africa, he was trampled, gored, and nearly killed by a charging elephant. He'd been near death with twenty-two broken bones. His spleen had been ruptured. Other organs were crushed. A helicopter flew him to a hospital, and from there he was flown back to New York. He'd left the local scene in the Hamptons after that. If this was going to be his coming out party, I wanted to see him again.

My wife and I arrived at the party at 9 p.m. Winding our way up a stone path through some beach grass, we entered this marvelous modern three-level house of glass, stone, and steel, designed by architect Norman Jaffe to look out over

PETER BEARD
(Photo by Davina Dobie)

the dunes to the sea. There were hundreds of people at this party, and they were upstairs and down, out on the terrace where an African band with native drummers and torches were holding forth. There were dancers, a barbecue of African food, and still more torches, which led down a path to the beach. It was a cool, still summer night. Beard's photographs, some of them very familiar since they had appeared in *The New Yorker* or other places, were all around.

I was introduced to Jenna Bullock, who, it turned out, did not live in the house. This was at the time when real estate was going through the roof in the Hamptons. She had bought the house six months before for umpteen million. Now she was trying to sell it for umpteen and umpteen million more. We were really there for a house showing, and among others I chatted up out there by the pool were three Wall Street billionaires I knew who'd found each other and were probably eyeing the place to see if they could pick it up and take it up to even further levels. The photography was incidental, it seemed, a sort of bait and switch in an odd way just to sell the house. Peter, I learned, was upstairs in a bedroom.

I climbed the stairs two at a time, fearing the worst. Peter in bed? In a wheelchair? I found him standing upright in the center of a crowd of people in one of the bedrooms, an arm around one beautiful young woman on his left and another beautiful young woman on his right. Peter looked very happy and as handsome as ever. When he saw me, he smiled, and then turned his head to the girl on his right.

"Natasha," he said, smiling at her, "say hello to Dan. He runs the newspaper in town. A very good thing indeed."

She said hello in a heavy Russian accent. He then introduced the woman on his left. Now, I saw, there were at least two other young women in the room who were part of this entourage. I got introduced to them too.

I do not recall what else we said up in that room, but everyone seemed very happy—I was happy to see Peter so happy—and after a few minutes, someone else came in to congratulate Peter and he moved on. As that happened, however, Natasha smiled really friendly like at me and broke loose from Peter's arm and came over close to me. She wore, as did all the women, a very low-cut dress, and she seemed to have something in mind, though she was not saying so directly. She wanted to know more about the paper. Well, I thought, this would complicate my life. Time to go. My wife was downstairs.

I shouted over the din. "Peter, how can I get in touch with you?"

"Just stop by the house sometime," he said. "Anytime."

Then, I was gone, escaped from the grasps of the life-complicating Natasha and back down the stairs to reality. Going home, I came to think of another party, years ago, at Peter's home, that I have never, ever forgotten.

Publishing a newspaper as I did in those earlier years just in Montauk in the 1960s, I came to know every piece of ground in that town, including a very wooded section extending two miles to the lighthouse. At one time, the Montauk Highway went through these woods out to the lighthouse a few hundred yards inland from the ocean. In the 1920s, however, a more modern Montauk Highway was built further inland. But nobody tore up the old one. I'd go out there in a jeep. Once in the late 1950s, bumping along this rutted forgotten road, I passed an abandoned gas station, vines growing all around and over it, the gas pumps crooked and bent. Even the big sign was there. It had the word SINCLAIR on it, above a silhouette of a dinosaur.

Between this rutted road and the ocean in the mid-1960s, a large contingent of prominent and young and sometimes very outrageous New Yorkers bought oceanfront properties in this secluded area. They included Andy Warhol, photographer Richard Avedon, photographer Peter Beard, painter

Balcomb Greene, TV host Dick Cavett, and later on singer Paul Simon. Guests included Jackie Kennedy, Lee Radziwill, George Plimpton, the Rolling Stones, Viva, and other members of the Warhol crowd.

In my role as newspaper publisher, I became friends with some of these people. Peter had the last and most easterly oceanfront parcel just before you got to the park and the lighthouse. On a foggy day out there, sitting at Peter's house, the forlorn hooting of that lighthouse was so distracting you could almost see the sound waves stirring up the dust on the ground. Peter didn't live on the ocean, though, couldn't even see the ocean from his house. He lived and worked in a small cottage a few hundred feet south of the forgotten highway and a thousand feet further through the woods, to the cliffs at the edge of the sea.

Peter seemed to be always going somewhere. He had just returned from a safari. He was heading off to London. Born and raised in well-to-do circumstances, he was living the life of an adventurer. I'd sit and listen to him, fascinated. Besides being movie-star handsome, he was always tanned and relaxed.

In 1977, talking to him at a cocktail party for an environmental group raising money to put benches, flower boxes, and trees through the center of town, he invited me to a party.

"It's this Saturday," he said. "Can you come? I built a big new house and it's the housewarming."

"Out at your property?"

"Just come in and go past the cottage. It's right at the cliff." He grinned. "And bring your camera."

There must have been two hundred people there that night. Torches bordered the property, particularly where the lawn simply ended at that eighty-foot drop at the edge of the cliff going down to the beach. There was a band, a barbecue on the lawn. It was among the most sensational settings imaginable.

The new house, though, was off limits for the partygoers. It had not been completely finished in time for the party as it turned out. But it was amazing nevertheless. It was three stories high, made of glass, wood, and stone. A beautiful windmill took up most of one wall. This was quite a step up from anything that had been built until that time out that way.

Just as the sun began to set, a helicopter appeared to the west, came closer, and then set very noisily and delicately down on the property. Soon, out came the governor of the state of New York, Hugh Carey.

The governor mingled. He was launching a reelection campaign and, as it happened, his opponent would be Perry Duryea Jr., the Speaker of the House, one of the most powerful men in Albany and a resident of Montauk who owned a wholesale lobster business here.

About an hour later, with the sun setting, the governor asked Peter if he could have a private tour of the house. Peter then invited me to come too. We went inside. There was a winding metal staircase that went way up to what were the most amazing views of the Atlantic surf and, just a thousand feet off to the east, the entire panorama of the Montauk Lighthouse and the cliffs. Peter talked about this house. He'd loved building it. They'd be moving in next month. The party went on and on, with people finally drifting off about midnight. I left too, and thus did not know until the next day of the horrendous thing that happened out there after we all left.

In the darkness of 3 a.m., the house caught fire. Beard, by this time back in his cottage by the road, was unaware of it. Flames soon engulfed it. And by the time the fire department was able to get out there, it had burned to the ground. All that remained were the foundations and one stone chimney. It was the remains of a house never lived in.

In the years that followed, Peter Beard and I went off on our respective career paths. My little Montauk newspaper expanded to become *Dan's Papers*. I drew my cartoons and wrote my stories for it. Peter Beard married fashion model Cheryl Tiegs and then two years later they divorced. He went back to Africa, took more pictures on safari, and published coffee table books about it, including one called *The End of the Game*. He also famously came home with a six-foot, four-inch Somali woman—named Iman—a total knockout—whom he photographed naked draped over some rocks near the ruined house foundations on his Montauk property. She soon became a supermodel. On another occasion, he came out to Montauk with a baby African elephant that he somehow got onto his property to photograph. How in the world had he done that?

Ten years after the fire, he called me up and invited me to come out to his house for lunch. We were both in our mid-thirties by this time, and I went out there to the cottage.

He still had not done anything about the ruined foundations out by the cliff.

We had lunch, prepared by his new wife Nejma, a white African woman from Kenya, and as she tended her new infant daughter Zara, he took me for a walk out to the foundations. Among other things he wanted to talk about was this horrendous divorce he was suffering through after his brief marriage to Cheryl Tiegs.

"It's four years now and still going on," he said. "I tried to be the good guy. We split this property and since she really was a New York City girl and I wanted to live here, I got the oceanfront and she got the cottage. Then, I found out that the town would not let me rebuild the house that burned down. I couldn't believe it. There were new laws prohibiting the building of anything that close to the cliff's edge. So I moved into this cottage she owned. She still owns it. And I'm *stuck* with this, can't do anything and I'm going to sue the town. I want to ask if you could help me with this when the time comes."

I told him I would be there to help if I could.

One time I asked him if my wife and I could pitch a tent out by the ruins and spend the night there. It would be a very romantic place to be, I said. He told me come out anytime.

A few weeks later, we drove out there around 11 p.m., my wife and I together with my sheepdog, and we drove down the path to the cliff, pitched the tent, and snuggled in. It was a beautiful night, but then a huge thunderstorm with lightning and hail hit, the sheepdog commenced howling, and it was soon a dripping, cold mess with water flooding in under us. Thus we abandoned ship, packed everything up into the car, and headed back through the woods. As it was 2 a.m., I drove as quietly as I could past his cottage. We weren't going to be thanking him for his hospitality at that hour, obviously. Also, after all his adventures, I couldn't even do *this*.

To this day, the foundations of that ruin remain, the stone fireplace the only thing left standing. Somewhere, deep in the blackened center of the ruin, there's probably a burnt party hat from the fire. Peter, back in Africa, shot some of the most astonishing photographs ever taken of that continent. He was in films, he had gallery openings of his work in Milan, Paris, and elsewhere. His most famous book was *The End of the Game*—the photos of which were featured in 2004 at that party on the beach in Southampton—consisting entirely of pictures he took from low-flying planes of dead elephants in the jungle. All that remains of them are their skins, lying flat on the ground like vast carpets, eerily life-like in their two dimensions, bearing silent testament to the disgrace that modern man has inflicted upon that continent.

In March of 2005, my wife and I went on safari in Africa. We stayed at tent camps in Zambia, Botswana, and South Africa and were away for five weeks in March and April. In the open-air Range Rovers with rifles across the dashboards, our guides took us to watch migrations of zebras, grazing giraffes, burrows of meerkats, cougars, hippos, crocodiles, white rhinos, and all manner of screaming monkeys up in the trees. We even silently watched off in a field as two lions mated. At a camp called Singita, we ate out on a wooden deck where the management warned us not to feed the monkeys that were lurching around in the trees overhead.

"If you feed them, they will come back the next time you sit down," we were told. "And if you don't feed them the second time, they will bite you."

Everywhere we stayed, we were told not to go out of the tent after dark. Some places had whistles we could blow or bells we could ring if we needed help. We never had to use them, though. Occasionally, I would think of Peter Beard, or imagine myself as Peter Beard.

On the other hand, I did see Peter Beard there. Pictures of him, fully dressed for safari, were on two life-size posters attached to the tent walls of the main dining room in Jack's Camp, an arrangement of fifteen tents out in the middle of nowhere in the Kalahari Desert in Botswana. They caught me up short when I first went into that dining room. I approached the management, a couple from New Zealand, telling them I knew Peter Beard and that was indeed his likeness. They nodded and smiled. Peter Beard, yes.

After the party at the oceanfront home for sale in Southampton in 2007, I waited two weeks and then went up to see Peter at his cottage. I drove out there and knocked on the cottage door, but there was no answer. I walked around. There was nobody there. But it did look lived in. There was a Porsche out front.

A week after that, driving around with my son David, who was twenty-five that year, I tried again. This time Nejma was there, and she answered the door.

"Peter's in London," she said. "He spends most of his time there now."

I introduced my son. She insisted we come in and we did. A young man was doing dishes in the kitchen sink and we nodded to one another, then went into the narrow living room where Nejma sat us down on the single sofa and she sat in front of us on an elephant-foot stool. She offered us iced tea.

She's an extraordinarily beautiful woman. She wore jeans and a work shirt and smoked a cigarette as we talked that day, first about this and that, and then about how Montauk had changed since she had joined Peter here all those years ago.

"It's not as magical as it used to be," she said. "Back then it was this wild place where people could wander around wherever they wanted. We were these six families living out here in these woods. We'd walk to each other's homes. Now it's all fenced off. Everybody's got caretakers. It's not the same."

I told her what I remembered of the property and the fire and how after all the struggles, Peter had never been allowed to rebuild.

"Come with me," she said, standing up. She led us to the narrow stairs that went up to the sleeping loft. On the wall over the banister, there was a framed surveyor's map of the property. Nejma pointed out the dirt road and the foundation and noted that the cliff had crumbled away ten more feet over the years but was still a hundred feet or so from the foundation. Then she said this.

"You know what? I researched everything. I went through the back records at town hall. I spoke to the building department there. I spoke to the town attorney. With the new information I uncovered, it turns out all this time, Peter was wrong. You *can* rebuild that house."

We stared, looking at this map for a long, long time.

"So it was all unnecessary," I said.

"Yes," she said. "All of it. The whole last half of the twentieth century here in Montauk, as far as Peter was concerned, should never have happened the way it did." She paused. "But he's not interested in rebuilding anymore."

Jenna Bullock finally did soon sell the Southampton house at which the Peter Beard party was held. And in the spring of 2008, this magnificent Norman Jaffe designed mansion was no more. The new owners had it bulldozed down to build something even bigger.

In the end, it's all ashes.

King of the Hamptons

~~~~~~

First thing every morning during the summer of 2008, a movie producer with a film crew would call me up to tell me where that day's filming was going to be. Some days it would be at the beach near my house. Other days it would be on a boat. Once it was at the late Andy Warhol's home at the beach in Montauk. I'd either drive my car to where we had to go or they would pick me up in an SUV and we'd all go off together.

It was an extraordinary thing. And it was all because in April, a businessman who said he was a filmmaker had walked over to me at Sagg Main Beach one sunny afternoon to tell me he wanted me to star in a movie. I was, at the time, alone there, sitting in a beach chair typing a story on a laptop computer. I don't like being bothered when I'm working. I didn't like him bothering me either. At first.

"I know who you are," he said. "You've done something really extraordinary."

"What's that?"

RIM, DAN, AND DENNIS LYNCH
(Courtesy of Dennis Lynch)

"You've been writing a newspaper for almost fifty years. You're good at it. And you enjoy doing it."

"Yes I do," I said.

"It certainly shows. Can I take up a bit of your time?" he asked, moving closer. "I won't be long."

This man then told me he would like to film a documentary about me and the Hamptons.

"It would pretty much be your life story, together with the newspaper and the celebrities. You certainly must know all the celebrities. And I'm sure you know this place inside out."

He was serious. He held out his hand. "My name is Dennis Lynch," he said.

A proper documentary had never been made about the Hamptons. Seven years earlier, Barbara Kopple, one of America's most celebrated documentary filmmakers, with two Academy Awards, took a crack at it. I often saw her that summer, lurking in the background with her camera crew, filming people at parties, by the town pond with the swans, on the lawns of some great estates, and even at the Artists & Writers softball game. Everybody had cooperated with her. But in the end, she produced an utter dog.

In her version, the Hamptons was a battleground between the local government officials and the party-hearty twenty-year-olds who put thirty mattresses on the floors of some of the mansions and sold shares to college kids, who then drank themselves into stupors. This was so far off base as to be awful. There were a few homes that had been reduced to this, but the Hamptons was overall one of the great fashionable resorts in America. Most who saw the film at the Sag Harbor Cinema the one night it played there walked out of the theater in silence. The film was also widely panned when it ran once on HBO.

And nobody had made one since.

"So where are we going?" he asked when he phoned the morning of our first shoot. I was supposed to take him around.

"Where? Well, there's Cyril's, a clam bar out in Napeague. It's a big hangout. Cyril's very colorful. He's from the Caribbean. Wears a headband. It's reggae, steel-drum music, and raw clams. There's a surfboard on the roof of the shack, and it's in the middle of nowhere."

"That's great!"

"I'm free until one. Then I gotta be at the paper."

Dennis Lynch was a completely unlikely candidate to be making a film about the Hamptons. He was thirty-eight years old, high-school educated, married with three children, and from Massapequa, Long Island, sixty miles away. He'd done video and Internet work. He'd never before made a documentary. And, like Kopple, he knew nothing about the Hamptons.

He was, however, the only guy who had asked me to help him make a movie about the Hamptons.

Cyril's was really rocking when we got there. And they loved having a film crew. Cyril himself sat in a director's chair and made thumb-and-pinkie wiggle signs with his fist for the camera. I thought he was drunk as a skunk. I have no idea if he even remembers us there.

I took the crew next to the Walking Dunes. The Walking Dunes, a hundred feet high, overlook Cyril's. Wind is blowing the dunes southward, and they are slowly heading toward the Atlantic Ocean. At some point, they will crush Cyril's, which I suspect would be perfectly all right with Cyril.

I loved making this movie with Dennis Lynch. It gave me a good reason to call all the celebrities I knew.

"What do you want me to do?" Mercedes Ruehl asked.

"I'll have him call you."

One of my friends said he thought this guy was just using me to make a film about celebrities in the Hamptons.

Great, I said.

One day, Dennis told me he had decided to call the film *The King of the Hamptons*.

"You are the King of the Hamptons," he said.

"No I'm not."

"Then the movie is a quest to find who is. Take me with you to some of the events, some of the fundraisers."

This was pretty lame. What was I getting myself into? Then I thought, *Idiot! We're making a movie!*

Alec Baldwin showed up on the town green in Amagansett at the appointed time and Dennis had me sit next to him in a wooden gazebo.

"So what is the Hamptons to you?" Dennis asked Baldwin from behind his camera.

"It's Gilligan's Island. It's the professor here," he said, pointing to me, "and the captain over there" (he pointed) "and Mary Ann. It's a place like many others, except people follow you around with a camera more."

Baldwin looked off to the side. "Now that's what's nice about the Hamptons," he said. Dennis swung the camera around. There were a dozen giggling girls on a sidewalk, all looking at Alec Baldwin.

Billy Joel told me to bring the film people to his house in Sag Harbor and he would serve Cokes and show them around. He met us at the door and we walked through the two-car garage where Joel had about a dozen antique motorcycles on display. A dog ran around. In several places there was dog poop on the floor. Billy walked out, came back with some paper towels, bent down, and cleaned it all up.

"Now *this* you can put in your movie," Billy said. "Billy Joel cleaning up dog poop. He's such a regular guy."

We filmed Christie Brinkley, filmmaker Ed Burns, anchorman Chuck Scarborough.

I took Dennis and his crew to one of the most remarkable parties anywhere—the summer party thrown by Robert Wilson, the world-famous performance and environmental artist, who has a twenty-acre estate in Water Mill. There were mimes out front, kids sitting amid bushes with paper bags over their heads, and alongside the entrance, women on stilts dressed in Raggedy Ann costumes making whimpering noises as you passed through the gates.

Hundreds of people were at this party, including Kim Cattrall of *Sex and the City*, and she came over to me. The cameras were whirring away.

"I'm so sorry I couldn't be in your movie," she said. "I just got back from England." She introduced me to her boyfriend. I introduced her to my wife. None had met before.

"Actually, you're in the movie right now," I told her.

"I am?"

After a month of this, all of a sudden, Dennis Lynch started to rise to the occasion. He was now bringing all sorts of new ideas to the making of this film, one of which was an actual plot. His idea was that he was having a midlife crisis and had come out to the Hamptons to break away from his family in Massapequa to find, with my help, the real Hamptons. Perhaps it would lead him to discover his true calling—which was to make films.

He also began to think of his being an outsider.

"I wonder what a cleaning lady from Ohio would think of all of this," he asked me one day, indicating the fundraiser and the big white tent we were standing under. I didn't think he was serious. He was.

He advertised on Craigslist for a cleaning lady from Ohio whom he could fly into the Hamptons to be in his movie for a weekend, all expenses paid.

Kate Broilin from Cincinnati flew in. Dennis picked her up at LaGuardia Airport and brought her out in a limousine. She stayed at a bed and breakfast. At the annual Artists & Writers softball game, somebody gave her a microphone and she became an interviewer for *Dan's Papers*, making wonderful conversation with Chevy Chase, Jimmy Lipton, and Bert Sugar. Dennis also flew over the Hamptons in a small plane with her, pointing out the homes of Jerry Seinfeld and Steven Spielberg. Seinfeld had a major–league-sized baseball field right on his property, for his children.

Some say the highlight of the movie is when my son escorted Dennis and his crew to an enormous castle in Mecox built by a New Jersey banker who holds wild, erotic parties nearly every weekend in the summertime.

"You won't believe this guy," David says as they drive up to the massive main gate of the castle.

"Looks like the gate in *Jurassic Park*," Dennis says.

Dennis presses the button on the intercom to ask to have the gates opened.

"Who is this?" a voice asks.

"Dennis."

"Sir Dennis?"

"Yes, Sir Dennis."

"This is Sir Ivan. Enter!" And the gates swung slowly open to reveal, down a long driveway, a massive castle with turrets.

The banker, Ivan Wilzig, is, besides a banker and a knight, a superhero rock star. His superhero name is Peaceman and as Peaceman he appears wearing a flowing Superman cape with a peace symbol on the back. He sings at his parties, he says, and he has records on the charts. As "Peaceman," the girls go wild for him.

In the film, Ivan Wilzig then shows Dennis around, and as he does, Dennis says, voice-over, "This guy is fifty-two. Now *this* is a real midlife crisis. But he's living his dream. And you just can't help but root for him."

Another highlight of the film is Dennis out fishing for thirty-six hours straight with two Montauk lobstermen. Billy Joel's song "The Downeaster 'Alexa'" accompanies this scene.

At one point, Dennis, manhandling a couple of crabs at 3 a.m., asks the fishermen holding the other side of the net, "Have you ever had a midlife crisis?"

"Why would I have a midlife crisis?" comes the reply.

"Are you having a midlife crisis?"

"Yes."

"How do you know?"

"Because I'm out on your fucking boat!"

Dennis began editing the film in the fall of 2008 at the nice suburban home with the white picket fence around it in Massapequa. I went to see it one day—driving from East Hampton to Massapequa took the better part of two hours—and I thought the film looked surprisingly good. Between what I knew from my fifty years in the Hamptons and what he knew about filmmaking, the film was turning into quite something.

"Better get ready to be going to twenty or thirty film festivals next summer," Dennis told me.

That summer, he sent a copy of it to Sundance, but he sent it after the deadline and they rejected it for that reason, which really pissed Dennis off. Then, three months later, going back to do further editing before sending it out again, he missed the deadline for the Hamptons International Film Festival for that year, and that pissed him off too.

"How many films get sent into film festivals?" I asked the director of the Hamptons film festival one day at a party.

"About four thousand," he said. I was staggered. They were choosing only about one hundred films. This was a very, very long shot.

Later, when I asked Dennis for a DVD of the film, he said it still wasn't ready.

"I just want to be able to show it to my kids," I said. At least *somebody* would watch it. Or maybe they wouldn't.

In early summer 2009, after everything from the summer before was behind us, I was surprised to find that nobody asked whatever happened to that film me and this other guy were making. It was just something absolutely forgotten, even by those who had been filmed in it. Maybe it would never come out. Oh, well.

During this time, I even lost contact with Dennis for long periods of time. We really were from two different worlds. He was this rough-cut thirtysomething Irishman, and I was now a seventy-year-old Harvard-educated Hamptonite of

Jewish descent. I could have been his father, but if I were, I wouldn't know what to do with him.

And then, in the fall of 2010, *King of the Hamptons* was shown at the Hamptons International Film Festival to a sell-out crowd.

As it turned out, what Dennis produced was beautifully filmed, funny, engaging, and a perfect slice of the Hamptons.

A reviewer for one newspaper wrote "albeit with a hand-held camera, Lynch does a fine job of scratching the surface and revealing some of the more unusual personalities who call the East End home."

Another reviewer wrote "the film stands as what it is: an ambitious, creative man's successful attempt to make a film about this incredible place."

The film is now out there. It is being distributed. And over the next months and even years it will have occasional showings all throughout the New York metropolitan area.

Alec Baldwin

~~~~~~

You hear this all the time—when does Alec Baldwin sleep? It seems hard to imagine that he does. He's everywhere. In the last year he starred in three movies, one Broadway show, the television show *Thirty Rock*, cohosted the Academy Awards, hosted the awards ceremony at the Kennedy Center in Washington, attended commencement and received an honorary degree from NYU, was a guest judge on the television show *Marriage Ref*, hosted a live television broadcast of the New York Philharmonic, and was on *Saturday Night Live* several times. He also, during this time, wrote a book about divorce law in America called *A Promise to Ourselves* and hinted, once again, that he might run for office, specifically, to become the mayor of New York, as he told CNN.

"On the other hand," the *New York Times* wrote, "Baldwin has just signed up for another three years in the role of Jack Donaghy on 'Thirty Rock' so nothing will happen until 2015, perhaps."

Many other celebrities are busy, too, but almost all, to a man or woman, come out to the Hamptons to hide out and

ALEC BALDWIN
(Photo by the author)

get a little well-earned rest and relaxation from the *Sturm und Drang* of their profession.

Here's something you don't know. Here in the Hamptons, where Alec lives year-round, he participates in local affairs with the same blizzard of energy he displays nationally. He's everywhere. Here's what he did *this* year. He starred in the revival of the play *Equus* at the John Drew Theater; he hosted two fundraisers; he founded a watchdog group to keep an eye on local politicians and their attitude toward saving the environment; he cohosted, with Billy Joel, a film called *Last Play at Shea*, about Joel's last performance there; he was an auctioneer for a charity; he funded a series of lectures and panel discussions at Guild Hall; and he even wrote the preface to my last book. And so local people ask—when does this guy sleep? It's like there are two people who get no sleep. Both are Alec Baldwin.

Needless to say, in my role as publisher and editor of *Dan's Papers*, our paths cross numerous times every year. Two years ago, he volunteered his time to be in the film *The King of the Hamptons*.

I was in the audience at *Last Play at Shea* when Baldwin piped up with this gem:

"How is it you are able to stay on such good terms with your ex-wife?" Baldwin asked Billy. He nodded to Christie Brinkley, who was right there in the audience watching her ex talk about the movie made about him.

This got a great laugh. Baldwin has now spent ten years doing a nasty divorce and then a custody battle with his former wife Kim Basinger, and there is no love lost there. The laugh lasted so long, Joel decided not even to try to answer.

Alec Baldwin is perhaps the most complicated and interesting person I've known. In fifteen years, he has changed quite a bit.

Fifteen years ago, he was a serious, dazzlingly handsome young man, highly focused and on the road to becoming one of the great male movie leads of our time. He had finished *The Hunt for Red October*, *The Ghosts of Mississippi*, and *Mercury Rising*.

I met him in a taxi cab. It was in 1998, and I had wanted to write a profile about him for the paper, with a formal interview that might take forty-five minutes. Instead, he offered me a cab ride.

"Meet me out front of the Public Theater tomorrow," he said, referring to the theater in Manhattan that the legendary Joseph Papp had developed.

I tried to protest that that would not be enough time, but that was the offer. I went. Maybe we could finish up at a coffee house or something.

All together, the taxi ride lasted twenty minutes. During that time, Alec talked about what was on his mind and I just listened to him.

The role he was playing at the Joseph Papp theater, he said, was the lead in Shakespeare's *Macbeth.*

"I could have been doing another film out in Hollywood, but then I was offered an opportunity to do this. It is one thing to be considered an actor. It is another to be considered a *great* actor. And it is here at Joseph Papp that reputations are made."

He talked a little while about the posters for the shows at the Papp, all of which were made in a recognizable and similar style by the same graphic artist, Paula Scher. Scher had been making them for years.

"When I was studying acting at NYU," he said, "I saw these posters, and I said that would be my goal, to be drawn like that on these posters and see myself around the city. That would be a mark of my having been a success. That would be something."

I asked him about the eighty-acre farm he and his wife had bought, north of the highway in Amagansett, and he said the two of them had just gotten tired fighting with the town about this chimney they had built, though pre-existing, that was two feet taller than was allowed, and so they had sold that house and bought this one. He said he was madly in love with his wife, that they had a crazy wonderful relationship, and that he couldn't imagine living without her.

He also talked about how he and his younger brothers, also actors, were strong supporters of the charity founded by their mother, a cancer survivor. He asked me if I would go to an upcoming event about it. I said I'd try. Or I would certainly send someone.

And then the taxi ride ended and I found myself in a part of the city I had never been in before, and about half an hour away from Second Avenue and East Seventieth Street, where I had a city apartment at that time.

I came away from that interview believing I had met an extremely active, talented, and personally open young man who was involved in a wide variety of things, and even then I wondered how he had time for it all.

Later that summer, President Clinton and his wife Hillary came out to the Hamptons to fundraise for the Democratic Party. They held a dinner at the home of Alan Patricof, the investment banker, and then the next day had brunch for about two hundred under a tent on the lawn of the home of Alec Baldwin and Kim Basinger. I tried to get in but hadn't done the proper pre-brunch paperwork, and so got turned away.

I did research on Mr. Baldwin. This was in the days before Google, so it was a harder business. But I came up with the basics to flesh out my article—he had been born and raised in Massapequa, Long Island, the son of a legendary football coach and history teacher at Massapequa High School.

There was something very unusual about his father. At a time when anyone in public life in that part of Long Island was a Republican and paid a part of their salary to the Republican Party if they knew what was good for them—this later became a huge scandal—Alec's father was a vocal and ardent Democrat. It kept him from getting promoted, but he stuck to his convictions. And he and his wife and their five kids got by. This made a great impression on Alec, people said. It was also said his father expected a lot from his eldest son. And then his dad died at age fifty-five.

As Alec and I continued to meet on occasion at this and that event or occasion, I wondered if he would be interested in having dinner with me. Turned out he would. We had one dinner at the American Hotel, one of his favorite places, and it went pretty well. It seemed we had a lot in common, at least as it concerned the Hamptons. We both were politically liberal and in favor of helping those less fortunate. We both cared about the beauty of the East End, and each of us in our own way thought we could do something to help preserve it.

After that, Baldwin began to talk about his endless divorce. One day in the summer of 2000, he came home to find that his wife Kim had left him—and not only left him, but actually cleaned out everything in the entire house in a moving van and taken it off to points unknown. I also heard—overheard, actually, from two local bonackers talking about it—that she had left him only one thing, a roll of toilet paper, and they knew this because it was they who had been hired to move all the stuff out. I never mentioned this little detail to Alec. Never will.

Alec also began, at this time, to write letters to the local paper about the beauty and history of the area and how he thought the local politicians were allowing it all to be ruined. He was very matter-of-fact about this, but also wrote his letters in a sort of take-no-prisoners way. He also became active in the Democratic Party, and it seemed clear that he and others were positioning him to run for office. Surely, he would be the white knight on the white horse coming in to clean things up. It didn't go over well.

The *New York Post*, providing everybody's daily yammering of gossip and New York City celebrity scandal, wrote something that Alec didn't like, which resulted in his writing something nasty back. He was, from that point on, and for quite some time thereafter, given very negative treatment by the *Post*, and in particular, given a nickname.

The *Post* during this era had begun to give nasty nicknames to celebrities they felt did not measure up. Monica Lewinski was "the Portly Pepperpot," Paris Hilton was "the Celebutard," Britney Spears "the Pop Tart," Mick Jagger "the Wrinkly Rocker," Robert Downey Jr. "the Rehab Regular," and Christina Aguilera "the Skanky Songbird." Now they began referring to Alec Baldwin as the "the Bloviator." It didn't seem to have an exact meaning. Maybe it referred to him being blustery and verbose, or maybe that as he was growing older, he became a little thicker around the middle. Whatever it was, it was not good. I never talked to Alec about that either.

During this time, Alec and I had a second dinner at the American Hotel. And this time it did not go well, although it was not for a lack of either of us trying. The thing was, Alec was getting ever deeper into the throes of his terrible divorce and custody fight and as he talked about it, it dredged up my old terrible divorce fight from some years earlier. I could sympathize with him about this, and by this time I felt close enough to him, particularly since we had polished off one bottle of red wine and were heading well into another, to begin to exchange divorce war stories with him.

I can't tell you what these were. We all know about them either firsthand or secondhand, but they involve the terrible things that one party can do to another when love turns to hate and when eager lawyers licking their chops and seeing dollar signs step in to "help out." It also involved denial of access to our children.

Anyway, the two of us were wallowing in so much pain that at a certain point we crossed over into this time zone where it had now become the entire conversation. I didn't care, but as we wallowed this way and that, it did occur to me that people at adjacent tables might be eavesdropping on our conversation, but I didn't care about that either. It was just so damned painful. In the end, we left the hotel, arms around one another holding each other up, and we headed our separate lonely ways, but I thought—oh this has gone too far and too deep and I think we can't be doing this again too soon. And we didn't.

About four years later, I was sitting at a table in a tent at a fundraiser for Bay Street, a local theater group, when Alec Baldwin hopped up on stage to become master of ceremonies of the event because somebody else who was supposed to do it did not show up. He was wildly funny. I had never seen this side of him before. It seemed to me that his pain, intelligence, and point of view had suddenly blossomed in some whole new way—into an absolutely incredible sense of humor.

I think the whole world has seen this by now. Alec cocks his head to the side, looks directly at you, and says something absolutely absurd and absolutely true but also absolutely hilarious. It is a sort of rabbit that has popped out of the hat, in my view. And it is Alec reborn.

So I guess it is fair to say that I don't know Alec very well, or that I know him about as well as any other local person in this community, which is to say, a lot.

The other day, I watched part of a show on the National Geographic Channel called *Great Migrations*. It was all about zebras and wallabies and penguins slowly making their ways across the savannahs and plains of Africa and Australia and Antarctica. The photography was simply stunning.

Then I heard the voice-over, doing the narration. I knew that voice. It was Alec.

"And so," he intoned, "the penguins march across the glacier in this great herd toward the Huckabee Shelf."

I could see him there, reading the script, a man committed to righting wrongs, to culture and the arts, to helping save the planet, to helping others enjoy their lives and I thought of him cocking his head to the side and thinking, as he proceeded to read what he was about to have to say, that this stuff in a certain way is pretty funny and look what they have me saying next!

Thus does the entertaining and complicated Alec Baldwin, following his instincts, march into his future.

ACKNOWLEDGMENTS

This book could not have happened without the help and encouragement of the following people. My wife Chris Wasserstein, my agent Scott Miller, David Rattiner, Alec Baldwin, SUNY Publisher James Peltz, Diane Ganeles, Fran Keneston, Marty and Judy Shepard, David Rattiner, Kelly Merritt Shelley, Andy Sabin, Mark Schneier, Dennis Lynch, Joan Hamburg, Billy Joel, John Roland, Charline Spektor, Betsy Carter, Mercedes Reuhl, Bill Henderson, J. Z. Holden, Jules Feiffer, Richard Burns, Joanne Harras, LeRoy Neiman, Melissa Levis, Mischa Brenner, Natasha Brenner, Adam Rattiner, John Keeshan, Darielle Watnick, Joan Baum, Cecil Hoge, Jerry Cohen, Henry Hildreth, Joslyn Pine, Richard Gollin, Bob Edelman, Jerry and Adrian Cohen, Maya Baker, Matt Cross, the late James Brady, E. L. Doctorow, Joan Zandell, Geoff Lynch and the Hampton Jitney, Kaylee Jones, Arthur Bloom and the Shelter Island Bridge and Tunnel Authority, Adelaide de Menil and the late Ted Carpenter, Richard Lewin, Mary Guillen, Paul "P. J." Jeffers, Ralph George, Nejma Beard, Ambassador Carl Spielvogel and Barbara Diamonstein-Spielvogel,

Bill Hattrick, Pia Lindstrom, John White, Jeff White, Red White, Stewart Lane, Leif Hope, Bonnie Gitlin, Eric Cohen and Gabriel Rattiner.

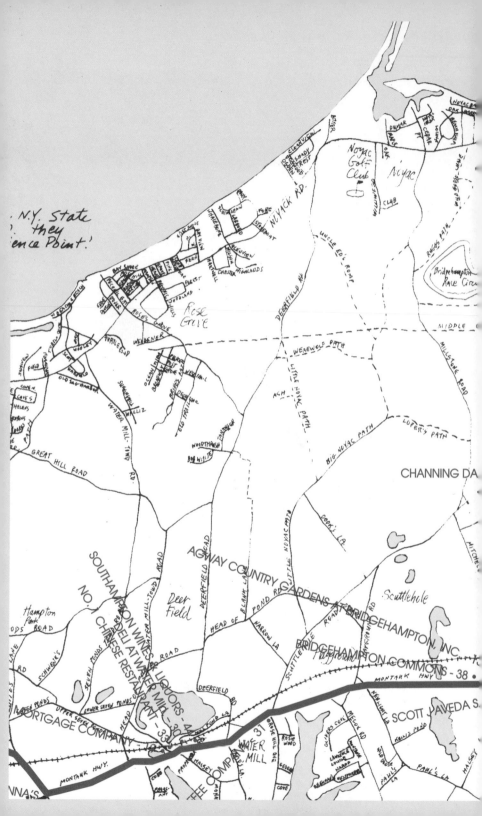